JUMPING
AT THE
CHANCE

JUMPING
AT THE
CHANCE

*From the court to the field, how NBA hopefuls
are changing Australian Rules Football*

Gil Griffin

JABberwocky Literary Agency, Inc.

I dedicate this book to Granddad and Fe.

Your eternal spirits live on in me.

Jumping at the Chance

Copyright © 2017 by Gil Griffin

All rights reserved

This paperback edition published in 2017 by JABberwocky Literary Agency, Inc.

First paperback edition published in 2016 by Nero,
an imprint of Schwartz Publishing Pty, Ltd.

Published as an ebook in 2017 by JABberwocky Literary Agency, Inc.

Interior design by Lisa Rodgers

Cover art by J Caleb Designs

ISBN 978-1-625672-87-2

JABberwocky Literary Agency, Inc.
49 W. 45th Street, 12th Floor
New York, NY 10036
http://awfulagent.com
ebooks@awfulagent.com

Contents

Foreword

by Martin Flanagan

The character missing from the writing of Gil Griffin is Gil Griffin. Mainstream American journalism, of which Gil is a classical exponent, insists on an "objective" method, which serves to erase the character of the narrator. I've never believed in it myself, but, in the case of Gil Griffin, it's a double pity because the man is a character and, in the Australian culture I grew up in, characters had a special place. People like me tell stories but characters are the people who make them happen.

Gil first approached me on the Internet: his profile showed a black man from L.A. wearing a purple Fremantle Dockers outfit. He asked if I would read something he'd written. I agreed, hesitantly. Reading manuscripts for strangers sounds like a generous thing to do but it can be a lot of work and lead to strange places. When I read what he'd written, however, I was glad that I had. He'd written about an African-American, a man like himself, trying to make it in the AFL. What struck me about the story was the clarity and precision of his prose, and his welcome absence of assumptions about Australia or the Australian game. In a word, it was intelligent. (I've since learned Gil has a master's degree in journalism from Columbia University.)

We arranged to meet when next he passed through Melbourne. I offered to give him my tour of the Melbourne Cricket Ground, when I show people what, for me, are its landmarks. We'd got about halfway round when it became clear that I wasn't telling this man much he didn't know. I had my first glimpse into the erudition that underlies Gil Griffin's passion for Australian football and Australia generally.

With time, I have come to understand that Gil is a polymath — a man with lots of knowledge about lots of things. One of his schoolmates told me that, in his youth, it was said of Gil: "Ask him the time and he'll tell you how to build a watch." I once pressed him for a list of his interests — they included the *New York Times* daily crossword puzzle (which he does on his iPad); plane watching (he's a huge civil aviation buff); taking in the annual two-week Pan African Film Festival in L.A. and watching African cinema by African directors; cats (Coco, his 2-year-old Siamese cat, is the third he's raised from a kitten); and sci-fi films and literature. He's a lifelong New York Mets fan and a rescue-level scuba diver (his favorite things to spot underwater are reef sharks, spotted eagle rays, clownfish and flamingo tongues). And this is without getting into his taste in music.

Gil talks a lot and thinks in American ways on matters I don't, but he's humble. He understands respect like it's in his bones, and he's an innately polite man. His mother was in the Carter administration and is an author. His father was a businessman with an endless list of interests. Gil attended the Quaker school in Washington, D.C., where Barack Obama sent his daughters. He then went to prestigious Brown University in Rhode Island. He first encountered Australian football as part of a wave of Australiana that hit America in the 1980s — Paul Hogan, Men at Work, *Mad Max*, *Picnic at Hanging Rock* ... "Anything Australian," he told me, "got my attention."

The clincher, as far as Australian football is concerned, was the young Aussie woman who, with her boyfriend, attended a yoga class in downtown San Diego that Gil was taking. She was a Collingwood supporter. She and her boyfriend came to Gil's place; over a pizza, they watched her video of the 1990 Grand Final. "She set the game's context, telling me about the Pies being known as the "Colliwobbles" for their previous Grand Final failures. I watched and was transfixed. It was like I'd spotted the woman of my dreams and joyously yelled out to her the cliché, 'Where've you been all my life?!'"

In 1999 Gil was working as a features reporter for San Diego's daily newspaper, the *Union-Tribune*, when he decided he was going to Australia for his vacation. He got on the Internet and found the AFL website, trying to see if there was a match he could attend. It took him several days to figure out that he needed to click on "Fixture" to see what Americans would call a "schedule" of games. Having learned that Sydney was at home against Port Adelaide on his last full day in Australia, he called the Swans' media department and "arranged a credential." The very first piece of literature he bought in Australia, at Kingsford Smith airport, was a copy of the *AFL Record*'s 1999 preview edition, "with Carlton's Craig Bradley and St Kilda's Troy Schwarze on the cover, showcasing the league's oldest and youngest players."

He wrote a story about the Swans-Port match, and the *San Diego Union-Tribune* even published a photo he took "from just outside the players' [tunnel] of Tony Lockett and Paul Kelly leading the Swans out." He also wrote a column about it for the *AFL Record*. When he got back to San Diego, he discovered the city had an amateur footy club, the San Diego Lions, and he became mates with quite a few of the players. Then, says Gil, "I really did meet the woman of my dreams." Some of their first dates were watching AFL matches on Fox Sports World.

Gil's wife, Arlene, is a remarkable woman. She is, among other things, highly intelligent and forthright in manner. Gil showed her a Swans match. Arlene saw a Swans player who was forthright in manner and highly skillful. His name was Tony Lockett. A Swans jersey signed by the man called "Plugger" now hangs on the wall of their L.A. apartment. I once said to Arlene, "Gil's different." "Gil's very different!' she declared. Shaking her head as if to further express her incredulity, she cried, "He's a black man who can't dance!"

Together, Gil and Arlene attended the 2000 AFL Grand Final. They've been all over Australia — Uluru, Rottnest Island, the Great Barrier Reef, Tasmania, Adelaide and Cooktown in Queensland. (While living in New Mexico in 1995, Gil was captivated by an image he found of a pub, the Cooktown Hotel, "draped in tropical foliage." He made a promise to himself that he'd visit it one day and, five years later, he did.) At Gil's first Fremantle Dockers home game, one of his favorite players, Michael Walters, kicked a goal in the first 30 seconds of play that landed three rows in front of where Gil was sitting. And where do you think he was sitting? With the official cheer squad, of course. Gil talks about "the footy gods" and how they have pre-destined his journey. He also does a great Australian accent and can quote any number of lines from *The Castle* or the car ads on 6PR, which he hears when he rings in from L.A. to have his say after Dockers games. I think Gil Griffin gets me as an Australian. I think he gets our game. If I were to describe Gil Griffin simply, I'd say he's `wa good bloke. He's genuine and he's on to something important. In my home state, Tasmania, Australian football has shrunk and is shrinking. Relative to our three major competitors — soccer, rugby league and rugby union — our vulnerability is our limited talent pool. This book is an American perspective on a serious discussion Australian football needs to be having.

Martin Flanagan
February 2016

An Open Letter

to American Sports Fans:

An Author's Appeal for Adventurous Thinking

There once was a time, long ago in my life, as a teenager in the 1980s, when I felt as you might right now about American sports. The full scope of professional spectator sports consisted of the big four — Major League Baseball, the NFL, the NBA, and the NHL. If that plate wasn't full enough, there also was NCAA football and basketball. At least that was what I once thought.

Soccer? That was a fringe sport played by kids who weren't tough enough to play football. Golf? That was a leisure sport played mostly by rich old guys. Auto racing? That was only a boring alternative to bridge the gap (the "dead period") between the end of football season and the beginning of baseball season. I once had all these uninformed misgivings about these "other" sports.

But then, one strange summer wee-hours morning during the early '80s, after my father and I returned home after spending one of our many nights at Shea Stadium, cheering on the New York Mets, something truly magical happened. I flipped the TV channel to that new cable TV network, ESPN, which would show just about any sport at any time of day. What I saw looked bizarre. It wasn't quite outdoor basketball on grass, or soccer, or American football, but it looked like an odd combination of all three.

Was I hallucinating?

The commentators' had Australian accents and the players were wearing basketball uniforms. Officials were standing behind parallel goal posts without crossbars and dressed in white lab coats and hats. They'd stand ramrod straight and point their index fingers like Old West gunslingers when the egg-shaped ball went through the posts. The confetti and toilet paper raining down from the stands only added to the intrigue.

I wasn't hallucinating. I was watching Australian Rules football. I couldn't bring myself to turn the channel. Neither then, nor any other late night thereafter, whenever I found it. It was as if I was picking up some strange broadcast transmission from a planet in another dimension and I was trying to decipher the message. I couldn't have imagined then that these "transmissions" would change my life. But they did.

After a few years, ESPN stopped showing "Aussie Rules" as it was nicknamed, but my memories of it lingered, refusing to fade away from my consciousness. About 15 years later, in my adulthood, when I was planning my first Australia vacation, in 1999. I wanted to attend a live sporting event while there. Only one would do. I attended an Aussie Rules match at the Sydney Cricket Ground — a season-opener on my last full day in the country. I returned to America totally hooked. Thankfully, a new American TV network, Fox Sports World, showed weekly live matches, which fed my growing habit.

As I'd learned, Aussies call their national game "footy" and I have religiously followed it ever since.

For whatever reason, many Americans I meet still mistakenly think, when I'm telling them about my love for Australian Rules football, that I'm talking about rugby, or soccer. They often ask me, "What do you love so much about Australian football?"

My answer never wavers: "What's *not* to love?"

The ball appears to have a mind of its own when it bounces, making for a continuous, ferocious fight for its possession and the very idea of choreographed plays, as found in most American sports, ludicrous. With no timeouts, the action never stops. Aussie Rules is an unscripted, spontaneous action adventure. If American football were a tune, it would be classical: highly structured, with orchestrated melodies, phrasing and harmonies. Footy's rhythm is mercurial and improvisational, like freestyle a cappella freestyle rap or a be-bop jazz or punk rock jam session.

If you don't believe human beings are capable of flying, just watch footy players make magnificent grabs of the ball by catapulting off the ground onto the backs and shoulders of other players, then defying gravity by hanging in the air before clutching their prize and triumphantly tumbling to the ground. Fans of AFL clubs are as tribal, if not more so, than American fans, with family loyalties to some reaching back to the 19th Century. Rivalries between AFL clubs boil over in intensity.

Yet, there's a childhood innocence about some AFL clubs' time-honored traditions, not found in the more jaded world of American professional sports. Every week, on the field, just before the start of a match, players run through a giant crepe paper banner decorated in big letters, spelling out a timely, playfully boastful slogan that their club's biggest boosters — members of the official cheer squad — has spent the week making. During matches, footy players don't preen for the TV cameras, literally beat their chests, or engage in other attention-seeking antics, as many American athletes do after executing the most routine or biggest plays.

In the locker room immediately after a match, Australian footballers on the winning club will link arms and joyously belt out the words to their club's anthem, to tunes sounding like they were borrowed from Broadway musicals. At the end of the season, players pitch in and take a trip together. The absence of surnames on the backs of player jerseys reinforces the notion that this is a team, not an individual sport. All these elements make the game culturally and uniquely Australian.

I never envisioned I'd ever open my heart and mind to embrace the Australian Football League as much as my first love, Major League Baseball and come to cherish one of its clubs, the Fremantle Dockers, as dearly as my beloved Mets.

But both things happened.

Footy has taken me back to Australia a dozen times, led me to make special, lifelong friendships with both footy-loving Australians and Americans (yes, there are a few thousand!) and even played a part in my courting my my American wife. I found American men and women — some of whom had never before played any sport — spending their weekends playing alongside homesick Aussie expats who had brought the game with them, in the amateur United States Australian Football League. As a teacher, I've introduced the game to enthusiastic boys and girls, armed with yellow and red Australian footballs and a library of YouTube clips.

In doing so, I've eliminated their many misconceptions about Australian Rules football. It is not, by nature, a violent game. Footy doesn't have American football's body armor and hard plastic helmets with metal bars that can be, and often are, used as weapons. Australian football, whose physical demands require players to run the equivalent of seven to nine miles a match; have pinpoint accuracy in kicking off both feet; play offense and defense; tackle and break tackles; and make intelligent decisions while possessing the ball, is arguably, the world's most challenging sport to play.

Finally, after almost 120 years since the rules were first codified, American athletes are making their first marks in Australia's great game. In 2015, Jason Holmes, the first born-and-bred U.S. athlete played in a regular-season AFL match. In 2016, Kim Hemenway and Katie Klatt became America's first two women to play in an AFL-sanctioned women's match. Later that year, Mason Cox debuted as the second American AFL player and was the first to kick a goal in an AFL regular-season match. Thanks to the AFL's recruiting in America, and its partnership with the USAFL, more talent may be on the way.

This breakthrough has happened only because these athletes opened their hearts and minds to learning about an international sport they'd never before heard of. Now I invite you to do the same. If the extent of your sports universe is "the big four" plus "the NCAA two," I challenge you to expand it by reading this book. The American men and women whose journeys I've closely followed the last few years have incredible stories to share, of sacrificing everything to become professional athletes — taking up an unfamiliar game in an unfamiliar land. After reading this book, maybe you'll fall in love with footy. Maybe not.

But you may certainly be inspired by a group men and women who followed their improbable dreams.

Prologue
Australian Rules Football 101
It's Not Rugby!

Reading this guide will guarantee you one thing: You'll never again mistake rugby with Australian Rules football. Ever.

The two sports are about as different as basketball and volleyball. How the myth started that Australian Rules football and rugby are the same — and persists in the United States — is anyone's guess. Rugby is English in origin and made its way to Australia, Australian football was, and remains, uniquely Australian, with its variant invented and played by its Indigenous people, perhaps a few thousand years ago.

Basics: Games are played 18-on-18 by competing teams. (Each squad has four reserves that can be brought on at any time, as temporary substitutes, as in basketball or American football). Matches are played on grass oval fields that, like Major League Baseball fields, vary in dimensions. The average oval size is 180 x 150 yards — much wider and longer than American football fields.

The teams try to outscore each other by kicking a leather football more egg-shaped than an American one, through a pair of parallel, crossbar-less goal posts at the oval's opposite ends, which are 20 feet high and 21 feet apart, for goals.

Matches start much like an opening tipoff or jump ball in basketball, but with a "field umpire" bouncing the ball in the middle of the oval, in the "center circle" inside the larger, "center square." Then, the two teams' ruckmen — the tallest players — battle to tap the ball to a smaller, more mobile teammate, who attempts to advance it toward goal. "Ruck contests" between these players take place during the center square bounces that begin each of the four quarters of play, or in "boundary throw-ins" by the umpire after the ball goes out of bounds, or in "ball ups," after the umpire blows the whistle and determines no player has clear possession of the ball.

Players are positioned are in the forward line, back line and midfield, but may go anywhere on the field. Depending on which team has possession of the ball, as in basketball, all players play offense and defense.

Rules: Players may only pass the ball to their teammates by "handballing" (holding the ball in one hand while striking it with an opposing closed fist) or kicking. Throwing or handing off the ball is illegal. So is running with it for more than 15 meters (16 yards) at a time, without bouncing the ball or touching it to the ground. As with traveling, in basketball, players violating that rule are penalized for "running too far."

If a player's kick travels at least 15 meters, the player "marking" (catching) it on the fly may either back up from the spot where they've marked — which, if an opponent steps over, concedes a 50-meter penalty — and kick or handball the footy, unchallenged, or may immediately "play on," by running, kicking or handballing.

Tackles are legal, but can only be made between a player's shoulders and knees. Tackling outside those areas are illegal "high contact" or "tripping" infringements, penalized by a free kick to the illegally tackled player. If a player has prior opportunity to kick or handball before getting tackled and doesn't, the player is penalized for "holding the ball," with the tackler winning a free kick. This is the most highly disputed rule interpretation in the sport, which is why in every footy match you'll hear the home team's fans roar, with gusto, "BALL!" in an attempt to convince the field umpire to penalize a visiting player.

Players may not intentionally kick, handball or paddle the ball with their hands toward the boundary line, with no teammate in the vicinity, so that the ball will roll out bounds to stop the clock, gain territory for their team, or avoid getting tackled. This penalty is called "deliberate out of bounds," or more commonly "deliberate." It's similar to NCAA and NFL football's "intentional grounding" rule, penalizing quarterbacks for intentionally getting rid of the ball to avoid losing yards from getting sacked.

Similar to the NFL's pass interference rules, AFL defenders attempting to "spoil" (bat or punch away) balls in flight that their opponents are trying to mark may not push them in the back, chop their arms or hold them. Similarly, players may not jump on others' backs or shoulders to use them as springboards unless they're making a legitimate attempt to mark the ball. For unsportsmanlike or other egregious physical actions, there is no penalty box, no yellow or red cards, no technical fouls and no ejections. An offender is sanctioned with a 50-meter penalty and an AFL umpire may "report" the player to the league's Match Review Panel for a hearing the following week.

Scoring: "Major" scores are six-point goals, which may only be kicked between the two tall goal posts, either through the air or on the ground. If the ball hits either of the goal posts, or a player touches it before it goes through them, or if a kick goes between one of the goal posts and one of two shorter, adjacent "behind posts," the kicking team scores a "minor" one-point "behind."

Defenders may concede a behind by carrying it through the goal square, between the goal posts. This is called a "rushed behind," and is legal, only if, in the umpire's judgement, there's no option to pass it to a teammate. This is similar to an NFL player conceding a safety by running the ball out of his own end zone.

A team's total score is its tally of goals, plus behinds. Thus, Australian football final scores read with the goal number, then a period, then the behind number, with the total reached by multiplying goals by six, then adding one for each behind. Example: In the 2016 AFL championship match, the Grand Final, the Western Bulldogs defeated the Sydney Swans, 13.11 (89) to 10.7 (67).

Statistics: The most important statistics for a ruckman, the position Australian scouts are recruiting most American former college basketball players to play, are "hitouts," "hitouts to advantage" and "marks." Statisticians credit ruckmen with hitouts when, against their direct opponents, they successfully tap the ball toward a teammate during a center bounce or boundary throw-in. A hitout to advantage is even better, as it shows how successful a ruckman is in providing a teammate "first use" of the ball. A team in attack mode, in the forward 50 meters of the ground often will deploy two ruckmen — one for potential ruck contests and another to "rest" in the forward line, to be a tall target for a teammate to kick to, close to the goal square, so that the resting ruckman can mark, then attempt to kick a goal. Teams also use this strategy in defense, with one of the ruckmen stationed in the backline, to spoil an opposition kick to the goal square, or serve as a tall target to kick to, up the field, for a counterattack. Midfielders and ruckmen have a symbiotic relationship; midfielders depend on ruckmen to tap the ball to them in ruck contests.

Unlike American sporting culture, in which individual performances in team sports often are measured by one's scoring tallies, Australian football metrics most highly value the number of possessions a player accumulates. Possessions or more commonly called "touches," or "disposals," help denote which players have the most influence on a match. To put it in an American context, if the NBA were to view its players through an Australian Rules football lense, the league's most valuable player wouldn't be the scoring champion; it would likely be the player averaging the most assists, combined with offensive and defensive rebounds.

The Australian game has become dramatically more athletic and strategically complex since the late-1990s, when it wasn't uncommon for the league's top goal kickers to amass in excess of 100 in a season. Center half forwards or full forwards were celebrated and idolized for their brute strength in marking contests and their goal-kicking prowess. But since the turn of the 21st century, midfielders, because they follow the ball wherever it goes, run the most and rack up the most possessions, are the AFL's glamor boys. Fittingly, midfielders, also known as "on-ballers" are responsible for steering their team out of defense and into attack and vice versa, their domain is colloquially known as the "engine room" or the "coalface." To use a baseball parallel, just as a team never can have too many good pitchers, a footy club can never have too many good midfielders.

Umpires working the field and boundaries see much more of the midfielders compete than other position players, so when it comes time for umpires to vote on a match's best players, midfielders are the most likely to garner votes. The player who accumulates the most umpire votes in matches wins the coveted Brownlow Medal; the equivalent to a North American pro sports league's most valuable player.

Timing: Matches are played in four 20-minute quarters, with "time on" (stoppage time) progressively added throughout each (as in soccer's halves), for when the ball goes out of bounds, or after a goal has been kicked and then returned for an ensuing center bounce. There are *no* timeouts — only 6-minute breaks after the first and third quarters, with a 20-minute halftime intermission. Tie scores at the end of regular season matches result in draws, but in post-season "Finals," scores are settled after two additional 5-minute periods. Until 2016, if the AFL Grand Final was a draw after four quarters, the two sides replayed the game the next week. Under the new AFL rules, two additional five-minute halves, plus time on, are played after a draw. In the event of a tie after that, the final siren would sound after the next score, whether a goal or a behind.

Gear: Players' team uniforms consist of "jumpers" or "guernseys" (like sleeveless basketball jerseys), shorts, socks and "boots" (cleats). Pouches inside the backs of players' jumpers, below the neck, contain GPS monitoring devices that record — among other metrics — their speeds and distances. In a long upheld tradition that epitomizes team, not individual focus, players' surnames aren't on the backs of jumpers. Players tend to favor lower numbers.

History: Though "footy," as Australians affectionately call it, was first codified in the 1850s and predates the first professional American football league by more than a half-century, a growing number of Australian scholars cite historic anecdotal evidence to illustrate its ancient origins with the indigenous Gunditjmara people of southwestern Victoria, who developed *marn grook* ("game ball") using a ball made of possum skins.
Leagues were organized in Victoria in 1858 and the first known recorded match happened. Historians recognize Australian cricketer Thomas Wentworth Wills — a man who grew up in southwestern Victoria among Aboriginal people and spoke at least one Aboriginal language besides English — as inventing modern footy as a way for his fellow cricketers to remain fit during the off-season.

Organization: The Australian Football League (AFL), the sport's nationwide, elite competition, has 18 clubs — 10 of which are based in the state of Victoria and nine of those 10 in the Melbourne area. The imbalance is a result of the league's evolution from its beginnings as the Victorian Football League (VFL) before its 1980s expansion to other Australian states. The VFL exists today as a minor league feeder to AFL for affiliated clubs, whose reserve players compete there.
AFL clubs draft teens from top statewide under-18 leagues. Australian universities do not have sporting competitions like America's NCAA. Some minor league footy clubs, though, may carry the moniker "University" in their nomenclature, as homage to their origins. AFL teams play a weekly, 22-game season, from late March/early April through late September/early October, only catching a breather during rotating, consecutive mid-season bye weeks. The top eight clubs play four Finals (playoff) rounds. The top four clubs enjoy a "double chance," in which they may lose a first round "qualifying final," but not be eliminated until losing a follow-up match. The two surviving clubs square off in the Grand Final — traditionally, the last Saturday in September — at the 100,000-seat Melbourne Cricket Ground (MCG).

Though many Americans mistakenly assume Australian Rules football is rugby, footy may not be as obscure in America as you might think. In fact, there's a very good chance a group of amateur men and women are playing it in your city.

The non-profit United States Australian Football League (USAFL) has been around since 1996, played its first matches the next year and today boasts about three-dozen clubs across the country in multiple divisions. Some men's teams, like the Orange County (Calif.) Bombers and Austin Crows and women's clubs such as the Boston Lady Demons and New York Lady Magpies share nicknames with AFL clubs. Other USAFL clubs, such as the Minnesota Freeze, St. Petersburg Starfish, San Francisco Iron Maidens and Columbus Jillaroos created completely original identities.

The USAFL season runs through the American spring and summer, with teams competing in an annual national tournament two weeks after the AFL Grand Final, in mid-October. Most teams are coached by Australian expats and players are a mix of people of varying ages, skill levels and experience, from both countries.

An American national men's team, the USA Revolution and a national women's club, USA Freedom, compete around the world in international tournaments, including the International Cup, in Melbourne. The next such event is scheduled for August 2017.

Introduction
The Collingwood Cowboy's First Rodeo

Hollywood couldn't have scripted a dreamier debut.

It's ANZAC Day, 2016. This annual holiday is sacred in Australia, on which citizens commemorate soldiers who either perished in or survived past foreign wars and those who continue to serve. And ANZAC Day also is sacred in Australian Football. The Melbourne Cricket Ground, whose iconic status as a sporting cathedral parallels Yankee Stadium's to Major League Baseball, annually hosts a standalone Anzac Day match between the Collingwood Magpies and Essendon Bombers, two stalwart Australian Football League clubs. The match-day crowd averages about 85,000, second only to the league's championship game, the Grand Final, which packs in about 100,000 fans.

The match's biggest story, though, isn't about either team's chances. It's about the debut of an American player — whose maiden appearance today follows the historic debut of one of his countrymen the year before. In 2015, Jason Holmes, a former Morehead State NCAA basketball player, became the first American born-and-raised athlete ever to play in a regular season AFL match. Today, it's Mason Cox's turn.

Cox attended Oklahoma State University. But unlike Holmes, Cox's school didn't recruit him to play basketball. Cox was focused on his engineering studies and joined the Cowboys as a walk-on player late in his college career. In 2014, Cox was all but certain to accept a position as a mechanical engineer with ExxonMobil and report to work in Houston. But an unexpected email that at first he wondered was a joke, inviting him to try a sport he'd never heard of changed all that.

Now here he is, all 6-foot-11 of him, dressed in the black-and-white-striped Collingwood Magpies uniform, trotting into position, ready for action.

That action happens quickly. Less than two minutes after the umpire bounces the ball to start the match, Cox finds the footy screaming toward his chest, kicked to him by his teammate and former roommate, Darcy Moore. Cox sprints to meet the ball. He lunges and marks the ball on his chest. He is 20 meters from goal and promptly walks back from the place he marked to line up to attempt to kick a goal. The Collingwood faithful, sensing history, unleash a roar that reverberates throughout and beyond the cavernous venue. Cox's family members, including his parents and two brothers, who are sitting in the stands next to Holmes, all anxiously await his next move — the run-up to a few feet before the spot he marked, where he'll then drop the ball onto his boot and attempt to kick a goal.

It's something no American born-and-bred player ever has accomplished in the century-and-a-half that professional Australian football has existed.

"This could be fairy tale," legendary Australian footy TV commentator Dennis Cometti intones, to a nationwide audience. "He's a long way from Oklahoma State...he's a cowboy, as they all are at that university..."

As Cox drops the footy onto his right boot and kicks, Cometti continues the Old West narrative. He declares, as the ball sails through the two big posts for a goal, "and he rides it home!"

The roar at the MCG is deafening. Cox's teammates rush from everywhere to mob him, burying him under a zebra-striped avalanche of affection.

But Aussies aren't the only ones witnessing and revelling in this historic moment.

So are a batch of 18 American athletes who recently played their last NCAA basketball games for their respective colleges and universities. They're watching very late at night, inside a Redondo Beach, California hotel conference room, with the live picture being projected on a wall from someone's laptop, streaming the match. These young men are the AFL's latest recruits, here at its 2016 U.S. Combine. The AFL hopes the next Jason Holmes or Mason Cox is among them.

Even it its wildest dreams, the AFL couldn't possibly have imagined a better sales pitch for its newest recruits. Finally, the league has indisputable proof that a footy dream for these guys isn't just possible, but with the requisite perseverance, plausible.

"*Two years*," a mesmerized Denis Ryan, the Australian-born, USAFL president loudly announces to the recruits, holding up two fingers, after he high-fives his two American USAFL colleagues. "Only *two years*. That's how long it took for [Cox] to get there."

As the mighty roar at the MCG abates and Cox finally emerges from under his teammates, the American footy neophytes in the hotel conference room are transfixed — even if they can't fully comprehend the moment's significance. The game quickly becomes a rout, with Collingwood winning by 69 points. While his performance barely gets a mention in the American media, in Melbourne, Cox quickly and literally becomes the talk of the town — and all of Australia.

"I was imagining myself there, watching him," Brandon Nazione, a 6-foot-8 former Eastern Michigan University basketball player, says later, of Cox. "It was impressive to see him come out there and play the game well. I thought, if he can do it, I can do it."

Cox would go on to play 10 more matches in the 2016 season before succumbing to a hip injury, requiring season-ending surgery. Along his way to cementing a role on the team, he kicked 16 more goals and in one match even earned a vote from the umpires for the Brownlow Medal, the AFL's highest individual honor for a season of play. Cox's greatest growth came not in the ruck, where other U.S. former college basketball players are being trained, but in the forward line.

With his recovery from injury complete and a strong 2017 pre-season, Cox appeared rested and ready. This former Oklahoma State Cowboy was trotting into the sunrise of his new, unexpected professional athletic career.

1

The American Experiment

Genesis

American sporting history was about to be made — in a small Australian town called Ballarat. The moment wouldn't go down in the annals of American sports history. It wouldn't be Jesse Owens, at the 1936 Summer Olympic Games in Berlin, gracefully smashing track and field records and punching a hole in Adolf Hitler's Aryan "master race" rhetoric. It wouldn't be the David vs. Goliath drama of the U.S. Men's Olympic hockey team at the 1980 Winter Games in Lake Placid, New York, in which a group of baby-faced, college aged Americans miraculously defeated an older, powerhouse, battle-hardened Soviet Union squad.

Only the hardiest footy fans gathered at Eureka Stadium on a wintry afternoon in 2014 to witness this VFL match between the North Ballarat Roosters and the visiting Sandringham Dragons. The match wouldn't even rate a blip on the American sporting radar. Still, one man from the American Southern Bible Belt and another from a Chicago suburb were about to achieve an athletic first for their home country.

Eric Wallace, of Winston Salem, North Carolina, and Jason Holmes, from Elk Grove Village, Illinois, were facing each other, wearing their customary sleeveless jerseys and shorts, just as they did in their previous sporting lives as American college ballers. Much like a basketball referee at the opening tipoff, an official was standing with ball in hand, ready to retreat and watch the two men vault upwards, furiously trying to tap it to a teammate. But the red, oblong ball the umpire holds aloft inside a chalk-lined circle on an enormous oval expanse of grass snaps the two Americans into their new reality: Australian Rules football.

Only a couple of years before this ruck contest, Wallace had never heard of it. Holmes had only caught fleeting glimpses in America while late-night TV channel surfing. But here they were in the center circle for this VFL match, with Wallace donning the gear of the home team, the North Ballarat Roosters and Holmes in a visiting Sandringham Zebras' kit. In more than 150 years of football in Australia, no two Americans had ever played in the same match, let alone directly against each other. At that point in its history, the AFL had had one Canadian player and a handful of Australian players with American fathers; in the past there were a handful of players born Stateside but raised in Australia. Wallace and Holmes were battling for their respective clubs, but also, and more importantly, they were competing to become the AFL's first-ever born-and-bred American player.

Wallace, at 6-foot-6, and Holmes were once basketball forwards in the NCAA's Big Ten and Ohio Valley Conferences — Wallace for Ohio State and Holmes for Morehead State. They were reinventing themselves as ruckmen. And as rare as American ruckmen are in Ballarat, African-Americans, as both men are, are even rarer. To the curious crowd of several hundred, it was unusual, to say the least, seeing them playing Australia's game.

Probably unbeknownst to most of them, though, Ballarat's most famous historical moment — the bloody 19th-century rebellion of gold miners against their British rulers — actually has an African-American connection, albeit a small one.

In 1854 — the decade in which footy was born in Victoria — a Melbourne newspaper, *The Argus*, described an African-American who had journeyed to Australia, seeking to change his fortunes. He was John Joseph — like Wallace and Holmes, "a tall and powerful man." Joseph sought wealth at the Victorian goldfields. He ensconced himself in a stockade, alongside Aussie gold diggers, rebelling against the exorbitant mining license fees charged by the colonial government, which also denied them voting rights.

On December 3, 1854, while troops were killing 30 diggers, Joseph fatally shot a British officer. The Crown charged him with high treason. But in a trial that riveted the entire town, a jury acquitted him. The *Ballarat Star* reported that 10,000 people attended the verdict's reading, and many celebrated it by cheering Joseph. Some even hoisted him on their shoulders through the city's streets.

There's no doubt Wallace and Holmes would get the same love from fans of their respective AFL clubs, North Melbourne and St Kilda, if they were to kick the match-winning goal in the AFL Grand Final, equivalent in magnitude to the NFL's Super Bowl. But right now they're striving simply to earn their new teammates' and fans' respect. To win their hearts, they had to prove themselves in this unfamiliar sporting culture. If they could, they'd be all right.

Six weeks after the Ballarat match, the Collingwood Magpies — the AFL's most popular and wealthiest club — would sign another American former college basketball player, Mason Cox, a 6-foot-11 man-mountain who played at Oklahoma State University. In 2015 Alexander Aurrichio, a Columbia University graduate, journeyed to Australia to have a crack at a footy career and despite not being signed by an AFL club, earned his way onto a VFL team's roster. The same year, the league's Carlton Blues signed Matt Korcheck, a University of Arizona product and in 2016, the AFL's Gold Coast Suns signed Brandon Kaufman, a former NCAA football player who nearly made the NFL's Buffalo Bills roster after a pre-season run.

Footy in the 1980s had its initial "Irish Experiment," in which Ron Barassi, the AFL's Melbourne Demons' star player-turned-club executive recruited Gaelic footballers, such as Sean Wight and Jim Stynes, who carved out famous footy careers. In the 2010s, beginning with a handful of players who preceded Wallace and Holmes on AFL rosters, it has been America's turn to have its athletes under a microscope in the AFL's laboratory. An American college basketball guru has steered collegiate basketball players with size, athleticism and limited pro hoops opportunities to scouting combines in the U.S. run by the AFL. The prospective players must first impress the scouts with their speed, agility and basic footy skills. Then they must survive the AFL's two-week Draft Combine, in Melbourne, where they compete against top-tier Aussie teenage talent. Finally, if they make it that far, the American hopefuls must prove they can adjust to Australian life and find a place within a sporting culture that values humility and a team-first ethos. Only then might they make history.

At Eureka Stadium, Wallace and Holmes take their stances: legs apart, knees bent, arms free. In team meetings leading up to this standoff, the Zebras' coaches, in true Australian spirit, had some fun with Holmes, showing a spoof slide show of the two Americans, hyping their anticipated clash.

The umpire now holds the footy high overhead, one hand at each end, then lunges forward and slams it down.

Thud!

The ball rises high and so do the two Americans — not only to win this ruck contest and the game, but also, as Cox and the others to follow would soon learn, to meet their biggest athletic challenge yet. They've literally jumped at this chance to become professional athletes, and are now striving to make their mark.

Three hours and four quarters later, after the final siren sounds to signal the end of the match, Holmes and Wallace's encounter concludes. With 29 hitouts, four marks and two tackles, Wallace, who played as the Roosters' number one ruckman, wins this battle. He earns a vote from his coaches as one of his team's best performers. Holmes mostly plays as an understudy to his team's number one ruckman, but he still amasses 14 hitouts, takes two marks and makes two tackles. And it is Holmes's team that takes victory, 18.9 (117) to 12.10 (82).

Through the course of their improbable journey, the two Americans have bonded. Hours later, back in bustling Melbourne, they'll text each other to see about catching up. But right now, as they walk towards each other on the field, their muscles, like their minds, are drained. They're exhausted. They're still building their tanks. Footy to them is still so new, and they're so very far from home. With a quick handshake and a smile, they silently acknowledge how far they've come and how much further they have to go. It is all the two countrymen can muster.

*

American Footy aficionados of a certain age may remember the long history of footy and the United States intertwining, but in thin, sporadic strands. Australians first formally introduced the game to Americans in 1963, near the shores of Pearl Harbor, on the Hawaiian island of O'ahu. Ask who made this introduction and the Geelong Football Club will say it did. After all, the club sent precisely this message in bold, white letters on the red Qantas carry-on bags its players carried as they travelled for their exhibition match against the Melbourne Football Club. "Introducing Australian Rules Football to the USA," the words read.

The match took place on October 20, 1963, a couple of weeks after the Cats' coronation as Victorian Football League (the league's name would change in 1990, to the Australian Football League, shortly after it expanded into a nationwide competition) Premiers and only four years after Hawai'i officially became America's 50th state. The match was played on a hardscrabble pitch at Hickam Air Force Base that included a baseball pitcher's mound and yard lines from an American football field marked in chalk. As proof that Americans then knew practically nothing about Australian football, an American-produced souvenir program for fans featured a cover with an illustration of an American football player, in helmet and uniform, kicking. A crowd of 1,500 — quite impressive for a Sunday night — turned out to see Melbourne win by two goals.

Six days later, on a Saturday afternoon, the two clubs were at it again, this time on the American mainland, in San Francisco. This contest was held in the open expanse of Golden Gate Park, at Big Rec Stadium, on an improvised oval significantly larger than Australia's most famous one, the Melbourne Cricket Ground.

The park is just west of the city's Haight-Ashbury District, the de facto capital of the decade's hippie movement. But there was no "free love" felt between the two teams. According to Australian news accounts, Geelong's travel bag slogan incensed the Melbourne players. As they saw it, Geelong was dismissing the Demons' shared participation in this international venture. At one point in the match, a brawl broke out between the clubs, with combatants including players, trainers and officials. An estimated crowd of 4,000 watched Melbourne win again, this time by five points.

Besides watching a competitive and contentious match, fans could purchase, for just 50 cents, a program that was far more accurate and authentic than the one printed for the Honolulu game. This one had on its cover an action photo of Geelong's most valuable player that year, Graham "Polly" Farmer, with the words "First Exhibition of Australian Rules Football Ever Played in North America."

That match, though, would be the last glimpse of Australian football in America for nearly 20 years — until the advent of cable television networks and the rise of televised sporting events. In 1979, out of a small studio in, Connecticut, the TV network that would in a few years revolutionize the way sports fans worldwide would watch sports took flight. When ESPN was launched, the network had eager American sports fans hungry for live events, but no contracts with any of the major U.S. leagues. As a result, it was a challenge for ESPN to fill 24 hours of programming.

"We had Irish hurling, billiards and anything else we could come up with," recalls Bill Rasmussen, the network's first CEO and president. "Our mission statement was that we'd provide sports anytime, anywhere."

One of Rasmussen's lieutenants was Chet Simmons, who had previously served at two other American TV networks and who, Rasmussen said, "had the pulse of what was happening in sports around the world." When the opportunity came up to cover the VFL, Simmons told Rasmussen, "Let's do a deal." What did ESPN have to lose? With the massive time difference between the two countries, most live VFL matches would take place in America's weekend wee hours, so airing them would be an easy way to fill hours. ESPN wasn't expecting its VFL coverage to gain a following, but it did. Many current American footy fans in their 40s and older — and assorted insomniacs — likely remember getting their first taste of Australia's game this way.

"It was so early in our evolution as a network and [Australian Rules] was something Americans had never seen," Rasmussen says. "It became very popular. The Nielsen Company didn't measure our ratings until the late-'80s, but a lot of people weren't happy years later when it went away. A lot of people wrote letters to us, wanting it back. They were an avid audience, but they didn't represent a big audience."

ESPN's airing of VFL matches was one element of a coalescing storm of Australian popular culture that swept across America in the early 1980s. Aussie films such as *Mad Max* and its sequel, *The Road Warrior*, released in the States in 1980 and 1982 respectively, gained critical acclaim and a cult following. Rock band Men at Work owned the American pop music charts in 1982 and 1983 with two best-selling albums, including the group's seminal song, "Down Under," which alone sold 2 million copies. Independent American TV stations snapped up and aired *The Paul Hogan Show* late at night on the weekends. By the end of the 1980s, Hogan's comedy, especially his two *Crocodile Dundee* movies, had saturated America, while his signature phrases — "Come and say g'day" and "Throw some shrimp on the 'barbie'" — were well known from the Australian Tourism Commission's relentless marketing campaign to American TV audiences. Foster's beer, packaged in motor oil-sized cans, became staples in American liquor stores. ESPN also televised the hotly contested America's Cup sailing races throughout the decade.

While Australiana continued to resonate in America by the end of the 1980s, the foothold Australian Rules had established had faded. By 1984 ESPN was televising American college football, as well as the new, professional United States Football League, of which Simmons was the inaugural commissioner. In 1987 ESPN landed the ultimate American TV prize: broadcast rights to the NFL.

Still, if not for the exposure Aussie Rules had enjoyed via ESPN, it's highly doubtful that four VFL/AFL clubs would have organized U.S. exhibition matches. In 1989 the Essendon Bombers and Hawthorn Hawks entertained 10,000 fans at Joe Robbie Stadium in Miami. The next year, across the country in Portland, Oregon, nearly 15,000 watched the North Melbourne Kangaroos take on West Coast Eagles at Civic Stadium.

In 1996 Essendon's head coach Kevin Sheedy recruited Dwayne Armstrong, a scarcely known former Iowa State University defensive back as Australian Rules football's first American athlete. That same year a combination of Aussie expats and Americans who most likely had first seen footy played on ESPN launched the amateur United States Australian Football League (USAFL). The competition today boasts around three-dozen men's and women's clubs from every region of the country, and hosts an annual, national tournament. In 2002 and 2003 it began selecting players for a national men's team, called USA Revolution, and a national women's side, USA Freedom, which would represent the country at the AFL's International Cup, played in Australia every three years.

Some men's teams, such as the Orange County Bombers and the Kansas City Power, and women's clubs the Boston Lady Demons and the New York Lady Magpies, derive their nicknames from the AFL clubs that have donated to them jerseys, shorts, balls and other equipment. Other USAFL clubs, such as the Tulsa Buffaloes, the St. Petersburg Starfish, the Los Angeles Dragons, the San Francisco Iron Maidens and the Columbus Jillaroos created original identities.

The USAFL season runs from April to September, with the annual national tournament held in a different city each year, usually two weeks after the AFL Grand Final, in mid-October. Most teams are coached by Australian expats, and players are a mix of people of varying ages, skill levels and experience, from both countries.

*

In the early 1980s some forward-thinking VFL clubs began looking to other corners of the world for talented recruits. The Melbourne Demons famously signed Sean Wight and Jim Stynes, while Sydney later unearthed a Premiership player in Tadhg Kennelly. But arguably it was Paul Roos who should get credit for launching the American Experiment, in 2009.

Roos retired after the 1998 season from a brilliant playing career and was living the next year in the U.S. with his American wife, Tami, and watching a lot of college basketball. Through the Swans' former owner and avid sportsman Basil Sellers, Roos met and befriended the legendary NCAA basketball coach Richard F. "Digger" Phelps. While watching basketball games and admiring the players' athleticism, Roos had a proverbial light bulb moment. With their extraordinary height and athleticism, could American college basketball players possibly become AFL ruckmen?

The question continued to linger in Roos's mind after he returned to Australia and in 2002 was appointed the Swans' head coach. Through his continuing friendship with Phelps, Roos — even while coaching Sydney to the 2005 AFL Premiership — was always looking for ways to improve the club, so he periodically picked Phelps's brain about whether American hoopsters might have the skill set to adapt to footy. So about four years after winning the 2005 flag, he asked Phelps if he knew of any athletes who might fit the bill. Phelps then phoned a cadre of other college coaches, who all told him of one young man they thought could: Shae McNamara. He had just finished his amateur basketball career at Marist College, in New York, and was getting set to play a season with a German pro team. McNamara had no idea he was being watched from afar, or that soon he would become the trial subject in the AFL's American Experiment. Ultimately, Collingwood drafted him with pick 47 in the 2009 AFL Rookie Draft.

Being the AFL's leading proponent of the idea of recruiting American basketball players, Roos may have been disappointed not to have drafted McNamara, but he wasn't deterred. By 2011 he had convinced Sellers to fund a Swans scouting combine for a handful of American collegiate athletes at Velocity Sports, an athletic testing facility in the Los Angeles suburb of Redondo Beach. One of the invitees, Alex Starling, made a big impression. At 22, he was a basketball standout at Bethune Cookman University, a small, historically African-American school founded in 1904 in Daytona Beach, Florida, by Dr. Mary McLeod Bethune, a teacher and activist whose parents were former slaves. Roos and the other Swans recruiters were blown away by Starling's athleticism and drive to perfect the basic skills he was taught.

The Swans utilized an AFL recruiting rule called the International Scholarship Scheme, which allows clubs to train overseas recruits in their home countries and in Australia as they finished their studies. Sydney quickly registered Starling in the program.

With Starling and McNamara both in the AFL system, it became clear the American Experiment was yielding some initial success and uncovering a potentially enormous untapped reservoir of talent. As the AFL's international and national talent manager, Kevin Sheehan, says, "We have a massive shortage of talls, and it's hard to get anyone at that height with elite athleticism."

So in August 2012, the AFL sent Sheehan, with AFL Academies Development Manager Mick Ablett (a former player and coach of the USAFL's Las Vegas Gamblers), International Development Manager Tony Woods, and Kennelly, to Velocity Sports to preside over its inaugural two-day U.S. Combine.

The AFL brought together athletes from all over America: 19 former NCAA basketball players, four former NCAA football players and two who actually had footy experience, playing in the USAFL. The prospects ranged in age from 22 to 26, and in height from 6 feet to 6-foot-9. A month later the league would fly the best three athletes to Melbourne, where they would compete with Australian amateurs in another combine and attend the Grand Final.

The candidates were an eclectic mix. One, Spencer Perrin, had never seen or touched an Australian Rules football. But he had experience as an international professional athlete, having played the previous two years on basketball teams in Slovakia and Hungary.

Another, Yannick Crowder, a former Florida A&M University hoopster, grabbed a footy, looked at it quizzically and attempted to bounce it — with two hands. Former Boise State University gridiron player Derrell Acrey, unfamiliar with the routineness in footy of marking a kick, would beam and whoop for joy every time he caught one of Kennelly's drop punts.

"The ball was different, bigger," Acrey says. "At first I started throwing it like [an American] football. The [marking] part is easy, but my bouncing needs work."

Tyler Mounce, of the USAFL's Orange County Bombers and Emmanuel Moody, a former University of Florida Gators' halfback, had become a half-forward for the USAFL's Dallas Magpies, seemingly had an advantage over their peers — especially after Moody ran a 20-meter sprint in under three seconds. But after the two-day trial, neither Moody nor Mounce — a 6-foot-3 ruckman who has for years captained the Bombers and been a multiple winner of its "best and fairest" award — was picked.

Instead, the AFL chose Crowder, B.J. Shearry, a 6-foot-7 candidate from the University of California Riverside, and a quietly confident, chiseled basketball player from Seattle University, for whom bouncing the footy seemed as natural as taking a breath — Eric Wallace.

The AFL filmed some parts of its first formal experiment, showcasing the results on its website. The scouts who ran the combine left with a good feeling that they were on to something. Woods expressed the league's desire to make the U.S. Combines annual, saying, "Elite athletes have an extraordinary desire to be successful. We'd be remiss as a sport not to reach out across the world."

2

The Prime Specimen

"Dazzling" Dwayne Armstrong

At first, it was a joke. Just a man playfully pulling a friend's leg. But at that moment, in 1995, if the AFL's most powerful and influential figure had only known how his remark to a fellow footy heavyweight would completely transform another man's life, he would've been "gobsmacked."

It was halftime at the MCG, where a crowd of about 95,000 was witnessing the inaugural blockbuster match between Collingwood and Essendon to commemorate Anzac Day. After each team kicked six goals in the first quarter, the Bombers were leading, 9.7 (61) to 7.3 (45) at halftime. The Bombers' Gary O'Donnell, Che Cockatoo-Collins and James Hird were pacing their attack, while the Magpies' Nathan Buckley was influential and Saverio Rocca was on his way to booting nine goals.

Inside the MCG's Legends Room, at a formal luncheon, AFL CEO Ross Oakley approached Melbourne Demons icon Ron Barassi's table. Oakley had in tow a 27-year-old guest whose African-American ethnicity, foreign accent, muscular 6-foot-2, 200-lb. frame — and T-shirt and blue jeans — made him stand out from everyone else in the room.

"Ron," Oakley began, "this is Dwayne Armstrong. He's an American gridiron player we're going to convert to play our game." The comment was no more than a put-on, and both Armstrong and Barassi laughed as they shook hands. Then Barassi introduced Armstrong to other assorted famous footy old-timers.

Armstrong intrigued Barassi and his mates, and they peppered him with questions about his American football background. Australians at the time were taking greater notice of American football because, a year earlier, the NFL's San Diego Chargers had lured Darren Bennett, a former Melbourne Demons' full forward, to the U.S. to be their punter. At the table, the men asked Armstrong why he had come to Australia and what he planned to do while there.

The engaging and outgoing Armstrong told them he'd only been in Melbourne a short time. He was planning to sort out his professional life and wanted to see a new country.

Three years earlier Armstrong had graduated from Iowa State, where he played football and earned a bachelor's degree in marketing and advertising. He dreamed of an NFL career. Although no team drafted him, Armstrong hoped the Los Angeles Raiders, who retained him on their practice squad, would one day activate him. Armstrong was living at home with his mother, Kathryn, in Costa Mesa, California, earning a living managing a valet car parking service.

A night out with his cousin in nearby Newport Beach, during the Christmas holiday season would forever alter the course of Armstrong's life. At a festive nightclub, he locked eyes with a young, attractive blonde woman and they started a conversation. She told him she was Australian. She had just been crowned the winner of the women's Australian body-shaping championship and had come to America on an extended, working holiday. Her name was Melanie Oakley.

The pair was immediately taken with each other. They chatted that night and soon afterwards began dating — but their time together was limited. She had to return home to Melbourne. Though the distance between them was vast, love was blossoming and they both wanted to see where their new relationship might lead. With her parents' blessing, Oakley invited Armstrong to visit her and stay with her family in an upscale Melbourne suburb.

In March of 1995, Armstrong arrived in Melbourne, and Melanie introduced him to her father, Ross. Armstrong didn't know anything about Australian Rules football or the AFL, but he and Oakley fast became friends. Oakley grew to admire Armstrong's interest in business and nurtured his entrepreneurial spirit.

Because of Armstrong's athletic background, Oakley thought he'd enjoy a day at the footy, so he took his new protégé to the Anzac Day match. Thinking his colleagues and Australian fans might enjoy hearing a visiting American athlete's impressions of footy, he invited Armstrong to address a gathering of 250 people at a pre-match function. Armstrong was a hit. Perhaps because all eyes had just been on him, he wasn't at all nervous when chatting at halftime to Barassi and the other footy luminaries.

The group enjoyed beers and wine, and heard the crowd's occasional roars from behind the windows of their viewing box. As Essendon and Collingwood battled to a famous draw, the conversation flowed.

"What do you think of our game?" Barassi asked Armstrong.

"It's great," Armstrong answered. "It's like a giant game of basketball. TV doesn't do it justice. There are lots of things happening off the ball. These guys have to be fit, because they never stop running."

"Why do you gridiron players wear helmets and pads?" another man at the table asked Armstrong.

"You'd *need* equipment if I ran through you," Armstrong replied with a grin.

"How do you reckon you'd go in *our* game?" Barassi challenged him.

"If you put me out on the field," Armstrong said, playfully upping the ante, "in three years I bet I'd have you cheering for me at this stadium."

Barassi wasn't taken aback by Armstrong's brashness. "You ought to give it a crack," he said matter-of-factly. "You've got the right physique."

The wheels in Armstrong's mind began turning. Later, he told Oakley he was seriously considering Barassi's challenge. Two days later, Oakley called the Bombers' head coach, Kevin Sheedy, the one man in the AFL who might just be audacious enough to try out the American. Sheedy soon phoned Oakley back, and asked to chat with Armstrong.

"I heard you were here," Sheedy told him. "I heard that you're fit, so why don't you come down, meet the boys and have a go?" Armstrong couldn't refuse an athletic challenge like this, which whetted his competitive appetite. It was just what he did. Because his father, Welton, who had served as a technical sergeant in the U.S. Air Force, had died when Dwayne was just 4, his athletic older brother Kevin had become his proxy dad. A few months after Welton's death, Kathryn Armstrong had moved the family from Ft. Belvoir, Virginia, to the Los Angeles suburb of Carson, near where her younger brother lived. She is a seamstress by trade, but Kathryn Armstrong supported herself and her children by working for an insurance company. In Carson and, later, Santa Ana, another Southern California city, Dwayne often played sports against Kevin's friends.

After Kevin Armstrong was enshrined in his high-school hall of fame, he won a scholarship to Princeton and co-captained its football team. He earned a molecular biology degree, and then a medical degree from the University of California Los Angeles, after which he worked as the NFL's Pittsburgh Steelers' assistant team physician.

In Dwayne's teenage years, in addition to playing football, he showed promise as a baseball centerfielder. Armstrong likened Barassi's footy challenge to the time he learned how to surf, which he did as a teenager, while living three straight summers in Hawai'i with a friend and his family. After cutting his surfing teeth on Waikiki Beach waves, Armstrong participated in several California competitions.

When Armstrong arrived at his first Essendon training, he discovered he wasn't the club's only novelty player. Werner Reiterer, the Austrian-born, Australian-raised, 28-year-old, two-time Olympic Games discus thrower was also trying out for Sheedy.

The two new recruits' presence didn't surprise Gary O'Donnell, Essendon's captain, who in club's 1993 premiership season was voted its most valuable player. "'Sheeds' was ahead of his time," O'Donnell says. "He has been a pioneer in the game in recruiting Indigenous Australians, as well. There were always five or six Aboriginal fellows with us. They added life and unpredictability to the list."

One of them was Che Cockatoo-Collins, whose Indigenous heritage includes the Yupangathi tribe, of Australia's Cape York Peninsula, and the Gangalidda, of northwest Queensland. Cockatoo-Collins, who had kicked three goals in the Anzac Day match Armstrong attended, quickly became the American's new best mate, both at the club and away from it. Cockatoo-Collins, who arrived at Essendon the year after the club's 1993 premiership, and later retired from the Port Adelaide Power the year before winning the 2004 Premiership, now lives on Queensland's North Stradbroke Island. He still treasures the moment he first saw Armstrong attempt a kick.

"He couldn't kick for *shit!*" Cockatoo Collins says, and then explodes in prolonged laughter — the kind only two close mates can share, at the other's expense. "He was *terrible*. He didn't know what to do. I thought, 'What are we gonna do here?' He held the ball in a way that his leg was reaching for it. I didn't want him to feel bad, so I grabbed him after the first training session to practice with him. It was like a child not being able to read. He needed to know the fundamentals — to feel good about himself and gain some confidence. He wanted to learn himself. We practiced over and over." Sometimes that was an hour before or after training — or both.

"We had to start from the absolute basics," Cockatoo-Collins recalls. "He might've gotten one out of 20 kicks that was right. We just had to be patient with him, to tell him to put his head down and move forward and to maintain the technique."

Cockatoo-Collins today works for the Australian oil and gas producer Santos, as an adviser on the company's engagement with Aboriginal communities. This means helping bridge the cultural gaps between white corporate interests and the land's Indigenous traditional owners, so he often travels to remote Northern Territory communities. Cockatoo-Collins's cross-cultural bridge building may very well have started with Armstrong.

"If I were going to the US, it'd be very hard if I didn't have anyone who cared for and valued me," Cockatoo-Collins says. "We kinda clicked."

While Armstrong says the entire team embraced him — James Hird, whose illustrious playing career would make him the face of the Essendon franchise — occasionally drove him to training. While other teammates invited Armstrong to their weddings and bachelor parties — he and Cockatoo-Collins became brothers.

Cockatoo-Collins was living near the Bombers' training facilities, so he often had Armstrong over to his home. He introduced his new mate to his two younger, twin brothers, Don and David, who were playing for the Melbourne Demons. They'd often watch American sporting events or dissect AFL matches on TV, but they closely bonded by sharing their experiences of being men of color who lived in mostly white countries.

Cockatoo-Collins told Armstrong his father Leslie named him after South American revolutionary Che Guevara. Armstrong was surprised, though, when Cockatoo-Collins told him his father had been a member of the Australian Black Panther Party, which modeled itself after the group African-American militants started.

"We exchanged a lot of notes on the history of our peoples that we were aware of," Cockatoo-Collins says. "We would say that what happened in America is the same as what happened here."

Besides the soul-searching and deep discussions, the two men occasionally ventured out to Melbourne nightspots. "But he didn't ever go silly on alcohol and there were no drugs, so I had no concern about his being unpredictable," Cockatoo-Collins says. "That's how we connected — our values were pretty similar."

*

Armstrong spent some months travelling in Australia as the 1995 AFL season played out, but after it ended in September, his training began in October, ahead of the March start of the 1996 season. In addition to learning the basics — kicking, marking, handballing and the rules — Armstrong was coping with a strenuous physical regimen unlike what he experienced in the US

"I wasn't fit enough," he recalls. "I was a sprinter. With gridiron, it's anaerobic, not aerobic like footy. I had to learn to swim, bike, and run, in training. I'd never had that sort of fitness. U.S. football is explosive running. You look at AFL footballers, they're like horses. They have to run, kick and handball for four quarters. The tackling isn't as hard as in the NFL, but you still get knocked around. You're more fatigued. In the NFL, you run for 10 seconds and rest, but AFL is an extreme contact sport. It's a lot of work for two hours and at the end, there's no lactic acid left in the body."

While Sheedy was playing Armstrong in intraclub practice matches, his new pupil was being tested mentally. In small town Ames, Iowa, Armstrong had been far from the limelight, but in Melbourne he was in the spotlight glare of the big-city footy media, most of whose members doubted his footy prospects.

One scribe, Nic Bideau, wrote a column headlined "Nice idea, guys, but don't quit your day job." Armstrong, he said, "with his great strength, 10.40 sec 100m speed and natural athleticism, would be useful running around the ground shepherding [blocking] for his teammates, but I can't imagine how he would ever get the ball. And if he did, I can't imagine him spinning on to his left foot and snapping [kicking] a goal."

While Armstrong was in his first preseason, another international recruit, the Demons' Irish ruckman Jim Stynes, was preparing for his 10th AFL season. After struggling at first and even incurring a crucial onfield penalty which many observers felt cost his club a 1987 Grand Final berth, Stynes steeled himself and went on to win the 1991 Brownlow Medal. Because Stynes had set such a lofty benchmark for any aspiring international Aussie Rules footballer, comparisons to him — perhaps unfairly — were inevitable.

Indeed, in his column about Armstrong, Bideau wrote: "Only Melbourne's Irish import Jim Stynes has been able to transform his athleticism from another game to football. And he came from Gaelic football, probably the only other sport in the world similar to Australian rules. Perhaps 30 years ago, when football was based around a distinctive mark and kick style ... Armstrong could have made a fist of it."

Instead of retreating from media criticism, Armstrong not only read Bideau's column, he kept a copy. "I was known only as 'the Kevin Sheedy experiment'," he says. "I used the article as motivation."

In February 1996, a month before the start of the AFL season, Sheedy — ever the promoter of the Essendon brand — was eager to showcase his team throughout Australia. He knew the club had supporters in Perth. The Fremantle Dockers, the AFL expansion club outside of Perth, that had just completed its first season but was playing under the shadow of its local rival, the West Coast Eagles, wanted to win new fans in rural Western Australia. So the two clubs' officials booked a preseason match at a ground 60 miles east of Perth.

Back at Essendon, after a training run a few days before the scheduled match, Sheedy found Armstrong. "Listen, Dwayne," the coach said, "we want to take you to Fremantle."

Armstrong was over the moon. The Bombers added Armstrong to their supplemental players list and Sheedy made the selection official at a team dinner, announcing the move to his troops, who broke out in applause and cheers.

The Bombers' assistant coach was David Wheadon, a disciple from afar of the legendary 1960s Green Bay Packers' coach Vince Lombardi, who famously got marginally talented players to perform above their capabilities. Armstrong had clear limitations: he had strength and speed, and he could tackle, but both his kicking and his reading the action on the field were poor. Wheadon decided to play him in the backline, where play would unfold before his eyes and he could react to what his opponent did.

Nevertheless, Armstrong faced a tough match-day assignment: guarding the Dockers' speedy and electrifying half-forward Winston Abraham. The previous season, he'd kicked 23 goals in just 12 matches.

What do I have to lose? Armstrong thought. *If I do the right things, who knows what'll happen?*

With the summer temperatures reaching near 100, the clubs agreed to shift the match to Fremantle Oval. There, the clubs hoped, the customary Indian Ocean afternoon breeze which locals affectionately call "the Fremantle Doctor" would cool things down by the 3:30 p.m. opening bounce. The heat even made officials from both teams consider shortening the quarters, but instead the start time was pushed back to 4 p.m.

On match day, the Bombers issued Armstrong with their famous black and red jersey, with number 20 on the back. As he ran out onto the field with his teammates, Armstrong noticed a group of local Aboriginal men near the tunnel, who launched into a chant he'd often heard at home, but at this moment seemed incredibly out of place: "U-S-A! U-S-A!"

Armstrong started the match on the bench — until, early in the first quarter, as if from the heavens, the footy gods reached down and touched him. An Essendon half-forward twisted his ankle and came off the ground. Sheedy, thinking quickly, saw an opportunity. He called out to Armstrong from the boundary line. "Dwayne!" he yelled, "go to the forward pocket!"

Armstrong stood up and looked at his teammates on the bench. "Guys," he asked, "where's the forward pocket?"

Quickly — and discreetly — they told him it was the area deep in their forward 50, to either side of the goal posts.

"If the ball comes to you," a teammate in the forward line told Armstrong, "handball it, or run and kick the goal."

If the ball comes near me, Armstrong was thinking, *I'm gonna beat my guy to the ball.*

Uncannily, that scenario played out exactly. A loose ball careened towards Armstrong, who was in the pocket 25 meters from goal. He pounced and grabbed it, then looked around.

"*Gimme the ball!*" yelled his teammate Matthew Lloyd, then just a second-year player with greatness ahead of him.

Armstrong got a handball away, but just as he did a Freo defender, whose hip-and-shoulder bump sent him sprawling to the ground, hit him hard. The umpire blew the whistle and ordered Lloyd to give him the ball, which he then handed to Armstrong. Again, Armstrong looked around, searching for answers.

"It's your kick!" Lloyd called out to Armstrong.

His club's immediate fate was now literally in Armstrong's hands.

"You could sense an apprehension on his face," recalls Les Everett, the Fremantle Dockers' official historian, who produced the match program and covered the event for the old *Fremantle Herald* newspaper. He was watching on from against a fence under the shade of the grandstand. "It was an expression like, 'Oh, *shit*! What am I gonna do?'"

O'Donnell ran over to Armstrong. "Steady," he told him, "just like in training. "Line up and kick the ball straight."

But that was exactly Armstrong's problem. Even all the work he'd put in with Cockatoo-Collins hadn't helped much. Armstrong hadn't yet had a kick in this match — in fact, in *any* match.

Meanwhile, the crowd of about 3,000 was buzzing.

"With practice games, there isn't the intensity amongst the crowd and Fremantle was in control right from the start," Everett says. "But the novelty of having an American playing for the opposition definitely interested the crowd. People were really aware of Dwayne and his situation. The crowd was on his side."

Armstrong walked back from the mark. In the distance beyond the goals to which he was kicking towered Fremantle Prison, the grim colonial-era building where almost four-dozen convicts had been condemned to death. Armstrong took a deep breath. He trotted towards the mark, cradling the ball vertically in his hands. He steadied. He dropped the ball over his right boot and, not smoothly, swung his right leg.

As the footy took flight, the kick didn't look great, but it rose toward the goalposts. A few seconds later, the goal umpire marched up to the goal line, preparing to signal the result to the crowd. As he drew both arms up to his waist, he extended them and pointed both index fingers forward, meaning only one thing — goal! A loud roar reverberated through the grandstand.

The Essendon players, from those on the ground to those the interchange bench, laughed and cheered. Dwayne Armstrong, the first-ever born-and-bred American to play in an AFL-sanctioned match, had just kicked a goal — from his very first kick.

Armstrong jogged back to his position, his right fist raised in the air. O'Donnell was the first teammate to greet him with a high-10 — a millisecond before his other delirious, celebratory teammates mobbed him.

"They told me later it was the longest kick, in terms of time, they ever watched," Armstrong reflects, laughing at the moment's improbability. "After that, it was full on. There were so many skirmishes. Fremantle were like, 'We're not gonna let this USA kid beat us up.'" But if any opponent harshly bumped Armstrong, away from the umpires' watching eyes, the Bombers responded in kind. "From then on," Armstrong says. "I knew every game, the boys had my back."

The Dockers would win the match by 54 points. But a match report published in the now-defunct magazine *Sports Weekly* trumpeted Armstrong's feat with a splashy headline: "Dazzling Dwayne."

"The highlight in a lackluster match was the performance of the league's only exchange student, American gridiron player Dwayne Armstrong ... [who] booted a goal with his first kick in an AFL match," the article read. "Is this another recruiting coup from Kevin Sheedy, or are the NFL trying to repay us for Darren Bennett?"

The goal was Armstrong's only impact on the match. He still had loads to learn and the coaches didn't play him in any other preseason games. The Bombers assigned him to their reserves squad, where he played all 22 games, many of which were "curtain raisers" against other clubs' reserves squads, before the varsity clubs' matches, which often took place at the MCG. Armstrong's role mostly consisted of "tagging" — attempting to negate one designated, impactful opponent for entire matches.

"We used him as a tagger to run with blokes who were good players," O'Donnell recalls. "He was like a blanket. There was no daylight between him and his opponent. He played his role to the letter."

*

A few months into Armstrong's first season, a notable and curious fan turned up at a handful of Essendon's reserves matches: Dwayne's mother, Kathryn, who flew to Australia to spend a few weeks with him at the Oakley home.

"Dwayne called me and said he was gonna play footy, but I didn't know their football existed," says Kathryn, a retiree who now lives in Las Vegas. She was born and raised in the American Deep South, in a rural paper-milling town called Bogalusa, Louisiana, about 70 miles north of New Orleans. 'My daughter and I started researching it and then I took off and went to Australia. I fell in love with the Oakleys. They were welcoming and down-to-earth and made me feel like a member of their family. Ross was like a surrogate father to Dwayne."

Armstrong was buoyed by his mother's visit. Towards the end of his first campaign he was excited to be joining his teammates on another tradition footy players at all levels engage in — an end-of-season trip. But the Bombers' players still hadn't yet picked a destination. One day in the rooms, Armstrong asked a group of them, "Hey, boys, where are we going on the trip?"

Wheadon, who was standing nearby, overheard Armstrong. "I know where *your* trip is," the coach told him. "You're going to the Northern Territory. You're gonna go up there and get some skills under your belt. We've already got a place for you to stay."

That place was the city of Darwin, on Australia's "Top End." Armstrong would stay in a room in the home of the general manager of a team called the Wanderers, one of the two clubs that in 1916 founded the Northern Territory Football League (NTFL). Russell Jeffrey, who forged a 50-game AFL career with St Kilda and Brisbane, was the Wanderers' player-head coach who was tasked with training Armstrong further.

"This'll be interesting," Jeffrey remembers thinking.

But when his new recruit turned up, Jeffrey was impressed.

"Straightaway I could tell he was there to learn," he says. "He was willing to listen and didn't do a lot of talking."

But his kicking?

"Shocking," Jeffrey recalls with a laugh. So was his marking. "I almost went off the ground in the first training session when I first saw him mark," Jeffrey says. "It was hysterical. It was freaky to watch. He was marking the way NFL players do, clamping down on the ball with one arm on top and the other coming up from the bottom. No one had seen anyone mark the ball like that. It was hilarious! When he was playing, he was *still* doing that."

So Jeffrey, born into the Woolwonga Aboriginal tribe, took a similar tack to coaching Armstrong as he did with many of the Indigenous players who spoke Tiwi, Yolngu, Yolngu Matha and Creole as their primary languages; English was often their third or fourth. "Everything had to be done by showing and not talking," says Jeffrey, who now works for Indigenous Construction Resource Group (ICRG) North, a mining, gas and oil resources firm that partners on projects with Aboriginal communities. "That's the approach I took with Dwayne. I didn't want to confuse him with terms he might not have known."

Jeffrey envisioned exploiting Armstrong's speed. "Our game is based on evasion skills, and I told him about the pace of the game. He said, 'Good, man, I'm *fast*,'" Jeffrey says. "Then, in his second or third game he goes, 'Oh, *man*, these guys are fast! I can't *believe* how fast these guys are!'" Jeffrey continues, playfully impersonating Armstrong's voice in a tone that sounds like African-American comedic actor Kevin Hart's. "That blew him away compared to the AFL, where the leg speed wasn't as pronounced."

Armstrong became a decent enough kick, Jeffrey says, that he was accurate when passing the ball short distances. Over the course of the Wanderers' 14-match season, the players became aware of that and used it to their benefit.

If Armstrong wasn't "Dazzling Dwayne" on the field in Darwin, as he was that one day in Fremantle, he certainly was dazzling off it. He relished the formal and informal speaking engagements the club arranged for him: he met Aboriginal children and adults, and was able to travel all over the Northern Territory, including one visit to remote Arnhem Land.

Jeffrey vividly remembers one occasion at a Darwin school. "Lots of these communities hadn't ever seen an African-American, except on TV, so here was this well built athlete who was a black man who spoke totally differently," he says. "His accent alone was enough to get a laugh. They were extremely captivated by him. He got asked a hell of a lot of questions. People from the club and our supporters gravitated to him. He was always willing to tell his story."

Armstrong returned to Essendon in 1997 for his second season, the same year Oakley was transitioning out of the AFL to focus on his own business, Oakley Enterprises. That company's acquiring the license to sell NFL products in Australia would shortly impact Armstrong's footy future — but not before Armstrong would be part of another attention-capturing moment on the field.

In a match against the Richmond Tigers, the Essendon reserves had just kicked a behind, meaning Richmond would put the ball back in play from their defensive end, "kicking-in" from the goal square. For whatever reason, the ball lay idle in the goal square, waiting for a Tiger player to send it back into play. Armstrong was playing forward that day, but in his role as a defender he'd been practicing kick-ins. So when he saw no one going near the ball — and even though he was at the wrong end of the ground — he picked it up. In front of his bemused teammates and opponents, he attempted a kick-in. An umpire blew his whistle and restored order.

"Dwayne thought maybe we were kicking in," recalls Mark Williams, then the Essendon reserves senior coach. "Even he laughs about it now."

Armstrong also laughs at some of the taunts rival fans aimed at him. "I remember playing Carlton at the MCG," he says, "and I heard this 'Steeeerooooids!' chant when I ran out — from the Carlton fans."

Despite Armstrong's work ethic, perseverance and magnetic personality, as a smaller player he just couldn't master kicking in his two years well enough to earn a spot with Essendon's first teamers. "If you're smaller and can't kick, that reduces your chances," Williams says flatly. "Smaller blokes have to kick the ball and do it accurately." Nonetheless, Armstrong had moments of triumph in his second season. In another match against Richmond, again playing forward, he kicked three goals. But Armstrong says he's proudest of playing on experienced AFL opponents and holding his own.

*

Off the field, Oakley introduced Armstrong to the concept of NFL Properties, for which Oakley Enterprises had a product licensing deal. He hired Armstrong part-time, while he continued his footy. In the 1997 season Oakley reached out to Armstrong with something even more promising: a full-time gig as his company's NFL development manager. The company would arrange a work visa for Armstrong; his first assignment would be to organize an NFL exhibition game in Sydney.

Armstrong, who was making about $230 Australian (about $165 US) in match payments as an Essendon reserve, plus income from a part-time AFL marketing department job, occasional modeling work and freelance NFL contract jobs, couldn't possibly decline the offer. Accepting it also allowed him to stay on in his adopted home.

"I had an opportunity to build a career, make real good money and travel the world," he says. "To Essendon, I was like, 'Thank you guys very much, but I need to move on.'"

The Bombers players and coaches were sad to see him go, but they understood. Even though he hadn't played a regular season AFL game, after nearly 60 with the Essendon twos and the Wanderers combined, Armstrong left a lasting impression on his teammates.

"Dwayne brought unbelievable attention to detail and the desire to learn the basics," Cockatoo-Collins says. "He increased the work ethic of the other players. He gave everyone a reality check and made players better for it."

In his six years with Oakley Enterprises, Armstrong helped bring over the San Diego Chargers and the Denver Broncos for a 1999 exhibition game. He helped get the NFL broadcast on Australian television and introduced flag football to Australian schoolchildren. With Bennett, the Demon-turned-Charger, Armstrong ran "Superpunt," an Australia-wide talent search for NFL punting prospects. At a Superpunt event at Waverley Park, a large AFL stadium outside Melbourne, Armstrong discovered Mat McBriar, who for his kicking skills earned a football scholarship to the University of Hawai'i, and afterwards played 11 NFL seasons.

But with Armstrong's professional success soaring, one aspect of his personal life nosedived. After their six-year romance, he and Melanie Oakley broke up. Cockatoo-Collins was the mate who comforted Armstrong. "He was quite down," he says. "It was heartbreaking. She was really the reason he got started in footy."

By 2003, though, Armstrong had moved into a loft in Melbourne's Fitzroy neighborhood and again fallen in love. This time it was with a Kiwi woman named Tracy Coutts, a Christchurch-born flight attendant. Armstrong signed on with Dickies Sportswear and later worked in sales and marketing positions in Australia with American Apparel and his current employer, Silver Crystal Sports Inc., a Canadian-based apparel retailer. One of Armstrong's ongoing projects is working with AFL clubs' retail stores, enabling them to customize the backs of their jumpers for fans, using on-site touch-screens to add names and numbers.

A little more than 20 years after her son first departed for Australia, Kathryn Armstrong remains pleasantly surprised by the turn of events that changed Dwayne's life. "Never in my wildest dreams did I think he'd stay," she says. "I didn't think he'd leave America. It just wasn't in the plan, ever. But he's a real go-getter."

Dwayne Armstrong and Tracy Coutts now live comfortably in the Melbourne suburb of Preston, and have two sons, Tyler, 9, and Maddox, 8. They both play in the under-10s for Strathmore Football Club. Like his dad, Tyler also plays in the backline, and in 2015 was the club's runner-up most valuable player. Both Tyler and Maddox have won medals in track and field competitions.

Armstrong, now 48, takes his sons to the footy a few times each season. He barracks for Essendon. "It's still my club," he says. "They gave me my first opportunity."

He feels for his old teammate Hird, whom he says was publicly and unfairly scapegoated after a "supplements scandal" in 2013, in which he was Essendon's head coach. The AFL and an independent, international doping agency found the club guilty of running a program in which players were injected with banned drugs. "It's hard for one guy to take the brunt," Armstrong says. "He wasn't the one injecting the players."

The AFL suspended Hird after the 2013 season, but he was reinstated for 2015. Hird again coached Armstrong's old club, but subsequently resigned after the club won just five of its first 19 games into the 22-game season. In January 2016, the AFL banned for a calendar year, an astonishing 34 Bombers players who had been injected. In January 2017 Hird, in virtual exile from the footy world, again made Australian headlines — for his emergency hospitalization after a life-threatening incident authorities called a drug overdose.

Even though Essendon once employed her son, oddly enough, Kathryn Armstrong, through her many visits to Australia over the years, has become an avid Collingwood supporter. A friend she made on one of those trips recruited her into the Magpie Army while attending an MCG match. Kathryn became such a fan that she adopted Andrew Krakouer as her favorite player; "I loved the way he kicked and hustled around the field," she says. Even today, she lovingly refers to him as "my Andrew" and has a badge with his face on it. She sometimes wears a Collingwood 2010 members' cap, while a Collingwood pillow adorns her sofa.

Dwayne Armstrong, meanwhile, still looks fit enough to have a run with a club. He still eats right and recently hit the gym and began running again. He never had much hair when he was a Bomber, and these days Armstrong is mostly bald, with small flecks of grey above his silver-studded ears. A small black soul patch covers part of his chin. Armstrong has become an Australian permanent resident, and has an eye towards citizenship. His accent — which decades before earned friendly laughs from people he met in the Top End for its uniqueness — now sounds like a hybrid of his new and old countries. Yet he has kept his Californian mode of dress — T-shirts and blue jeans.

In his home office, Armstrong moves and shakes, wheels and deals. One afternoon he's preparing to attend a car show at the Melbourne Museum, where he'll drop off T-shirts and other merchandise of an American brand he represents. Another day he answers a phone call and chats up a South African business associate.

"He's very personable," says Ross Oakley, Armstrong's long-time champion. "He's convincing in the way he puts things together. He catches on quickly and has a way to get people to do the things that he wants."

And he has a way with preserving old friendships. Armstrong and Cockatoo-Collins remain close. Whenever the two hang out and Cockatoo-Collins has his own three sons, around him, they call Armstrong "Uncle Dwayne". "In our people's way," Cockatoo-Collins says, "you have to earn that title."

Armstrong isn't completely disconnected from America. CNN is on TV all day when he works from home, so he can monitor the 2016 presidential race. Besides business trips to Asia, Africa and Europe, he goes home when he can, to visit his mother and his sister, Karen, a financial analyst living in Culver City, a Los Angeles suburb.

If Armstrong were 25 years younger, would he join the likes of Eric Wallace, Jason Holmes and Mason Cox and strive to play at AFL senior level? He scrunches up his face and mulls over the answer. "It's like sliding doors," he says. "If I signed up for AFL now, I would play. In hindsight, if I had the same opportunity, I would've run quite further."

3

The Headhunter and the Exporter
Jonathan Givony and Zach Frederick

In his office in Brooklyn, a man keys in digits on his mobile phone to a number in Detroit. He knows the person on the other end will greet his cold call with surprise at best, derision at worst. The caller is Jonathan Givony, a college basketball junkie and founder of the worldwide professional basketball scouting website DraftExpress. Since 2009, he's been an AFL consultant on the side. Givony attends hundreds of college basketball games and practices each year.

It's early April 2014, Givony is doing what he does every year at this time, just after the end of the NCAA's March Madness period. He's contacting about 100 NCAA Division I basketball centers and forwards he's tracked on an Excel spreadsheet and inviting them to the latest AFL U.S. Combine. If 60 or so respond to his calls, emails or Facebook queries, Givony considers it a success. Even better if 20 of the players actually attend the combine. Today, Givony is ringing one of those young men on his spreadsheet: Evan Bruinsma, a 6-foot-8 former University of Detroit basketball forward, who averaged 13 points and eight rebounds per game in his senior year.

Inside a classroom of 20 to 30 students in a strategic business policy class, Bruinsma's mobile phone suddenly and unexpectedly vibrates. He discreetly takes the phone out of his pocket; he peeks at the screen but doesn't recognize the area code.

Who can it be now? He ducks outside, into a hallway to take the call.

"Hi, I'm Jonathan Givony," the call begins. "I'm with the Australian Football League. I invite college basketball players to a scouting combine in Los Angeles to try out. What are your thoughts?"

This must be a prank, Bruinsma thinks. A guy with an American accent asking him, a basketball player, if he'd be interested in trying some Australian sport he's never heard of? *Yeah, right.* An awkward pause follows.

"Have you got the right guy?" is all Bruinsma can think to ask. "Are you sure you have the right number?"

"Yes," Givony says.

Givony assures Bruinsma that his call, the sport and the combine all are legit. He tells Bruinsma he'll send him YouTube links so he can see how Australian Rules is played, and how there are already some American former college hoopsters playing footy in Australia.

Another pause. "Maybe I'll get back to you," Bruinsma says. Then he ends what seems like a weird conversation. But for the 22-year-old, who hails from the small farming town of New Era, Michigan, the offer of a free trip to L.A. is pretty exciting. His long shot at playing a new sport in Australia might be better than playing in a low-level basketball league in a country with more language and cultural barriers.

Givony contacts more college hoopsters who are contemplating going pro in Europe or Asia, great athletes who nevertheless have just about reached their basketball ceiling, offering them an unconventional, yet intriguing alternative in pro sports. He makes his pitch to Marvin Baynham, a 6-foot-6 former forward at Georgia Southern University.

It was Paul Roos who first called Givony in 2009, at the suggestion of iconic Notre Dame basketball coach Digger Phelps. Then, Roos made what might have seemed a strange request to some: would Givony keep his eyes open for athletes who might be able to make a transition to the sport of Australian Rules?

"I didn't think he was crazy at all," Givony recalls. "There's not much size coming out of Australia these days. Where's the size gonna come from? There's an unlimited supply of American big men. There are 350 colleges with 12 guys on the roster and four of them will be

6-foot-7 or taller. There are tons of guys graduating every year and only a handful will be drafted. Some will have meaningful basketball careers and have shelf life. For others, there's not much of a future." While some Americans might earn hundreds of thousands of dollars annually playing in Europe, and a handful will top US$1 million, in lesser leagues the pay is far more modest. One American in 2014 signed to play for a Spanish third-division club for only $1,500 U.S. a month.

Bruinsma eventually buys in. Baynham also comes on board. After excelling in vertical jump, agility, sprint and footy skills tests at their LA auditions, the AFL flies both men to Melbourne in late September for its Draft Combine. The AFL pays for their accommodations and meals, and also hosts them at the Grand Final.

"I had nothing to lose. Plus, I could get a picture with a kangaroo," Bruinsma deadpans.

Givony himself knows a few things about living abroad, having split his childhood between Brooklyn, Miami and Israel, where he rode the bench as a teenager for a youth team in Moshav Ein Yahav, a rural Israeli village. But the man really knows his college hoops, and has quickly learned Australian football. Before he found the currently active footy players — Jason Holmes, Mason Cox, Alexander Aurrichio and Matt Korcheck — he also recruited other college basketball big men: Eric Wallace, Mark Cisco and Patrick Mitchell. All these young men gave footy a go, travelling to Australia to test their abilities, but in the end couldn't quite reach the level of an AFL senior list player and didn't get an AFL game.

In Melbourne, in September 2014, Bruinsma didn't get his planned selfie with a kangaroo. But at the Draft Combine, he recorded the highest running vertical jump of any of the hundreds of footy aspirants — just over 3 feet. Only the AFL's star ruckman, Nic Naitanui, of the league's Perth-based West Coast Eagles, achieved better at an AFL Draft Combine. Bruinsma also made some new friends among the young Irish recruits the AFL brought over. He left without getting an AFL offer, but North Melbourne would invite him and Baynham to its Utah high-altitude performance camp.

By then, though, Bruinsma was over his footy foray. He signed a deal with a Maltese pro basketball team. He later played back in Detroit in a five-on-five basketball tournament for a team called Eberlein Drive, which competed for a $1 million grand prize.

Those odds of attaining such a big reward might seem slim — as are the chances of former college basketball players succeeding in an international sport they'd never previously heard of, that they must start from scratch to learn. But it's precisely that Herculean challenge that motivates American recruits. Indeed, they might feel as though they've won a lottery of sorts if they get signed to AFL deals. In a whirlwind seven months, the uninitiated basketball recruits can transform into bona fide prospects in another sport's highest level.

"It's very rewarding," Givony says. "Anytime a guy gets signed, that's great. But then my first question to the AFL people at the combine is, 'What about this guy? What about that guy?' I keep pushing. Someone's gotta go to bat for these players."

*

Between 2012 and 2015, the U.S. Combines have produced four athletes who have landed AFL contracts — Wallace was the first, followed by Holmes, Cox and Korcheck. But that's not enough for Givony.

"I always feel like we could've gotten more," he says. "When AFL teams look back, 15 to 20 years from now, some will kick themselves for not getting on board earlier and for letting other American prospects slip through the cracks."

Counting the most recent U.S. Combine in April 2016, the AFL talent evaluators have tested 92 athletes. Doing the math reveals that an American athlete attending the combine has about 20 to 1 odds of eventually landing an AFL contract.

"It's a process," Givony says. "We knew it wasn't gonna be an immediate thing, that it would take a few years. We're getting there. It's gotten easier for sure, to recruit athletes. Every year, there's a little more awareness of the AFL among the recruits and when someone gets signed, I have more articles to send them. I now have athletes reaching out to me."

Givony says the key for more Americans getting offers from the U.S. Combines is having representatives from more AFL clubs attend. Just two AFL clubs, North Melbourne and Richmond, attended the 2016 combine, but in 2015, North Melbourne, Richmond, Essendon and Carlton sent representatives to the combine held at the IMG Sports Academy in the Tampa Bay area. Ablett, Sheehan and Kennelly have collaborated with Givony and the USAFL since the beginning of the U.S. Combines to make them work.

While Givony has a financial stake in getting players signed by AFL clubs, he also has a genuine interest in their adjustment to their new career and workplace. "I was at the AFL Draft Combine in Melbourne in 2013 and sat with Jason Holmes on a couch and convinced him to sign," Givony says. "I remember earlier, his trip to Sydney to work out at the Swans' academy overlapped with his brother's wedding, which he missed. His parents really tried to convince him not to miss it."

In Melbourne, before Holmes and St Kilda's head of football at the time, Chris Pelchen, fronted the TV cameras to announce the deal, Givony was on the phone with Kevin Holmes, assuring him that his son was indeed making the right career move.

"His dad had a lot of questions," Givony says. "He wanted to know details about the sport and the league and the combine and what we were looking for and why Jason. I don't know that he was skeptical, but he was a concerned father and wanted to make sure Jason wasn't suckered into something."

Givony also gives athletes as much insight as he can on the subtle differences between Australian and American culture that could help them in their auditions with AFL scouts. Making it in footy, he tells them, isn't only about athleticism. While Americans face no language barrier and the Australian culture seems so familiar that it may even seem like America in a parallel universe, it's not. Slight miscommunications and seemingly innocuous gestures can trap Americans in the same awkwardly tense situations that many American baseball players experience while playing professional Winter Ball in the Dominican Republic or Venezuela or in high-level leagues in Japan, Taiwan or South Korea.

"American athletes are very individual," says Chris Johnson, the AFL's national talent diversity manager, and a three-time Premiership player for the league's Brisbane Lions and member of the league's Indigenous Team of the Century. "Footy relies on teamwork."

Another factor is that American athletes might easily fall prey to Australia's "tall poppy syndrome" and be cut down to size by clubs, fans and the media if they were to self-promote, self-indulge or complain. Australians would take pleasure in piercing an American pro athlete's hyper-inflated ego. While onfield choreographed celebrations and emotive histrionics may make great TV in the US, they don't play in Oz. Or at least they haven't for decades, since the days of freewheeling footy showmen like Mark "Jacko" Jackson. With his signature platinum blonde-dyed hair, brawny frame and loudly yells of "Oi!" he firmly entrenched himself in American popular culture after his playing days, as the TV pitchman for Energizer batteries in campy 1980s commercials.

So Givony spreads the word among his American recruits. "I tell the players, 'Bring it down a notch,'" he says. "Be modest. The purpose of their game is not to talk yourself up."

Ablett, Sheehan, Kennelly and the other AFL scouts at the U.S. Combine concentrate on talking up the game. And they usually leave Givony with a couple of Aussie footballs to pass on to any athlete he might want to recruit for a future combine, or for an attendee to practice with while he waits to hear if the league is interested in testing him further.

One of the beneficiaries was a Columbia University soccer goalkeeper and baseball player, Alexander Aurrichio. He heard about the U.S. Combine from Cisco, who attended the same school and had been trialed by the AFL in 2013. Aurrichio called Givony and then made the short drive to Brooklyn from his home in Long Island City. There, they watched an NCAA basketball tournament game, and Givony pivoted to tell him about footy.

"Alex was sitting in my living room and I handed him his first footy," Givony recalls. "He was so persistent. He wouldn't take no for an answer. He's a great dude."

Givony added Aurrichio to the list of invitees for the 2014 U.S. Combine, even though, at 6-foot-6, and not having college basketball experience, he isn't the target physical and skill-set specimen for the American Experiment. Aurrichio started training with the USAFL's New York Magpies, and a few weeks later was flown to Los Angeles for the combine, where he tested in the same group as Baynham, Bruinsma and Mason Cox. Aurrichio tested well, Givony says, but the AFL scouts saw him as the eighth to 10th best prospect.

True to the persistent form Givony describes, however, Aurrichio continued playing in the USAFL, then, with the help of contacts at that club, moved to Melbourne and trained with a handful of VFL clubs. Eventually he earned his way onto the Northern Blues' senior list.

"By all accounts he had a tremendous VFL season," Givony says. "If he did that, how many other guys from our group could've also been playing in the VFL? Footy clubs in Australia are underestimating the ability of our American athletes to make the transition. Yes, the Aussie athletes are incredibly skilled, but it's only a matter of time before the floodgates open for American athletes to make it in footy."

For that to happen, Givony says, it's simple math. If more AFL clubs send scouts to the U.S. Combine, then more American athletes will get signed. So far just a handful of clubs have. And although Holmes's debut as the first born-and-bred American AFL player was a win for the American Experiment, Givony says he didn't see interest spiking since then, among AFL clubs, to attend the 2016 U.S. Combine.

But when he reflects back to that first U.S. Combine, Givony feels pride. Even though, after the 2015 AFL season, North Melbourne delisted Wallace — the first man ever signed from a U.S. Combine —

after three VFL seasons, Givony recognizes Wallace's importance in the American Experiment.

"Eric was a pioneer for us," Givony says. "He was the right guy to lead the charge. He had the personality and the charisma. But it comes back to height. North felt he was a little short. He's a bulky, chiseled guy and it's hard for someone of that type to build up the aerobic base to play in the AFL. Eric never really built up that endurance base. You're not going to see his body type as much in the future of combines."

Sure enough, before Givony conjured up candidates and invitations for the 2015 U.S. Combine, the AFL organizers gave him a mandate that all invitees had to be a minimum of 6-foot-7. All 15 who turned up were.

"This has been a learning process for all of us," Givony says. "It's fun. I'm not disappointed by anything."

*

About 1,800 miles west of Givony's Brooklyn office, in the shadow of Colorado's Rocky Mountains, where fortune hunters once flocked seeking riches via gold panning and silver mining, Zach Frederick goes prospecting for American athletes to play AFL football. But while Givony taps into a perpetually rich vein of NCAA basketball ore, Frederick dips into the NCAA gridiron and NFL free agent talent pool. Although the AFL has been targeting ex-NCAA hoopsters to fill a niche role in the ruck, a few AFL clubs are embracing Frederick's idea of testing former NCAA football players, who might instead transform into tall defenders, tall forwards or even midfielders.

As head of the Denver-based Frederick Export, Frederick ships to the world, including Australia, a plethora of American consumer goods. In 2009, while Frederick was visiting Melbourne, a local importer of musical instruments took him to an AFL match at the MCG. Both the sport and the possibility of infusing American talent into it fascinated Frederick.

"It doesn't take a genius to know we have a certain caliber of athlete who could excel [in Australian Rules] if he learned the game," Frederick says. "I thought, *Let's make this a reality.*"

Frederick took an unconventional route into the footy world. In 2011, before he had recruited a single American athlete, he made his own brand of history. After rigorous studying and testing, he became the first American to earn accreditation as an AFL player agent, hoping he might one day represent some American AFL players. In 2012 Frederick returned to Australia for an agents' conference, where he met AFL Players Association representatives, AFL club list managers and league officials, and it was then he made his pitch. Tony Woods, who then was the AFL's International Development Manager, was in the audience.

"He sat there with very little to say," Frederick recalls. "For him, the idea was coming out of left field. Then, within two weeks, he helped organize the first U.S. Combine. It seemed like the AFL didn't want to be perceived as being on the back foot and saw [that] someone was seriously trying to organize talent."

While most of the two dozen American athletes at the AFL's inaugural 2012 U.S. Combine were basketball players Givony had found, four were former NCAA football players who had been recruited and were represented by Frederick. Emmanuel Moody, Draylen Ross, Derrell Acrey and Quinn Porter had all attempted NFL careers. Moody, who had played in the University of Florida backfield with quarterback Tim Tebow, had even started playing for the USAFL's Dallas Magpies. Frederick believed then, and still maintains, that "American football translates the best [to AFL]." Judging from the combine results, though, the AFL scouts disagreed. All three players the league invited to Melbourne to test alongside top Australian footy prospects were ex-hoopsters.

In 2013, when Frederick realized that the timing of the AFL's U.S. Combine in April conflicted with the NFL's annual Scouting Combine — a must-attend event for American pro football hopefuls — he tried a new strategy. First he hired Tom Ellis, the American head coach of the USAFL's Denver Bulldogs, part-time, to help scour the NCAA and NFL landscape for any hidden athletic gems. They'd have to be short on pro opportunities, and they'd have to have the following attributes: speed, height, a high vertical leap, ball receiving skills and backgrounds playing multiple sports. Just as Givony was doing with basketball players, Ellis would have to convince the gridiron guys the Australian game was indeed real. Then the recruits would have to be willing to learn it and, if they earned the opportunity, be willing to relocate halfway around the world.

Ellis's credibility in American footy circles was — and remains — unmatched. From 2000 to 2012, Ellis played on four Bulldogs USAFL championship-winning teams, and he was a club's player-head coach senior coach for its three other titles. Only a pre-planned family vacation to Disneyland kept him from playing in the club's eighth championship-winning match. As of 2016, Ellis was the only American head coach ever to win a USAFL championship. He hails from Dublin, Texas — a town of 3,700 people — and discovered Aussie Rules as a teenager in the 1980s, while catching part of a late-night televised VFL match on ESPN at a high-school football teammate's house.

Besides Ellis, Frederick got an AFL club's endurance coach to devise a running regimen for his gridiron prospects, and he brought to Denver Sean Clarke, a coach at Kick Builders, an Australian-based footy kicking program. Clarke and Ellis trained the players in basic skills and implemented the running program at an informal, improvised combine in late August, the time of year NFL franchises are making their final roster cuts. Team Frederick's 2013 NCAA football group included players Josh Chichester, Preston Pace, Lucas Reed and DeAndre Thompson.

Months later, having completed the Denver camp, all four registered for the 2013 AFL Draft. Frederick tried to sell the players' potential to all 18 AFL clubs, but none was willing to take a punt on them. Essendon did trial Reed and Chichester — who Ellis says had become a very good kicker — in Boulder, Colorado, during its December 2013 high-altitude training camp, but nothing came of it.

Reed — whom the NFL's Denver Broncos released from a preseason camp shortly before Frederick and Ellis found him — decided to continue his footy training. The AFL invited him to its 2014 U.S. Combine but he didn't make the Melbourne cut, leaving him, Frederick and Ellis frustrated.

"[Most] AFL scouts don't think an American can amass the game knowledge to play any other position besides ruckman," Frederick says. "If a coach trains them properly, players can acquire those skills and that knowledge. The [gridiron] defensive backs and wide receivers could be transformational players — much more so than a big, slow ruckman. In order to get AFL scouts to get beyond 'the ruckman headspace,' we have to get athletes in front of them that have a higher endurance base and can actually kick."

So Frederick, Ellis and Clarke persisted. In late 2014 Ellis formulated a list of about 100 talented NCAA gridiron players, then whittled it down to 10. In 2015, after extensive talks with their college and high school coaches, Ellis used social media to track down and invite two athletes to another Denver training camp. They were John Peters, a tight end who months earlier saw NFL preseason action before being let go, and Brandon Kaufman, a former NCAA wide receiver coming off a lengthy preseason trial with a Canadian Football League (CFL) team and a 2013 NFL preseason run.

After years striking out, Frederick finally got an AFL club, the Gold Coast Suns, to show genuine interest in his gridiron players. After the Denver camp, the Suns agreed to further train and evaluate Peters and Kaufman in Queensland, in January 2016, at a two-week trial.

"We have as an ideology that we want our tall athletes to be combative and have someone within that position that's used to catching the ball and judging the flight," says Dom Ambrogio, a Gold Coast development coach. "Because of their aggression and experience in a receiving position, we were looking for an NFL player."

At the Suns' camp, Kaufman's blue-collar work ethic, drive and athleticism won them over. Gold Coast signed him to an International Scholarship contract just before the start of the 2016 AFL season and assigned him to the Labrador Tigers, its minor league affiliate. After five years, Frederick, the exporter, had finally shipped an American athlete to Australia.

He's thrilled by Kaufman's signing, but tempers his excitement.

"I've resigned myself to the fact that [getting American gridiron players signed by AFL clubs] is not going to be a big cash cow anytime soon," Frederick says. "But I remain passionate about bringing a transformational American athlete to the game."

4

The Beast

Eric Wallace

For most people, the eyes are the windows to the soul. That's not necessarily true of Eric Wallace. The portals to his spirit might well be his Twitter and Instagram accounts. That's not to say the hoopster-cum-Australian-footballer is shallow; it's quite the opposite. Wallace isn't "most people". And that's not to say he's an odd duck. Not at all.

Wallace is just a young man of diverse interests, many passions. He plays piano. He loves the music of rapper J. Cole. He likes Formula 1 racing and in 2015 ticked an item off his bucket list by attending the Melbourne Grand Prix. He loves the Japanese anime TV program *Dragon Ball Z*, and superhero sci-fi movies like *Avengers: Age of Ultron*.

Wallace's American agent, Dwon Clifton, describes him as a renaissance man. Wallace describes himself on his Twitter profile as a "full time polymath". It's no wonder, then, that in 2012, when he first heard of Australian Rules football, through an email inviting him to the AFL's first-ever U.S. Combine, his interest was piqued. After a 10-day trial with the North Melbourne Football Club, Wallace signed a two-year Category B International Rookie contract, arriving at the club in December of that year. One of his new teammates, Jack Ziebell, known for his ferocious tackling, saw Wallace in the gym and called him "an athletic beast". The moniker stuck, and from that moment on, Wallace became "The Beast".

"I don't think I've heard my first name the whole time I've been here," Wallace says with a chuckle on a July 2015 afternoon after a midweek training session. He's relaxing at Toast, an Abbotsford Street cafe near the Kangaroos' headquarters, eating a plate of bacon and eggs and drinking a caramel-vanilla milkshake. "I love being called 'The Beast'. It has an intimidating connotation."

Awestruck North Melbourne fans quickly got on board. In and around the city, some residents who spot him would approach him for conversation. "I'll be walking around, not expecting to be recognized," Wallace says. "Some people will come up to me and ask, 'Do you play basketball?' and I'll say, 'I used to.' But some people see me and they'll come up to me and say, 'Carn the Roos!' or 'Beast! When are you gonna get a game?'"

Wallace wears the nickname proudly — he even uses it as part of his Twitter handle — but it would be hard to find a gentler athlete off the ground. He's also a deeply spiritual man. Wallace often "likes" and re-tweets messages from the Twitter address @AthletesForGod. A week after his four-year footy foray with North Melbourne officially ended after his 2015 season, Wallace re-tweeted: "Retweet if you play for Him!"

Faith is Wallace's bedrock, especially in adversity. He was raised in Winston-Salem, North Carolina, in a devout Christian family. Of his great-grandmother's 13 children, six are pastors. His grandfather is a bishop. So when Wallace entered North Melbourne's headquarters for his 2015 year-end meeting with the club's general manager, Cameron Joyce, and head coach, Brad Scott, he tapped into his spiritual center.

"I was calm," Wallace reflects. "I was ready for anything."

Having his small family in town with him likely helped him stay centered. His September 24 Instagram post, "The Wallaces down under!" which featured a touching photo of Wallace surrounded by his mother, Nikita, his sister Taylor and his father, Tremonteo ("Monty"), says it all. Wallace, wearing a gray sweatshirt, a blue Toronto Raptors NBA cap, black-framed eyeglasses and a newly grown beard, is holding his mobile phone in his hands — perhaps pushing out another

Tweet. His countenance shows a man at peace, having been relieved of a heavy burden.

The meeting inside the Kangaroos' offices lasted 10 or 15 minutes. Scott, who Wallace says genuinely loves his players, began to speak but struggled to get the words out. "You've showed great improvement," he said. "You've made us better as a club. But we have to delist players …"

Although Wallace says it wasn't a big shock — and when discussing his delisting, he is characteristically calm and reflective, thinking a higher power ordained it — the news still stung. It was the culmination of a year of frustration and angst, uncertainty and upheaval, both on and off the ground.

*

Wallace finished 2014, his second VFL season, as the North Ballarat Roosters' number-one ruckman — in fact, its *only* ruckman. He averaged 35 hitouts per game, kicked seven goals, and in one match even picked up a vote for the VFL's J.J. Liston Award for the league's best player. His coaches were pleased.

"He's come a helluva long way," said Gavin Brown, North's development coach — and a man who worked closely with Wallace — shortly after the season. "He just needs to bide his time."

That would be tough. Wallace turned 26 in the off-season, and entered the 2015 campaign on a one-year contract. He was on the rookie list of a deep, strong AFL club — only a Preliminary Final thrashing at the hands of the Sydney Swans had prevented North Melbourne from making the Grand Final the previous year. In particular, the Kangaroos boasted one of the AFL's best ruckmen in Todd Goldstein, and were developing his tag-team partner, the promising 22-year-old Ben Brown. Wallace would have to build his fitness and lift his own game to greater heights.

At the Roosters, Wallace played under "Fitzy" — North Ballarat's fatherly head coach, Gerard Fitzgerald, a six-time VFL Coach of the

Year and a man known for his skillful development of young and inex-
perienced players while still managing to win three VFL premierships.
Fitzy, whom Wallace calls a "great man," championed him, empathiz-
ing with his ruckman's challenge of facing a steep athletic learning
curve while living so far away from home.

Wallace developed a comfortable routine before home games in the
rural Victorian city. While making the 90-minute game-day commute
to Ballarat from his apartment in Melbourne's CBD, he would get
in the zone. He'd mix opera, gospel and hip-hop playlists on his car
stereo, all the while focusing on the task ahead.

One of Wallace's matches for North Ballarat saw him all over Australian highlight reels for several days afterwards. The Roosters were
on the road at Simonds Stadium, in Geelong. As a booming kick from
fullback arced towards a pack of three players, Wallace charged forward from the middle of the ground. In one motion, Wallace soared,
planted his left knee on an opponent's left shoulder, rode the pack
of players beneath him and extended his arms, unaware of another
opponent's swinging fist directly behind him, trying to bat away the
incoming ball.

"*Ohhhh!*" the awed crowd roared a second later, after Wallace —
hanging in the air above everyone else — snatched the footy with
both hands, clasping it to his broad chest. Then these *opposing* fans
did something entirely unexpected: they burst into robust applause.

Wallace landed hard on his back, but with no fuss he rolled up off
the ground and handpassed the ball to a teammate to keep the play
moving.

"He took an absolute screamer," recalls Melanie Whelan, the
Roosters' beat writer for Ballarat's daily *Courier*. "Geelong's fans are
very parochial. Normally when a rival player does something great,
they're quiet. It was a big respect thing."

By the 2015 season North Melbourne had ended its affiliation
with the Roosters. Wallace was reassigned to its second VFL affiliate, the Werribee Tigers. There, he would play for senior coach John
Lamont, with whom he had a good relationship. But Wallace was

now sharing the ruck duties with the more experienced Daniel Currie and Majak Daw. Because Daw and Wallace wore uniform numbers 38 and 39, respectively, the two men were locker neighbors. Daw, a Sudanese-Australian who himself had made history in 2013 as the AFL's first African-born player, became Wallace's closest mate at North. But friendship aside, the presence of Daw and Currie, plus North's flurry of other off-season player moves, hurt Wallace's chances of a call-up.

The Kangaroos had used picks in the 2014 National Draft and Rookie Draft to bolster their tall stocks with younger players with ruck experience: 18-year-old Sam Durdin and Braydon Preuss, a 20-year-old who stands about four inches taller than Wallace. Then North Melbourne upgraded its forward line by signing a highly sought-after free agent who also could pinch-hit in the ruck when needed.

"It wasn't a shock to me to see them bring in those guys," Wallace says, letting slip a sly smile. "The American in me was like, 'Cool! Bring it on!' Then I saw it as having other guys to learn from."

With all those circumstances weighing on him, preseason started. Wallace was looking to have a massive one. Even with the competition, in Wallace's mind this season was to be his breakthrough. But then the injury bug bit him. Hard.

With pain in his left shin already flaring up and nagging him during training, he tore his right calf, a malady that footballers ominously call "the old man's injury." Wallace suddenly was out for six weeks. With a possible call-up and a new contract riding on his performance in the 2015 season, Wallace would now miss the first three VFL rounds. From the sidelines, he yearned to be doing something he had dreaded when he first arrived at North Melbourne.

"It was weird," Wallace says, "but I actually missed running. I hate running. Three years ago, I couldn't run around the field at all. But when you can't do it, you miss it."

Wallace's mind went back to his college basketball career at DePaul University, outside Chicago, where one season he had broken his leg.

"I went through depression, hearing that I couldn't play," Wallace recalls. "You think to yourself when your team loses, *Man, I could've helped.*"

Wallace's new injury meant he'd now have to work his way into Werribee's senior team by playing in its VFL Development League side. This was the league in which Wallace had played his first year of footy, 2013, and he says that, while there, he felt "lost", competing each week against more experienced opponents. But rather than getting discouraged, Wallace got inspired. He began channeling his inner American.

"It fired me up," Wallace said. "I had to ask again, 'What does it take to play senior footy?'"

He would find part of the answer while playing his first six matches of the season. Weighing 227 lbs., his exact weight at the 2012 U.S. Combine, Wallace was fit. "Continue giving great effort," his coaches told him, "but double it. Throw your weight around more. Add more ferocity.'

He had to truly become The Beast.

"I'm not a guy who gets hyped before matches," Wallace says. "I'm laid-back until the ball bounces. Then I ramp it up."

Wallace's development coaches saw much more "ramp up" than usual in the Development League side's Round 9 comeback win over the Frankston Dolphins, in a night match at Avalon Airport Oval. Wallace says he played with more grit and "did more" than in previous weeks, including kicking a goal. He was named one of the Tigers' best on ground. Better yet, Wallace was immediately promoted to the Werribee seniors and collected 34 hitouts and laid seven tackles in his first senior VFL game. The performance helped Wallace maintain both his confidence and his hope for the future.

"Apparently, North sees something in me," he said at the time. "The AFL sees something. The development people tell you, 'You need to play good footy and make your case.' I've done everything I can. I've mapped out where I need to be."

Despite his ups and downs at Werribee, while training with his North Melbourne teammates, Wallace appeared completely at ease with his them, and they with him. Wallace relishes being the student and observer. At training he learned to pattern his goal kicking after his teammates Drew Petrie and Brown. He also absorbed advice from Waite as he tried to sharpen his forward craft.

"You're tall and quick," teammate Jarrad Waite, the free agent who signed with the Kangaroos, told Wallace in one session. "Never stand still as a forward, because that makes it easier for a defender to try and stop you from moving, running and jumping."

Wallace was also developing the improved game sense his coaches were teaching him. He teamed up with Daw to develop a rhythm as a strong ruck combination. Wallace initially made that discovery while playing in a match opposite a fellow American, Alexander Aurrichio of Northern Blues.

"It's the little things," Wallace says. "You learn in center bounces, ball-ups and boundary throw-ins as a ruckman that if your midfielders are even just a meter out of position, bad things can happen."

North's assistant coaches began to trial Wallace up forward in VFL games and as a tall defender in training sessions. Once, the coaches matched him up against Petrie. When asked how that went, Wallace pauses for a moment, then his eyes flash and he smiles. "He didn't get a sniff," he says.

North's ruck coach, Alex Ishchenko, noticed Wallace's shutdown job on the prolific goal-kicker. "You don't look at all out of place behind the ball," he told Wallace after the session.

*

At the time Wallace was working his way back from injury and into Werribee's senior team, he was reading online and hearing from friends about the grave social unrest in America. In mid-April 2015, Baltimore Police arrested Freddie Gray, a 25-year-old African-American man, who was just one year younger than Wallace. The officers claimed Gray had a knife and that he ran when he saw them. Several witnesses told the *Baltimore Sun* that officers beat Gray after he was put inside a van and shackled with leg irons.

Police denied that Gray was beaten, but conceded not giving him the medical attention he repeatedly asked for after he suffered a head injury after his arrest. At the police station to which the officers took him, Gray fell unconscious. Paramedics later transported him to a hospital shock trauma unit. Several days later, following a double surgery on his spine, Gray, who had lapsed into a coma, died of what an autopsy reported as a broken vertebra; Gray's attorney claimed that 80 per cent of his spine had been severed.

By this time Wallace was closely following the story, which now was making international headlines. Hundreds, then thousands of Baltimore residents, outraged by a staggering spike of police brutality cases involving non-white civilians, staged city-wide non-violent public demonstrations, demanding the officers' arrests. They continued for a week. When protests became violent, U.S. National Guard troops were brought in and the mayor ordered a weeklong nightly curfew, citywide.

In Melbourne, Wallace was conflicted. He had recently teamed with the U.S. Consulate in Melbourne, giving visiting American servicemen a tour of the Kangaroos' facilities. He also hosted U.S. Consul General Frankie Reed at a North home game. But he couldn't ignore feeling horrified by what was going on in Baltimore. Then-President Barack Obama himself had said justice needed to be served in the Gray case.

The discussion on the police brutality and the protesters' responses grew testy on social media, with millions, including Wallace, having their say.

"While I DO NOT condone violence in anyway, and pray for a peaceful and effective outcome to Baltimore & the minorities' USA, I understand," Wallace posted on Twitter. Another poster challenged his message, and Wallace then tweeted a comparison between the Baltimore protesters' anger at police brutality and the eighteenth-century Boston protesters' ire towards British colonial soldiers: "Food for thought: not long ago a great nation was built on resistance sparked by a 'Tea Party Riot.' Resistance was justifiable then huh?"

The day after Wallace's impassioned Tweets, investigators ruled Gray's death a homicide. Also that day, six officers — three African-American and three white — were charged in connection with it. In June 2015 a racially motivated massacre of nine people by a white shooter inside an historically black church in Charleston, South Carolina, hit even closer to home for Wallace. He was keen to continue his footy, but in Australia Wallace felt the same powerlessness to help his countrymen as he had years earlier at DePaul, while benched with a broken leg. And if Wallace wanted to discuss his country's crises in person, he would've been hard-pressed to find anyone where he was who could've truly understood.

"You want to be a proud American here and say about America that it's the best country in the world," Wallace says. "But when you see the racial and socioeconomic problems and the poverty, you wish we could put the right people in the right offices, so these problems could be solved and the easy stuff could get fixed. Thinking about how much money people make in America, you think people's time has to be worth much more than the minimum wage, when people running the companies are worth millions and billions. I think about the fact that if I didn't play sports in college [and get athletic scholarships], I would've owed $100,000 in loans."

Still, on a wet, wintry 4th of July in Melbourne, Wallace outwardly displays his American pride. He wears a tasseled red-and-blue beanie emblazoned with white stars. His navy blue and white jacket bears the iconic New York Yankees logo, and under it he wears the team's famous pinstriped jersey.

He's come to Victoria Park to watch Collingwood play Sandringham, a match in which Jason Holmes and Mason Cox will square off in the ruck against each other for the first time. Wallace doesn't stay long — he has his own match the next day. But his two countrymen later learn that he was there and appreciate his support.

Wallace's morals are driven by his faith. During his time in Melbourne, it was on full display, inside and out. On match days Wallace would wear shin guards on which he inscribed not only the names of his family members, but also Biblical passages that inspire him. One had "Isaiah 40:31" and the other had "Colossians 3:23," "Matthew 6:33," "Romans 12:12" and "John 3:16." Inside his sedan, a crucifix pendant hung from the rearview mirror, while the music of American gospel singers Kirk Franklin, Fred Hammond and John P. Kee was never absent from his car stereo for too long.

"This is music that speaks to me, more than just stuff on in the background," Wallace says as he drives past Princes Park, then through the suburbs of Princes Hill and Brunswick East. "It touches me where I need to be touched." The songs were especially comforting to Wallace when, despite the unrest in Baltimore, he longed for home and family.

Wallace is very close with his father, who for years worked an overnight shift for a battery manufacturing company. Like Tremonteo Wallace, Eric Michael Wallace has never tasted alcohol. Wallace never takes for granted the relationship he has with his dad. Too many African-American young men today, Wallace says, grow up without their fathers in their homes, or their lives. It's a societal ill with complex historical causes. Some leading American sociologists say the problem is rooted in the days of slavery, when black families were often torn apart.

"In our culture, most dads aren't around," Wallace says plainly. "But my dad came to most of my basketball games. My dad's a hero. Now, to be doing something big, I want him to be there when I'm doing something special. I want to share these moments with those who have been there the whole time for me — my dad, my mom and my sister."

On a good week, when he wouldn't be overwhelmed by on-field and off-field commitments, Wallace would phone home three days a week. Other weeks, it would be once, usually the day after a match. During his first year, the club sprang for his parents to fly over from North Carolina, hosted them in Melbourne, got them to Eureka Stadium in North Ballarat and even documented the visit on the club website.

Just as he'd do watching his son on the basketball court, Monty

Wallace closely observed Eric's play on the oval, and he didn't shy away from making some pointed comments.

"Dad understood footy the first time he saw it," Wallace says, smiling. "After he saw me play, he was telling me exactly what my development coaches did."

While Wallace was struggling to make it as an AFL ruckman, he was a natural at being a team guy. Wallace calls himself a homebody, so he wouldn't constantly be out and about in the city's bustling nightlife. He's not the type. Instead, he'd enjoy an occasional walk, taking in the multicultural vibe in Footscray, in Melbourne's west end, where many of his friend Daw's fellow East African refugees have resettled. Wallace participated in the Roos' group known as The Huddle, helping out with teammates at a skills clinic in Flemington, another immigrant-rich area for local kids — many from refugee backgrounds. Wallace also made a visit with teammates to the Royal Children's Hospital and participated in the "24 Hour Mega Swim," which raised awareness and money to fight multiple sclerosis.

Despite his goodwill off the ground, Wallace's form spiked and dipped while on it. Of the 18 games he played, half were in the Development League and half were with the VFL seniors. He struggled to build momentum. Whenever Wallace had a run of good form, it was interrupted by a bye week, an injury flare-up or an ordinary performance.

Wallace's good form also seemed to coincide with surges of homesickness. Two of his Tweets in the second half of the 2015 season tell the story. On July 11, playing as Werribee's sole ruckman, Wallace had a remarkable 78 hitouts in his team's 2-point loss to Geelong. Although he was named as one of his club's best, he tweeted after the match: "Post-game struggles. #footyishard #soreboy."

Two weeks later, there was an even more revealing Instagram post. It was an image of an elegant new pocket watch Wallace had purchased, open to show two circular panels. On one side was a clock he set to U.S. Eastern Time, matching where his parents and sister live. The other panel held two black-and-white photos: one showing his mother and sister, the other himself and his father. In his caption Wallace wrote: "Above the knocks, the bruises, the sore legs, the broken fingers, and whatever may come ... the toughest part about my journey is being away from the ones that mean the most to me, family ... my way of being able to take them everywhere with me." His post was accompanied by an audio snippet from the song "Coming Home," by the popular soul singer John Legend.

Wallace also occasionally reached out to his mentor and agent Dwon Clifton, who has known him since his pre-teen years. "He'd call me when he was homesick," Clifton says. "Sometimes I could hear it in his voice. I'd just listen to him. He missed the ability to be in the same time zone as family and friends, and not have to schedule talking to them. Sometimes I'd have to talk him off the ledge."

The first two weeks in August epitomized Wallace's schizophrenic season. In the first week he had one of his most memorable VFL matches. During a 28-point win over Essendon, he had 26 hitouts, took four marks — two contested — and kicked two goals. Wallace's first goal, a set shot from about 30 meters out, came after a strong contested mark.

For Wallace's next trick, his ruck partner Daw, the team's resting forward, was about to contest a ball a teammate kicked towards him just inside his team's forward 50. Wallace reacted as the ball bounced high in the air, bolting from the center square to the top of the 50-metre arc. Daw spotted his teammate and tapped the ball his way. Wallace overran the loose ball, then recovered, gathered, sidestepped a defender and slotted a running goal from about 35 meters out.

The North Melbourne media department highlighted Wallace's performance, posting the highlights on its website. But the next week Wallace wasn't named to Werribee's senior team. The Development League squad had a bye week, so he couldn't sustain his good form.

Then came Thursday, August 20. With his VFL prospects wavering, an AFL recall practically out of the question and a new contract offer iffy at best, Wallace and the rest of the footy community heard the breaking news. Jason Holmes had earned a promotion to his club's senior list and would make his historic debut two nights later as the AFL's first-ever born-and-bred American player.

"It was bittersweet," Wallace says. "You're thinking when you sign, you wanna be the first. But I'm happy for Jason. We're friends and he's a good dude."

Longtime Kangaroos' star Brent "Boomer" Harvey, who at 37 has had one of the longest-ever AFL careers, empathized with Wallace. He was one of The Beast's first teammates to chat to him about missing a distinction he once thought was within his grasp. "You're disappointed, but you're at a really good club right now," Harvey told Wallace. "You shouldn't get discouraged."

And of course Wallace still has a place in AFL history. He was the first graduate of the AFL's U.S. Combine to be signed by an AFL club. That only helped the league's American Experiment.

Wallace played his final VFL game in the first week of September 2015. Werribee ended its 2015 campaign disappointingly, with a 29-point playoff loss to Collingwood. Wallace backed up Currie and had a modest 11 hitouts. There were, perhaps, more bittersweet feelings for Wallace that day. Collingwood's Mason Cox, who graduated from the U.S. Combine in 2014, two years after Wallace, was wrapping up an impressive first season.

Wallace's season was over, but as North Melbourne was still in the race for the AFL Premiership, his contract discussions had to remain on hold. He faced a nervous three-week wait, but Wallace didn't brood. He passionately barracked for his North Melbourne teammates — players he had become brothers with over the previous three years. His Tweets said as much. On September 19, he celebrated the club's semifinal victory over Sydney, shouting out on social media to his goal-kicking guru: "Drew Petrie! What a Champ!"

The Kangaroos lost the next week to West Coast in a Preliminary Final. But whatever pain Wallace might have been feeling from that, or whatever anxiety he might have had over his immediate playing future, was soothed. His family, so precious to him, had arrived.

It was time to catch up with his dad and sister. Time to celebrate the fashion week event in Winston-Salem his mother, Nikita — a visual artist and clothing designer — conceived and staged, through her business Audacity Productions. As Wallace would tweet, "My family is here. All is well!"

After Wallace's delisting, the club posted a heartfelt send-off video on its website. Again, the American didn't let his disappointment trump his sense of camaraderie. After all, he says, "when I first got here, I said, 'I don't care where I play, I just wanna help us win.'"

The Wednesday following his delisting, Wallace took part in his last annual bonding ritual with his teammates — "Wacky Wednesday," a day in which players meet up at a pub, dress in costumes and blow off steam after a strenuous season. Wallace arrived in style, with a freshly cut Mohawk, and with his beard, denim jacket, gold chains and rings, he had resurrected Mr. T's badass "B.A. Baracus" character from the campy 1980s TV action adventure series *The A-Team*. Of course, Wallace posted the image on Instagram. He gave away his Grand Final ticket on Twitter.

Wallace stayed in Australia for a few more weeks. It was long enough for him to bid farewell to the new mates for life he'd made, both at North Melbourne and off the field. And it was long enough for him to stop by a Melbourne tattoo parlor and get some new body art on his left shoulder.

Wallace signed off from his Australian adventure with one last Instagram post. Although he borrowed the words from someone else — the late Ernie Harwell, the iconic Detroit Tigers' Hall of Fame radio broadcaster — they epitomize Wallace's temperament and outlook on life.

"It's time to say goodbye," he wrote, "but I think goodbyes are sad and I'd much rather say hello. Hello to a new adventure."

5

The History Maker

Jason Holmes

From his hips down, every joint in his tall, sturdy frame aches. Every muscle in his entire body is tight. For three grueling hours, he has been constantly in motion — stopping, starting, sprinting, jogging and pivoting — to the point that he has covered between eight and nine miles. He has been locked in seemingly endless strength contests, jostling, shoving and crashing into other young, strong men. His sides, abdomen and ribs have absorbed sharp knocks from his opponents' knees in fierce mid-air contests.

The previous night he had trouble sleeping — even though his team captain ordered him to go to bed earlier than usual. Finally, he fell asleep at 2 a.m., and awoke eight hours later. Earlier this afternoon he took a 90-minute nap, but arose with his mind racing. *What do I need to do? What does a good game look like for me?*

A few hours from now, after he lies down in bed in his apartment, he'll have more insomnia. Fortunately for him, getting to the front door won't involve walking up a flight of stairs. If it did, he'd have to pause every few seconds just to catch his breath.

Just as his body is right now, his mind is shot. He's completely drained. He's on edge. His mind feels as if it's in three different places at once — over-stimulated and hyperaware of everything around him.

The intense effects of the drop in adrenaline he now feels — after performing in front of 25,245 people in the stadium, and half a million more watching on television — is stultifying. It's damn hard to come down from that high. One painful step after another, he walks down the tunnel at Melbourne's Etihad Stadium. He lumbers into the locker room alongside his teammates on the St Kilda Saints, one of the Australian Football League's 18 clubs.

If the Saints had won this late-season match, the shocks to his body might have been more bearable. The cascading sports drinks his mates would've showered him with, as he stood in the middle of their hastily formed circle, might've washed away his aches. Together they'd jubilantly and breathlessly follow tradition and do as every Australian Rules football club does, from youth leagues to the pros, after winning a match — belt out the words to its club anthem.

If St Kilda had lost, the anguish of wondering what he might've done better might have been easier to set aside. There is solidarity in defeat, comfort in commiseration.

But on this August night the match ended in a tie, and the Saints' performance lies awkwardly in sporting purgatory. He and his comrades are bemused; each man lacks closure and is tortured by individual, unresolved questions. *What could I have done to make a difference? How could I have won the game for us?*

Inside this St Kilda player's mind and body, everything at the moment is insane and intense. He's just played his first AFL game, but Jason Holmes's debut has been unlike any other in the league's nearly 120-year history. It has been unexpected and extraordinary, but not because of any feat he's performed on the ground. It's because of his mere presence.

Holmes has become the first born-and-bred American to play an AFL game. He is, in the flesh, the first fruit of a carefully crafted experiment of a small group of radical thinkers in the AFL brain trust. Holmes's historic debut may be a harbinger of greater things to come. In Australia, unusually tall young men with extraordinary athletic gifts are rare. But NCAA Men's basketball is full of top-level athletes such as Holmes — and the National Basketball Association (NBA) has only a limited number of roster spots. In reaching out to these players, the AFL hopes American supply will meet Australian demand.

As far back as 2009, out-of-the-box Australian thinker Paul Roos, a legendary AFL player and head coach, recognized that. He believed American basketball centers or power forwards could transfer their skills in leaping for jump balls, boxing out, rebounding, pass catching and shot blocking to play the AFL position of "ruckman." The positions in the two sports aren't dissimilar. That year, Roos, at the time the head coach of one of the clubs for which he had starred, the Sydney Swans, actively scouted then-former Marist College basketball big man Shae McNamara, who in 2010 would become the first American former college basketball player to sign an AFL contract.

In 2011 Roos secured funding from the Swans to conduct an AFL team's first-ever scouting combine in America. From that, they signed Alex Starling, a 22-year-old hoopster from Florida's Bethune Cookman University, as an International Scholar at their academy, in the hopes of eventually promoting him to the team. By 2012, despite resistance and skepticism from some quarters, the AFL got on board with the idea, hosting its first American scouting combine — in Redondo Beach, California — where it tested two dozen athletes.

Inside the Saints' locker room, Holmes, a graduate of both the 2013 U.S. Combine and a three-week course Roos conducted at the Sydney Swans Academy, isn't basking in glory. He's too spent. But the footy debutant can't help reflecting on the rapid and transforming journey he's made to get here.

*

In 2012 Holmes was in Tennessee, a large ocean and a hemisphere away from Australia, playing basketball — the sport he loved, which his father once played professionally — for Morehead State University. He would soon be graduating, but his chances of joining an NBA franchise were so small that he was looking to follow in his father's footsteps and play overseas. But Holmes was still regaining full strength in his right knee, which had been operated on a year-

and-a-half earlier, after he dislocated his kneecap, sprained his medial ligament and tore his patella tendon.

Then one day he got an email that changed the trajectory of his life: an invitation to a scouting combine in California, where his skills would be tested in a sport called Australian Rules football. *Is this a scam?* he thought. *I've never heard of this sport. Does it really exist?* He asked around. Both the sport and the invitation were real, he learned. And a reward was dangling in front of him: perform well enough and maybe, just maybe, a professional team in the sport's top competition might offer him a contract. He thought about it and concluded that it was a classic low-risk, high-reward proposition. He wrote back and agreed to fly to the west coast.

After the combine, weeks passed without contact. Then Holmes got a phone call from a scout who had attended the combine. He was impressed. He issued another invitation: "Let us fly you to Sydney and *really* train you and a few other guys we liked from the combine for three weeks at an academy, with a coach from one of the league's top teams."

Of course Holmes accepted. He busted his butt for those three weeks. He hoped the other boys did well too; in a way, they became his teammates. They had a shared goal.

After the training camp, the team signed someone from the academy — but it wasn't Holmes. It was tough to take, because he had worked so hard, but he didn't give up. He realized he kinda liked this footy thing. The academy guys said the league might yet invite him to participate in another combine — this time in Melbourne — where he would compete against the best under-18 footy talent in Australia. So Holmes, by this time back in the States, went and trained with his hometown's amateur club, the Chicago Swans. He worked on his kicking and his endurance.

Holmes was invited to the Melbourne combine and dazzled everyone. A few days later, he was in front of the Australian media's TV cameras, smiling and wearing the red, white and black cap and track-suit of St Kilda, which had just signed him to a two-year, international rookie contract for $180,000 Australian (about $130,000 U.S) while the team's head of football enthusiastically introduced him. Then came the hard part. He survived a months-long pre-season that was more demanding, physically and mentally, than any other he had experienced. He always arrived at training earlier than everyone else to do extra skills work. Holmes was not only the team's new guy, he was also its least experienced.

Even though his football career was in its embryonic stage, Holmes was sent to play in the minor, Victorian Football League (VFL), just one rung beneath the AFL, with and against a fair number of players with top-level experience and aspirations. He often felt frustrated, as everyone around him — teammates and opponents alike — made playing this game look easy. The awkwardness of his early mistakes showed how much catching up he had to do.

Holmes tried not to be too hard on himself. He worked tirelessly to earn the respect of his teammates and coaches, who, he hoped, would be patient with him. Yet he knew that the club had signed him because they expected him to develop from footy infancy to adulthood at an accelerated rate.

While this new adventure was exciting and Holmes was making new friends, he missed the comforts of home. Sometimes he was downright homesick. With the enormous time difference, he had to carefully plan his calls home to family and friends. After training, matches and during bye weeks, his Australian teammates could go home to their families. Holmes couldn't.

He had a countryman in Australia, Eric Wallace — like him, a former college basketball player. A year before Holmes, Wallace got the same email. He'd graduated from the same combines, been signed by another AFL club and, like Holmes, was playing VFL and living in Melbourne. Holmes would have loved to hang out with him, compare notes, share some laughs and bond over their shared experience, but the mutual demands of their schedules made that hard. A post-match handshake and embrace and the occasional text message was the best they both could do.

As Holmes was cutting his teeth in his first season, 2014, his coaches said he still had work to do, but that he was impressing them. As the season wound down, he got hopeful news: the club was thinking of promoting him to the big club. Holmes didn't want anyone on to get hurt, of course, but he did want an opportunity. But it didn't happen. When Holmes went home in the off-season and spent some weeks with his parents, siblings and friends, he loved it. He thought about the loneliness of being in an unfamiliar country, no matter how much he was embracing its differences. He thought about his on-field frustrations, the embarrassing moments, the cultural misunderstandings and the toll this new sport had taken on his body and mind. He thought about the sacrifices he'd already made.

Was it really worth the effort? Of course.

Holmes would soldier on because he's a competitive athlete. It's in his genes. It's who he is and what he does. He would dig in, power through and give it his all — he owed it to himself, his teammates, his club and all the family members and friends who had supported him on this journey. In the process, Holmes knew, he might one day do what no one else from his country ever had.

He got back on the plane for another 15-hour flight. He endured another pre-season. He even got a taste with St Kilda's varsity squad in a couple of preseason matches. In one, early in the first quarter, he gathered a loose ball near the boundary and streaked just inside the 50-meter arc, known as a team's "forward 50." He dropped the ball on his left boot and fired at the tall goal posts. His kick was true. It sailed between the posts for the match's first goal. He loved the feeling when his teammates mobbed him afterwards, the camaraderie they shared. He dreamed of having that moment in a regular season match.

Now, another six months later, having played his first one for St Kilda, Jason Holmes is trying to make sense of what has just happened. He and his teammates have battled to a stalemate with the visiting Geelong Cats, 14.13 (97) to 15.7 (97). Holmes can neither celebrate nor mourn. Ties don't happen in basketball. The adrenaline crash he is experiencing is 10 times sharper in AFL footy, he is learning, than in basketball. All that is why the 25-year-old, 6-foot-7 ruckman is not thinking about the history he has made.

But the gathering media is quick to remind him. In the day leading up to the match, on social media, the U.S. Embassy in Canberra and U.S. Consulates in Melbourne and Sydney posted celebratory Tweets and Facebook posts. Now, reporters ask Holmes about his game-high 34 hitouts, three tackles and a mark, but they focus more on his etching a place in AFL lore. So it is they who crowd around him, not his teammates.

Someone from a major Melbourne radio station gives him a set of headphones and a microphone. He tells the on-air host: "It was really exciting to be out there. In the second half I was able to settle in and understand the ball movement a little bit better, reading it in the air."

Then the station puts Jason's father, Kevin Holmes, on the line. He's calling in from tiny Wilberforce, Ohio, where it's just past dawn. Kevin was working as an assistant basketball coach and resident advisor at Central State University. He rose hours ago, and went to his office in one of the school's residence halls to live stream the match on his laptop.

Somehow, it seems fitting that as a U.S. athlete made history in Australia's national sport — one that barely registers in America's consciousness — nearly all of his countrymen were soundly asleep. Most Americans also remain in the dark about the AFL's "American Experiment." It's a covert sporting operation. Maybe one day the Australian footy scouts in America will emerge from obscurity. Maybe Jason Holmes will be remembered as the man who first stirred America's footy consciousness. That's partly why his dad is so proud of him. "Hey, man, congratulations," he says on air. "I love you. You look like you belong out there."

That's when Jason Holmes, as well-mannered and polite a young man as there is, loses a little of his polish. He gets caught up in the elation of making his father proud. "I fuckin' love you, too, Dad!" Holmes roars, producing hearty laughter from both Kevin and the host.

Half-jokingly, Holmes then asks his dad a question. "What should I work on?"

"Stamina," replies Kevin, drawing on his own experience as a professional sportsman.

Jason's mother, Mary Holmes, also watched the match online at the family's suburban Chicago home. Her maternal instincts surged as she watched her son's body language in from the opening bounce and discussed the action on the phone with her husband.

"When I saw him rocking back and forth before the ball was bounced, it made me nervous," Mary recalls, chuckling. "You know it's an intense moment for him. I was thinking, 'Please let him win this first bounce.'"

When the umpire slammed the ball into the grass and the crowd's murmur became a roar, Holmes duly soared over Cats ruckman Nathan Vardy to win the first contest.

"The fans are on board already!" commentator Brian Taylor, known throughout Australia for his dramatic intonations, exclaimed, playing up a dramatic moment.

"Saints fans think he's a cult figure already, after one hitout," added one of Taylor's broadcast partners, Matthew Richardson, a former AFL legend.

Holmes racked up 33 more hitouts on the night — two more than Geelong's two ruckmen, Vardy and Mark Blicavs, *combined*. Holmes also made three tackles, one of them a chase-down that won him a free kick after the field umpire penalized his opponent for "holding the ball," producing another crowd roar. Later, Holmes took a relatively easy mark, drawing noticeably loud, warm cheers from his new fans.

His first post-match radio interview over, two overjoyed AFL officials, who, despite some resistance from their peers, have long championed the American Experiment, approach Holmes: international and national talent manager Kevin Sheehan and academies development manager Michael Ablett. Holmes's team may have tied, but they recognize that a number of victories have nevertheless been won —

for Holmes as a man, for the AFL as a competition, for footy as a sport and for America as a nation.

"His debut was very exciting for our footy club and even more so for the AFL," says Alan Richardson, St Kilda's head coach. "It's not often in footy we have someone who hasn't yet played a game but has already won the respect of his teammates. He's embraced everything we've thrown at him, then the poor bugger's had to deal with all the media attention. He's very well equipped to do the job."

After a fairly restless night, Holmes rediscovers his routine. He visits a favorite bakery and digs in to his customary post-match breakfast: a bacon-and-egg sandwich and a lemon-lime Gatorade. Having had some time now to decompress, he can reflect more thoughtfully on his first match.

"The first nine minutes of the game, I was running around thinking, *This is gonna be the longest day of my life*," Holmes says. "I was hoping it would pass quick and we'd get the win."

*

Just hours before Holmes's debut, as if inspired by it, Mason Cox of Texas booted five goals playing ruckman and full-forward at Victoria Park, a 15-minute train ride away from Etihad Stadium, to help Collingwood's VFL club smash its opponent by 72 points.

Around the same time Cox was lighting up the scoreboard, at Preston City Oval in Melbourne's outlying northern suburbs, New York native Alexander Aurrichio led all ruckmen on the ground with 36 hitouts for the VFL club, Northern Blues. Wallace of North Carolina played a game for the VFL's Werribee Tigers' team. And a month earlier, prospective American ruckmen Matt Korcheck, Kye Kurkowski, James Johnson and Jalen Carethers — all former college hoopsters and fresh graduates of the AFL's 2015 U.S. Combine — completed three weeks of intensive training in Melbourne, paid for and supervised by the league.

Holmes isn't the first American to make an AFL journey. But he is the first to reach the desired destination. One day he may be remembered as a significant footy figure in Australia, much like 1980s Gaelic football recruits, Sean Wight or Jim Stynes. Perhaps Holmes can rise to the level of Stynes, Australia's greatest Irish import, who, years after winning the Brownlow Medal, off the field ascended to the Melbourne Demos club presidency.

But tonight and for the remaining two weeks of the 2015 season, all that is far from Holmes's mind. He will concentrate on being the best footballer he can be, and on helping his teammates. Perhaps, after this regular season, or maybe several more, "Holmesy" (as he's come to be called by his teammates and newfound fans) might appreciate his unique accomplishment more fully.

"There's a reason why AFL clubs 'blood' [break in] their players and get their first game out of the way," Holmes says. "I had to have that whole roller-coaster experience. It still hasn't sunk in yet. I don't reckon it will for a while yet."

*

Stay focused. Stay in the moment. Don't focus on past thoughts.

With the afterglow of his historic debut two full weeks behind him, Holmes was running out onto the ground at Domain Stadium in Subiaco, West Australia, silently giving himself these strict orders. It was the last week of the 2015 season, and Holmes and his Saints teammates were about to take on the eventual Grand Final runners-up, the West Coast Eagles. A few minutes later, though, Holmes snuck a look over to the Eagles players as they ran up through the tunnel, then through the crepe paper banner made by their official cheer squad, as all AFL home and visiting teams do before each match. He caught a glimpse of the man who was a key reason he came to Australia in the first place.

Three years earlier, Holmes opened the email from Jonathan Givony that first introduced him to footy. In a video clip he saw a player starring in a piece of play that mesmerized him. The man looked a little like him — tall and black — but had long, flowing dreadlocks. He wore a yellow number "9" on his blue jersey and looked unlike any-one else on the ground. He soared over three other players, planted his knees on the shoulders of a teammate and an opponent and grabbed the ball. Even as the player was tumbling to the turf, Holmes's mind was filled by just one thought: *I wanna do that.*

Tonight, Holmes had his chance — but he would have to outplay his inspiration.

Geez, he's massive! Holmes thought when he first saw the Eagles' star ruckman and 2012 All-Australian, Nic Naitanui, doing a center bounce warm-up, flying high to practice his tapping. A few minutes later Holmes was lining up against him in the center circle. Again, Holmes's inner voice was active: *I have a HUGE task ahead of me. If I'm not on my game, he'll towel me up.*

Taking on Naitanui is difficult for most AFL ruckmen, but espe-cially so for one as raw as Holmes, who to date had just two AFL games to his name. The American had just short of two years of expe-rience in any kind of footy competition, and still had much to learn about the game's nuances.

From the opening bounce Naitanui schooled Holmes, playing the part of professor in this ruck-forward class. Not only did Naitanui win the hitouts battle against Holmes, 30 to 23, but he was also a force all over the field, from start to finish. Naitanui gathered 16 possessions, made four tackles and kicked three goals.

Naitanui took only one mark that night, but it wasn't too dissimilar from the one that awed Holmes three years earlier. At the doorstep of the goal square, the Eagle majestically catapulted himself off the back of one of Holmes's teammates and hauled in the football.

The Eagles' second ruckman, Callum Sinclair, also bested Holmes in hitouts, registering 27. The Eagles easily dismissed the Saints with a thumping 95-point win.

Coming off the ground, Holmes and Naitanui met.

"Keep up the good work," Naitanui told Holmes. "Keep at it."

"Thanks," Holmes replied. "I was excited to ruck against you. Good luck in the finals — I'll be barracking [cheering] for you."

Weeks later, with his season over, as if Holmes needed a reminder of Naitanui's dominance in the match, he learned the Eagle was awarded the maximum three Brownlow Medal votes from the umpires as the best on ground player.

"Early on, I competed well, but clearly he beat me all day long," Holmes says of his match-up with Naitanui. 'He wore me down and they wore me down. I was getting double-rucked and I couldn't run out the whole match. I definitely learned."

A couple of months later, after the Eagles' Grand Final loss to back-to-back premiers, the Hawthorn Hawks, Naitanui was moved to learn of Holmes's admiration and was complimentary of his game.

"It's very humbling to have guys to follow the game from afar and move to the other side of the world and say they were inspired because of vision of myself and my somehow playing a role in that," he says. "He reminded me of me in my early days. He's still learning. He's raw, but he's good. It takes a bit of time to develop the skills, to have the knowledge to get around the field. It was similar to when Majak Daw played against me years ago, with his athleticism."

Naitanui compares Holmes's skills to other athletic AFL ruckmen. Holmes might also be surprised — perhaps even flattered — to know how much effort Naitanui put in as he prepared to compete against him.

"I spent a week-and-a-half beforehand, watching vision of him every day," Naitanui reveals. "You can't take anyone lightly, especially if you've worked so hard to get where he has. You're more wary of the guys who are hard to read. He's a lot quicker than most ruckmen, especially considering the amount of time he's had in our game."

Naitanui, being of Fijian heritage, feels a special connection with Holmes and Wallace, both of whom say they readily identify with him. "The more color in the game, the better," says Naitanui, who is also one of the AFL's official Multicultural Ambassadors, promoting cultural diversity in footy. "It brings a whole new dimension to the game. There was no one who really looked like me or played similar to me, when I started. I thought, *Maybe there isn't a place for guys like me.*"

Naitanui learned his footy in the streets of Midvale, a working-class Perth suburb, playing with his childhood friends — which included two future AFL stars. As a young player, Naitanui idolized the Eagles legend Dean Cox — who first would become his teammate, then his ruck coach — for his athletic ability, and modeled his game on his. Now Naitanui is a role model for Holmes.

"His vertical leap is a lot higher than most, and he changes direction well and does good follow-up work," Naitanui says. "The biggest improvement for him will be using his body. The game smarts will come: understanding the throw-ins and ball-ups, and not using up too much of his energy."

Holmes admits he was gassed late in 2014, his first season of football, but he better managed his second. After the West Coast match he had a week off, before returning to Sandringham and rucking for the club in its VFL semifinal victory and its Preliminary Final loss a week later.

In addition to his first three AFL matches, Holmes played 18 in the VFL in 2015. In three of those matches he was voted as being among his team's best six on ground. Over the year Holmes averaged a respectable 32 hitouts per match, including a career-high 60 in one, and kicked five goals. His stats showed the step up he had taken since 2014, when he had averaged 29 hitouts over 19 matches and kicked one goal.

*

Beyond Holmes's VFL statistics and eventual AFL call-up, 2015 was a year of tremendous personal and professional growth. Holmes is a reflective man and a voracious reader; he has kept a daily journal of his Australian journey, from the time he first arrived.

"I'm a big fan of sports memoirs and one day I want to write mine," says Holmes, who when writing in his journal kicks it old school, preferring to put pen to paper in a leather-bound notebook rather than pecking away at a laptop keyboard. "My writing doesn't feel as authentic if I type."

Holmes has been a bookworm since childhood, and learns much about writing from his extensive reading. Off the ground, the 26-year-old wears a pair of Clark Kent-esque glasses. In the preseason, while on the massage table at the club's Seaford headquarters, Holmes broke routine — surfing social media on his mobile phone — to re-read one of his favorite books, *The Autobiography of Malcolm X*, which the African-American Muslim human rights activist co-wrote with Alex Haley. Holmes plucked the book from the basement shelves of his family's suburban Chicago home, which holds a stack of other books he's eager to add to his reading list.

In 2015, Gillian Flynn's novel *Gone Girl* was Holmes's favorite read, but sports memoirs are his preferred genre. Former professional American gridiron player Nate Jackson's *Slow Getting Up: A Story of NFL Survival from the Bottom of the Pile* and legendary NBA coach Phil Jackson's *Sacred Hoops: Spiritual Lessons of a Hardwood Warrior* and his *The Last Season: A Team in Search of Its Soul* are three of his favorites. Holmes so loves reading that — as his aunt Deidre Holmes tells it — as a teenager he turned down her offer of a back-to-school shopping spree for new clothes, insisting instead she buy him the latest volume in J.K. Rowling's Harry Potter series. Holmes likes spending some of his off-day afternoons at Dymocks, perusing the bookstore shelves.

Holmes is handsome, charismatic and affable. He starred in a 2 1/2-minute short film for Virgin Australia, which was part of the airline's 2014 film festival; the video lives on via YouTube. St Kilda, which occasionally features him in short pieces on its own website, undoubtedly recognizes their import's marketability.

Still, Holmes doesn't go out of his way to seek public attention. He lives in an unassuming house in a southern suburb of Melbourne, with Arryn Siposs, his teammate and housemate during his first two seasons. Holmes's room features a large poster of his musical hero, Bob Marley, which he bought in his freshman year at Cochise College in Arizona. His black and white practice basketball shorts from Mississippi Valley State and a pair of blue and gold ones from Morehead State — the two other universities he attended and for which he played basketball — are reminders of his previous athletic life. In fact, when it comes to long, complicated journeys, Odysseus has nothing on Holmes. In Holmes's early childhood, his father, Kevin, played pro basketball in Europe, Asia and the Middle East, so the family lived briefly in Europe and Israel, before settling in Elk Grove Village, Illinois.

But another souvenir Holmes has on a black mantelpiece in his room serves as a constant reminder of how he earned his athletic rebirth: a Sherrin Australian football (the AFL's official brand) mounted on a plaque, which is inscribed with the words "2013 NAB AFL DRAFT COMBINE BEST PERFORMANCE Best Running Vertical Jump Test." This is the reason he's so far from home.

In 2014 Holmes very nearly earned a promotion to the Saints' senior list and an AFL game. "If the season had gone another two weeks, he would've been promoted," says the club's head of football, Chris Pelchen. "We had inherited a difficult situation with an ageing list and our intention was to try as many young players as we could at the highest level. We were in a position where some players were injured, but we didn't want any player to be promoted and go in for just one game."

Perhaps for that reason, St Kilda's match committee named Holmes for the first two of its three NAB Challenge matches the following pre-season. In the second of these, against Essendon, for a brief moment Holmes had the footy world's attention all to himself.

Halfway through the first quarter, just outside the forward 50, Holmes marked a kick from the wing in full stride. He played on and fired a shot at goal from 40 meters. It went straight through the posts for the game's first major score, prompting a hearty roar from the small crowd gathered at Morwell Recreation Reserve. While Holmes's teammates bombarded him from every direction with hugs, Fox Footy commentator Anthony Hudson talked up the moment: "Jason Holmes, the American. Big, tall ruckman who had a first full year at VFL last year, and what a start for him in the year 2015."

But the beginning of the calendar year hadn't been as auspicious.

Holmes broke his right hand during a tackling drill during a preseason training session and had to miss several days of further workouts with the club in a small town on New Zealand's South Island. "I thought I'd dislocated it and I continued with the drill," said Holmes, whose hand was later set in a plastic mold cast. "In basketball, coaches want you to be able to dribble with both hands and in footy, I ruck with both hands. And I need to be able to use both of them."

As Holmes learned during his NCAA basketball days and two seasons of VFL footy, the aches and pains an athlete experiences while playing high-level sport are ubiquitous. He endured niggles with an ankle and his back in the 2014 season, and dealt with a sore shoulder. Holmes was also deeply missing home through the early part of the 2015 season.

"I miss home most when times are tough," Holmes says. "But I like it here, trying to build a career."

Pelchen attributes Holmes's homesickness to a condition many footballers wrestle with after their first year in the AFL system. "It's the 'second-year blues,'" Pelchen says. "It's a challenge for our local boys in their second years, too. The initial excitement and euphoria has passed and it makes the transition difficult when reality sets in. You're no longer stimulated by that initial excitement. But the local boys can go home to their families on long weekends and bye weeks. Jason couldn't."

The Holmes family is highly athletic, worldly and tight-knit. Holmes is one of three brothers playing three different professional sports on three different continents. Jason's younger brother, Mark, plays pro basketball in France, while older brother Andre is a wide receiver for the NFL's Oakland Raiders.

Jason's competitive edge was forged playing basketball and gridiron against his brothers on the gravel driveway and in the snow-covered front yard outside the family's two-story townhouse. "Jason always plays with fire," Andre Holmes says. "When he sets his mind to being good at something, he does well."

Halfway through the 2015 season, with his senior call-up still weeks away, Holmes started slowly coming out of those second-year blues. He began dating a young woman, with whom he grew close. His form improved and he gained confidence with each passing match. His body began adapting to the soreness that usually hit him two days — not one — after matches.

Hours after a hard-fought three-point win over the Footscray Bulldogs at the Zebras' home ground, in which Holmes was thoroughly tested by two opposing AFL-experienced ruckmen, he is weighing up his progress and footy future. He's heartily eating chicken parmesan at Poci's, an Italian restaurant a little over a half-mile north of the oval, where he sometimes has his post-game meal.

"You want to know about what kind of legacy you can create," Holmes says. "There's a glass wall at Seaford [club headquarters] with all the names of everyone who has ever played for the club inscribed on it. I want to get my name on that wall and be part of something special."

But Holmes will have to be patient if that "something special" is an AFL finals appearance, or a Premiership. The Saints are in a rebuilding phase, but Holmes is optimistic about the club's near future. "We're not that far from being competitive [for a finals berth]," he says. "I daydream about fighting for the flag at the MCG, to have that feeling where we've gotten to the end and there's no one better than us."

Mid-season, Holmes is still working on his game sense. At dinner he readily admits to sometimes "stuffing up" kicks from his defensive 50. Sometimes the mistakes lead to opposition goals. Other times, he kicks waywardly into space.

"He's a fierce competitor, and in that aspect he always finds some fault in what he's doing, and that's what makes him better," Kevin Holmes says. "He talked to me about what he should've done and what he could've done."

Though he's a tough critic of his own skills and progress, Holmes's Sandringham coaches say he has been a model pupil. "If you want to be a teacher and have a good student, he's ideal," says assistant St Kilda coach Peta Searle, who herself has made history as the first woman to be appointed to such a role in the AFL. "You'd love to have 25 players like him. He takes feedback well, he's a special student and he's been able to mentor the younger guys in mental and physical preparation."

On occasion at Trevor Barker Oval, the Zebras' home ground, besides hearing his own inner voice, Holmes kept hearing another influential one nearby. It would come from behind the goal the Zebras were attacking, when he was resting forward. It was the Saints' head coach, Alan Richardson, trying to get him to think about his positioning.

As the season progressed, Holmes heard much more from Richardson. But his senior coach's words never had quite the impact as they did in early August, before a Sandringham hosted Port Melbourne. The coach told the young ruckman to prepare himself; he might also want to talk to his parents about making some travel plans to come to Australia. Suddenly, getting a senior game was on Holmes's horizon.

But the coach's words didn't have the desired effect. Instead of feeling inspired, Holmes fell flat. "My first feeling when he told me was, 'I heard that a couple of times last year,'" Holmes says. "My parents got excited when I told them, but I had to tell them, 'Mom, Dad, chill. I haven't done anything yet.'"

Instead of buckling down and playing his game, Holmes lost focus. From a purely statistical standpoint, the 32 hitouts and five tackles he amassed in his side's 33-point win didn't look terrible. But his ruck partner Lewis Pierce had three more hitouts, while the opposing ruckman equaled Holmes's total. Holmes was disgusted with his performance. He says he allowed the news of his possible call-up to distract him.

"I ended up playing poorly," he says frankly. "I was caught up in what was going on around me. I knew then that I couldn't have two bad weeks in a row. I battled a cold and still played the next week."

That match was a 45-point victory over Northern Blues. This time, Holmes was dominant in the ruck against an AFL-experienced Cameron Wood. Though Holmes says he played only marginally better than in the previous round, the hitout count was solidly in his favor, 33 to 14. He also kicked a goal and took a couple of marks. Considering his mild illness, Holmes says he played better than he thought he could.

Three days later, Richardson called Holmes to his office. The wheels were in motion. Richardson told him that, finally, a senior call-up was being seriously discussed. "The match committee is meeting again today," the coach said. "I'll ring you tonight."

A couple of hours passed as Holmes anxiously waited. Then a few more. Finally his mobile phone rang and he recognized his senior coach's number on the screen. After he answered, Holmes's housemate Siposs could tell from the look on his friend's face who was on the line. The conversation was brief. When it ended, Holmes faced his mate, who had been alongside him on this journey for each step he had taken in Australia.

Holmes tried his best to keep his cool. "I'm playing."

Siposs couldn't contain his excitement. He jumped up and grabbed Holmes in a bear hug. "That's amazing!" he yelled. "I can't believe it — you did it!"

Holmes finally let go of his cool. Even Archie, Siposs's 66 lb., caramel-colored Hungarian vizsla dog was going mad, as if he understood the moment's significance.

"It gave me chills," Holmes says. "It *still* gives me chills. I just remember that moment and then, after that, I went about my day the next two days knowing, but not saying anything to anyone else. Going to sleep the night before the announcement, I thought I'd sleep okay. But when they made the announcement on Thursday, that's the day everything changed."

Holmes had told his parents and his girlfriend the news, but the rest of the world was hearing for the first time that he would make his senior debut against the Geelong Cats in a night match two days later. Every device Holmes had was getting non-stop notifications from well-wishers on three continents. On the Thursday night he couldn't sleep at all. By the time the Saints match committee selected Holmes, it was too late for his parents, Kevin and Mary, to arrange to fly over for his debut match, but they did travel to Melbourne to see him play the following week, a home game against Sydney.

The young Saints were hammered in that match by the perennial Grand Final contenders, the Swans, and their Canadian born-and-bred ruckman, former international rugby player Mike Pyke, got the best of Holmes. But Holmes, now a second-gamer, didn't embarrass himself.

On the Australian TV coverage, Dennis Cometti said Holmes and Pyke's meeting in the center square represented "the changing face of footy." His co-commentator, AFL Hall of Famer Leigh Matthews, meanwhile, was balanced in assessing Holmes's performance and his prospects as a quality ruckman. "He might be a really valuable asset in the future," Matthews says. "Athletically, he's magnificent and center bounces are his forte, but you only get so many of those a game. He's not finding much of the ball at ground level, so that's clearly an area of improvement."

But the technical aspects of Holmes's game were far from his parents' minds. On their whirlwind trip, Kevin and Mary Holmes landed in Melbourne on the morning of the match. Almost as soon as the wheels touched down, the proud parents did the media rounds: a pre-match radio interview, a TV appearance during the match, a previously recorded feature of them that aired at half time, then another radio interview post-match. Early the next morning they and their history-making son appeared live on a national TV news show.

Back home in America, there were small ripples of excitement. With some influence from the Australian Football Association of North America, an American organization dedicated to spreading awareness of the sport, the subscription TV channel Fox Soccer Plus — which, along with Fox Sports 1 and Fox Sports 2 broadcasts live AFL matches weekly, during America's collective graveyard shift, to very small audiences — ditched its planned coverage of another AFL match so it could air the Saints' one.

"It was really exciting," Kevin Holmes reflects. "We had been there before and Jason sat in the stands with us, but to be there and see *him* out there on the field was something special, seeing him competing at the top level of Australian footy."

Kevin and Mary became sudden celebrities. Some fans at Etihad Stadium even walked over to congratulate them. "They're Holmesy's parents!" shyer fans murmured, pointing at them.

The sense of occasion wasn't lost on Holmes's parents, who relish their son's history-making accomplishment. "I've told Jason it's something that can never be taken from him," Kevin Holmes says. He confesses that "a couple of tears could've dropped" from his eyes a few weeks earlier, when he got a photo via text message of Saints captain Nick Riewoldt presenting Jason with his number "45" jersey. "He's established a benchmark in his life he can one day tell his kids. He can be an ambassador for the sport."

The stress of playing in front of family and friends, plus the intensity of the match and the physical and mental exhaustion associated with it, affected the St Kilda ruckman. It took Holmes several hours to unwind after the match. His parents felt that stress as they stopped at a drive-thru restaurant on their way home from the match. In Jason's mind, they were taking forever to decide what they wanted.

"It was great to have them over and see a game and I'm always patient with my family, but they had to hear me crack the whip," Holmes says, laughing as he recalls the moment. "I said, 'You guys need to speed this up!' I really needed to get out of the car. I just wanted to get the food and go to their hotel and relax."

*

Holmes's AFL debut ratcheted up the demands on his time and for his attention, and he could barely leave home without people approaching him for a chat, a handshake or a selfie. The most awkward episode came the afternoon after his first game, when he was back at Trevor Barker Oval, watching his Sandringham teammates play Geelong.

In that match, Holmes saw his best mate Siposs get knocked unconscious in a head clash with another player. Siposs eventually regained consciousness but had to be carried off the ground on a stretcher. Holmes was concerned for his injured mate, so he started walking back to the rooms to be near him. As he did, a group of fans walked up to him. Although he felt bad for the fans, Holmes had to put his friend first.

"Arryn was out and some kids were asking for autographs," Holmes says. "You try to do the right thing at that moment, but I was looking out for my friend. I was distraught and was hoping he was okay."

If the incident had happened earlier in the season, Holmes likely would've made it back to the locker room with no fuss, to comfort his fallen comrade. But his elevation to the Saints had thrust him into greater prominence.

"Prior to his call-up, he seemed like his life was pretty under the radar," Kevin Holmes says. "But since the media explosion, he's known everywhere he goes. His life there has taken a turn, but it hasn't gone to his head."

The next week, as his parents returned to America, Holmes and the Saints departed Melbourne for Perth, for their disappointing match against West Coast, their final one of the season. There was still more work for Holmes to do, though. In his end-of-year meeting with Richardson, the coach reminded him that he needed to have a big preseason to consolidate the progress he had made in 2015. But he left Holmes with encouraging words.

"We didn't gift you those games," Richardson told Holmes. "You *earned* them."

Still, Holmes is far from satisfied with his effort. "I looked at the highlights of the Geelong game," he says. "I'll see it now and wish I could've played better. I wish my last couple of games had been better. There's obviously room for improvement. I wanna see improvement year to year. I'm happy that I don't look back and say, 'I'm proud of what I've done.'"

At the end of September, as Naitanui and the Eagles prepared for the Grand Final, Holmes headed home to Chicago. Besides checking out his personal library at home, Holmes had some fun with his father, who had started a new job as the head basketball coach at Francis W. Parker Senior High School, on Chicago's North Side, in the same neighborhood as DePaul University, his alma mater. Back in the day, when Kevin Holmes was helping lead a Swiss team to two national championships, fans gave him the nickname "The Smasher" for his thunderous slam-dunks.

"Jason likes to play devil's advocate with me and we had some great debates right in the living room," Kevin Holmes says, with a laugh. "We've had some good ones. But one day we came downstairs to watch some TV and he just said, 'Dad, I just don't feel like it this morning. I'm calling a truce.'"

There also was a family reunion with another professional athlete sibling. Holmes, his parents and about a dozen other relatives and friends piled into cars and headed to Soldier Field to watch Andre Holmes and his Oakland Raiders teammates play against the Chicago Bears. The Raiders had a bye week afterwards, so Jason was able to fly to Oakland and enjoy some quality time with his brother, sister-in-law and nephew. Meanwhile, Mark Holmes had begun his basketball season in France.

In November, after Jason returned to Australia for preseason training, breaking news of the deadly Paris terrorist attacks gave him an urgent reason to ring his brother. Mark plays for a team based in Châteauroux, about 170 miles south of Paris, so he was safely removed from the violence. When the brothers spoke, it was before dawn on Saturday in Paris, several hours after the attacks. They anxiously discussed what had just happened. The game Mark Holmes and his team were scheduled to play that day had already been cancelled.

The Paris attacks deeply concerned Holmes, not only because they touched his brother's life. They seemed to be part of a worldwide uptick in violence, from different sectors of various societies. While in Chicago in November 2015, Holmes and the rest of the city were riveted by police squad car dashboard video released to the public, which showed a white Chicago police officer fatally shooting a 17-year-old

African-American boy named Laquan McDonald 11 months earlier. The officer claimed he was carrying a knife. Holmes also watched the debates American politicians were having about admitting Syrians who were fleeing the violent disintegration of their country. These events inspired Holmes to do what comes naturally to him, besides play sports — read. That's why, before returning to Australia, he grabbed *The Autobiography of Malcolm X* off the shelf at home.

"Reading it in a different part of the world is eye-opening," says Holmes, who fondly embraces the dual ethnic heritage he inherited from his African-American father and white mother. "Especially with what's happened in Chicago and with the Syrian refugee crisis. As a black man and a white man, I have a dual mindset and I understand where people are coming from. I don't think of the world as black and white; it's more gray. Malcolm X was an amazing man. What's most amazing was his ability to change and adapt. He saw America for what it was, and then he goes to Mecca and learns the white man is not the devil. He knew his assassination was coming, but he was never afraid to stand up for what he believed was right."

Could an AFL ruckman become as well known for his book-ishness as his hitouts? Improbable, but not impossible. After all, not too long ago the idea of an American former college basketball player ever playing AFL footy might've also been seen as impossible in footy circles.

Holmes has travelled a difficult road, and has many more miles to go. No doubt he will be forced to make further physical, mental and emotional sacrifices as well. That's why he was so moved the night he watched the 2015 AFL National Draft on TV. With the rest of the nation, Holmes saw his newest teammate experience a rite of passage much like the one he had experienced months before.

"I saw the Brandon White video," says Holmes, referring to a You-Tube clip he saw which captured White's and his family members' joyful exultation at hearing his name being called out in the draft. "It moved me to see this kid reacting. It was one of the milestone moments for him."

Jason Holmes had a bunch of those in 2015, including manning up on Naitanui for the first time. That challenge was of a type Kevin Holmes knows very well, from his experience of an NBA preseason with the Philadelphia 76ers. Kevin found himself on court with the Los Angeles Lakers' great champion, Earvin "Magic" Johnson, a player he idolized.

Kevin discussed that game with his son, as well as the one Jason played, against Naitanui. "There's a lot of learning to be done from that game," the father told the son. "He didn't make you look silly. You held your own."

6

The Collingwood Cowboy
Mason Cox

He stands in a landscape of vast emptiness. As far as his eyes can see, the terrain is ivory-hued, flat, and so bright from the sun's glare that it's almost blinding. The endless sky above where Mason Cox is standing is cerulean blue. It's October 2015, about a month after his first professional footy season, and Cox has come to a special place, at the beginning of his off-season leave, to get away from it all. There's no Wi-Fi anywhere close, no phone signal and no TV. In fact, the only electricity available comes from a generator.

When you're the AFL's tallest-ever player and you play for its most famous club, and when your foreign accent makes you stand out in crowds even more, it's hard to find somewhere to escape the attention, reset your mind and feel completely insignificant while basking in nature's splendor. But Cox has found that place: Salar de Uyuni. It's one of the planet's remotest places. It's in Bolivia, at an altitude of almost 12,000 feet. With its area of about 4,700 square miles, it comprises the world's largest salt flat.

"I needed a break," Cox says, after returning to Melbourne for the 2016 pre-season, his second. "I needed to detox from footy."

For Cox, the Texan drafted by Collingwood in 2014 in the Rookie Draft and signed to a Category B International Rookie contract, the last year has been taxing. Having played NCAA basketball and soccer, he had to learn footy from scratch. When he began training with the club in September 2014, he was desperate to make a good impression on his new coaches and earn his teammates' respect. And not to embarrass himself with poor skills. When the 2015 preseason officially began in November, the physical and mental strain was at a level Cox had never before experienced. A full VFL season followed.

Afterwards, Cox was in pain. Beside the standard bangs and bruises, his right shoulder, which had been barking all year, wasn't right. For the first time in his life Cox would have to have surgery. He went under the knife to repair the damage.

So Cox plotted a brief escape to Bolivia, where a few American friends joined him. He went on to Chile's Atacama Desert, where from nightfall to dawn nothing could obscure his view of an infinite array of stars. He visited Peru's Machu Picchu and marveled at the ruins of the ancient Incan city. He explored the Argentine and Chilean region of Patagonia, feeling the below-freezing temperatures on his skin and hiking trails up sky-piercing peaks.

Nevertheless, Cox couldn't *completely* get away. In Cusco, Peru, his newfound fame as Collingwood's American recruit caught up with him. A couple of vacationing Aussies from Melbourne spotted him, introduced themselves and chatted to him about Hawthorn's Grand Final victory over West Coast. It was the first Cox had heard of the match's outcome.

Then, at a hostel in Punta Arenas, Argentina, while deep into conversation with Cox, a tourist from Sydney confessed: "I knew who you were, but I just didn't want to say anything."

"Thanks for treating me like a normal guy," Cox replied with a laugh.

Cox is fully embracing his unexpected athletic adventure in Melbourne: he enjoys playing footy, he cherishes the camaraderie of his teammates and he delights in discovering the urban wonders of Melbourne. But, he says, "it's tough to find people who don't see you only as a footy player."

Cox's whirlwind introduction to the footy universe began in the early months of 2014, when he was completing his senior year at Oklahoma State University. Cox, nearing the end of his bachelor's degree in mechanical engineering, was finishing up his senior year capstone project, overhauling a cutting process to help a metal manufacturer. He saw a better future in his degree than in his basketball, which had seen him compete in a modest total of 24 games in three years, in which he averaged just 2.4 minutes per game. Cox was preparing to enter the same field in which both his parents had made their careers. After graduating, he had planned a European backpacking vacation and then would return to Texas to take up a well-paying job in Houston.

Shortly after the basketball season, though, Cox got *that* email: the one from Jonathan Givony, inviting him to attend the AFL's U.S. Combine. The Draft Express headhunter had seen Cox play on TV. Givony also learned that Cox had formerly played soccer, too.

"Hey, dude," Cox said to Connor Schuman, his close friend and college roommate of three years. "You will *not* believe this."

"What the hell?" Schuman said, looking over his buddy's shoulder to read the email. "What do they want?"

Cox and Schuman took some time to fully digest the message.

"Should I do it?" Cox asked.

"Hell, yeah," Schuman told him. "Why not?"

The next thing Cox knew, he was in Los Angeles with other American potentials, getting used to the feel of the unfamiliar leather oval ball. When he put on his standard-issue black compression top, he was pleased to see he'd been given number 17, the same number he wore on his Edward S. Marcus High School jersey when he was a defender on its state champion soccer team.

After Cox killed it at the Combine, the AFL flew him to Melbourne for a different kind of job interview — one that didn't involve fronting up in a jacket, tie and freshly polished dress shoes. This one featured follow-up ball skills tests and a timed 2-kilometre run in front of scouts from a handful of AFL clubs. Midfielders usually run that distance in six minutes; Cox finished in six minutes and 50 seconds. Considering Cox's size, his time was staggering.

The scouts also marveled at his vertical leap and his appetite for work. They even loved his manners. "We look for little clues," says

Collingwood's recruiting manager, Derek Hine. "We were out having a coffee with him, getting our first impression. We noticed he held the door open for a couple of women. He's very humble and very polite." Cox was equally taken with Collingwood and Hine. "Derek was on top of everything," he recalls. "He came to the airport to meet me, called me every day and was with me every step of the way. I saw it all in college, players getting wined and dined, but I felt like if Collingwood was gonna take care of me like that, they'd do it if I sign with them. It's a successful club culture. You can see it upfront. It makes you want to be successful."

One day during his visit, Hine took the potential recruit for a wander. They walked together the short distance from the club's state-of-the-art headquarters to the MCG, and continued out onto the field. From the center circle, Hine showed Cox what he envisioned as his destiny. "This is our home," he told Cox. "And this," he continued, spreading out his arms to highlight the ground's expanse, "could be your workplace."

Hine is known in the game as being devoted to the wellbeing of the club's young players. Marty Clarke, an Irish recruit Hine signed from professional Gaelic football in 2006, became part of Hine's family after the recruiter invited him to live at his own home. Clarke had six successful years at Collingwood, over two separate, three-year stints, playing 73 matches.

The Magpies made Cox an attractive offer. But there was another tempting contract dangling before him. It wasn't from one of the three other AFL clubs that had scouted him but from an American corporate behemoth. ExxonMobil, whose recruiters Cox had met at a job fair before he was invited to the U.S. Combine, had offered him a position in the company's project management exploration department, at its Houston headquarters.

Cox knew he had a daunting choice: move across the world from his suburban Dallas home and try a new sport he'd known about only for a few months, or take a plum corporate job for which most new college graduates would give their eye-teeth.

Schuman, who has accompanied Cox on camping trips to Arkansas's Ozark Mountains and on biking and kayaking excursions in Texas, knew which path his friend would choose. "He was never the type of person to sit behind a desk," he says. "He'd be miserable sitting there and putting on a suit every day. He sees life as one big string of experiences, and he wants to experience everything. He'd have a lot more fun and be a lot more fulfilled if he tried Australian football."

Ultimately Cox told the ExxonMobil recruiter what was in his heart. "I have this amazing opportunity," he said, "and I can't turn it down."

So instead of cramming himself into an office cubicle, Cox has spent the last two years fitting in with his new teammates, in a new city, country and sporting culture. "I didn't want to be behind a desk 30 years from now, thinking about what I could've done," Cox says. "This is the time of my life to take risks. I could've been making money for a big company, or making it for myself. I could've taken the easy way and gone the corporate route."

Collingwood's original plan was for Cox to work out with development coaches for a month, beginning in September 2014, and then to head home to Texas and return in time for preseason training in November. Cox, however, insisted on staying until Christmas. He got plenty of weightlifting in, adding bulk to his lanky frame, and the coaches gave him an insane amount of endurance conditioning to do. Even during 2014 Grand Final week, with his dream workplace, the majestic MCG, visible in the distance, Cox would often be out on the park for individual sprinting drills and kicking practice. And more kicking practice. And even *more* kicking practice, as late morning would become afternoon, then afternoon would morph into evening.

Cox, who speaks with more Texas droll then drawl, quickly got plenty of public attention in Melbourne. "Coxy!" a random footy fan once yelled to him, "you signed with the wrong club, mate!" Not a chance, from Cox's perspective. Long before the Collingwood Cowboy's fairytale debut on Anzac Day, the Magpies had made quite an investment in him. If you mentioned his name to anyone at the club, even as far back as 2014, before he'd even played his first VFL match, the response never changed: sly smiles, as if everyone was in on a secret plan to deploy a new weapon they couldn't wait to unleash on their opponents.

*

Craig McRae, Collingwood's head of development, has been a key player in the club's plot. In his on-field footy career, McRae kicked 232 goals in 195 games and was a three-time premiership player with the AFL's Brisbane Lions during their 2001-2003 Premiership dynasty. Off the field, he has been a development coach more than a decade, with three AFL clubs.

In his spacious office at Collingwood's Holden Centre, McRae flicks on two television monitors and excitedly says, "There's something I want to show you." The words "Mason Cox Progress Report" appear on the screens. Then video plays on each screen.

It's Cox kicking the footy. "Week 1" is written on one monitor and "Week 7" on the other. If the Week 1 footage seems a little odd, it's not only because Cox is out of uniform and awkwardly dropping the ball, tilting and slightly tossing it upwards before kicking. It's also because the picturesque, snow-capped Swiss Alps tower over him in the background. It's footage of Cox during his post-graduation European trip, filmed by a friend on a mobile phone. The Week 7 video, though, shows Cox in full Magpies gear. His body language is far more assured. His ball drop is no longer awkward and angular, and the laces face his target. The point of impact off his right boot looks good.

"We worked for six weeks every day," McRae says, beaming, as Cox — after a training session — sprawls on a nearby couch in his office. "I've said this to Mason, that in five years I've never seen anyone pick up the basics and knowledge that quickly — even more than the Irish guys. He's a problem solver. He could work out why he was missing when he kicked. He could be a serious talent in this game, if he perseveres and grows, as quick and agile as he is."

Sometimes McRae would break up the monotony of Cox's training routine. He'd set up several rubbish bins and toss balls into the air; Cox and his fellow ruckman, Brodie Grundy, would compete to tap the ball into the bins. In one of his first sessions, Cox matched Grundy tap for tap.

McRae lauds Cox for often coming into the club on his off-days to work on his ruck craft, and also to learn the particulars of forward play. The Magpies' top brass's vision is that the American will one day be capable of taking contested marks and kicking goals on the biggest stage of all.

The coaches' excitement did not lessen when it was time for Cox to test his skills in actual matches. After just one intrasquad match, Collingwood gave Cox a run against Carlton in its second 2015 NAB Challenge match, at Queen Elizabeth Oval in Bendigo.

The day before, Cox had celebrated his 24th birthday. Cox's teammates bought a cake in the club's black and white colors to celebrate his special day — but two-thirds of it was gone by the time he pulled it out of the refrigerator and cut a piece. When his teammates acknowledged Cox's birthday in a team meeting, star midfielder Dane Swan called for him to make a speech. Cox stepped forward and opened his mouth but couldn't get a syllable out: in a typical "haze the new guy" moment, another teammate yelled at him to "shut the hell up!"

The night before Collingwood's first preseason match against the rival Carlton Blues, Cox's head coach Nathan Buckley told him he might send him on just before the end of the first half. On match day, Cox was sitting on the bench at the time Buckley mentioned when an assistant approached him. "Start warming up," he told Cox.

This is it, Cox thought to himself. *This is what you've been working your butt off for, for the last six months.*

No sooner did Cox join the action than he sensed a navy blue blur shooting past him. It was Carlton speedster Chris Yarran bursting past from halfback with the footy, moving his team into attack. His blinding pace made Cox do a double take. A thought flew through his mind: *You've gotta be kidding me!*

Cox had only ever competed in about 20 center bounces before, all in intrasquad practice sessions. He was learning his new craft from his development coaches and his midfield mates. "You talk to them and they tell you where they want you to hit it," Cox says. "You have signals. But it's tough to judge where the ball is going to go. You find the ball and you protect yourself." Now, here he was, up against the Blues' two veteran ruckmen, including Robbie Warnock.

"When I went up against Warnock, he was about to hit me with an elbow in the gut," Cox recalls, "but I slipped out from under him."

When the day was done, Cox had racked up 14 hitouts in Collingwood's seven-point loss. "It was a good birthday present for him," Buckley recalls. "He didn't disappoint. The biggest challenge for the American boys is going into the ruck and knowing they've got people coming at them."

*

A steep learning curve did not intimidate Cox. Three years before Cox's metamorphosis from NCAA basketball center to AFL ruckman, he was learning how to compete in a basketball jump ball. Oklahoma State hadn't recruited Cox to play the sport, and he'd never played it competitively in high school. He was a walk-on.

Strangely enough, Cox hadn't looked for the opportunity to play basketball. Instead, it found him. The most experience he had was outside his family's home in a town called Highland Village, where he played against his two older brothers, Austin and Nolan. "Mason used to come out in the driveway and would play and get beat up on," Nolan Cox says. "He was super-competitive and he'd quit when he was losing."

Cox played for fun on an Oklahoma State intramural basketball team, but he soon found himself promoted to a far higher level: the Oklahoma State's women's basketball "scout" team. That squad is made up of players who are similar in size to the team's upcoming opponents, and they practice with the team.

The women had a big game ahead against Baylor and needed someone on the scout team to stand in for opponent Brittney Griner, a 6-foot-8 powerhouse center who was well on her way to establishing an NCAA basketball record of 748 career blocked shots — a total no player of either gender has bettered. Griner now stars for the Phoenix Mercury in the Women's National Basketball Association.

While Cox was shooting around during his women's scout team gig, Travis Ford, the school's men's basketball coach saw him. With the team down a few players due to injuries and suspensions, Ford offered him a tryout. Cox made the team and quickly became a fan favorite.

"He's always had a lot of friends," says Devon Sells, Cox's closest friend, who has known him since grammar school. "He was already friends with a lot of people on the campus, so that didn't shock me."

Sells and Cox's friendship blossomed from the moment their 9th grade biology teacher assigned them to sit next to each other — because they were the class's two tallest kids, Sells says. At 5-foot-11, she was especially tall for a girl her age.

"Our friendship has centered around us being ginormous," says Sells, who lives in Houston. "He's always been there. He's a really good, supportive friend. He's one of those friends you never lose that relationship with. He's like one of my brothers."

So while Sells was attending Louisiana State University, she twice made fairly long road trips to Oklahoma State to watch Cox and his Cowboys teammates play. She even created a T-shirt in Oklahoma State's orange and black color scheme, with a provocative slogan: "My Cox is 6-11. What's Your Excuse?"

In Cox's final year at college, in a game that saw the Cowboys pull off a major upset and defeat the University of Kansas, he earned rave reviews from Ford, his coach, for three minutes in which he blanketed Joel Embiid, a standout 7-foot center whom the NBA's Philadelphia 76ers would select at number 4 in the NBA draft a few months later. In his last home game, at Gallagher-Iba Arena, Cox brought the house down with his first-ever basket there — an authoritative slam-dunk — in a victory over Kansas State.

But even with these small victories, Sells says Cox's humility is his most valuable asset. "He's been able to accomplish so much with knowing so little [about footy], but he lets his friends and family be proud of him," she says. "He's still treating me and all of his friends the same and he's never let anything go to his head. I have lots of friends who play professional sports, from high school and college, but Mason's the one I know will always respond when I contact him."

Cox's friends have grown accustomed to seeing him as a ferocious competitor. Whatever impulses he once had to quit during the driveway basketball battles with his brothers are long gone. AFL scouts say he was relentless in his first VFL season, often playing against AFL-experienced ruckmen such as Majak Daw. The scouts also say Cox is rapidly mastering the fine art of "bodying" an opponent, a subtle aspect of both ruck and forward craft.

St Kilda's former head of football, Chris Pelchen, says Cox is more adept at this than other American AFL recruits. "Mason has the most competitive streak among them," Pelchen says. "He's initiating that contact in marking contests. He's softening his opponent's desire to resist. When the ball is in flight, Mason is willing to bump, bash, then come forward to mark. When you 'body' your opponent, then marking contests aren't 50-50. You're trying to get the advantage before the ball arrives."

Cox played 19 VFL games in 2015, averaging 22 hitouts per game and kicking 17 goals. Collingwood balanced his workload in the ruck and up forward so he could get considerable time playing both positions. Which does he prefer?

"I like whatever role's gonna get me a game first," Cox says with a laugh. "Being able to [be] versatile gets you more games. Being in the forward line is a little more difficult and mentally taxing, knowing where you have to be and learning everything from scratch, but as a ruckman you can follow your direct opponent."

*

Cox's first VFL season featured many memorable moments. He wasn't used to runners coming onto the ground to deliver messages from coaches. He hadn't experienced fans standing just a few feet away from the huddles at the end of the first and third quarters while the coaches addressed their players. On more than a few occasions, young fans asked Cox for an autograph during the quarter-time break, when he was trying to focus on the match. Once, after Cox kicked a goal, he even heard Collingwood fans chanting "U-S-A! U-S-A!" just as some had done a few years before for his countryman Shae McNamara, Collingwood's first American recruit.

And then there was Cox's best match. Perhaps fittingly, it came on the 4th of July. Even more fittingly, the Round 12 match against Sandringham at Victoria Park pitted Cox against Jason Holmes.

It was a bone chilling, rainy, Southern Hemisphere winter afternoon. In the first quarter, Cox led the Pies to a 20-point advantage, setting up one goal by kicking to a teammate in the forward 50. Holmes helped Sandringham stay in touch, kicking a set-shot goal from 35 meters out. Ultimately, Collingwood held on for a 10-point win, despite Sandringham's spirited comeback that fell just short. Cox accumulated 29 hitouts, four marks and seven tackles, while Holmes registered 30 hitouts and laid two tackles to go with his goal.

One passage of play epitomized Cox's effort. He flubbed a kick in the forward 50, missing a target and — it seemed — gifting the ball to the opposition. *What the hell was I thinking?* he fleetingly thought. Before he could answer his own question, though, he put to use a skill he had displayed in his initial Australian audition, when he had run a 20-meter sprint in an even three seconds. Twenty meters was about the distance Cox was from the Sandringham player who pounced on the loose ball, and three seconds was all it took for Cox to emerge out of nowhere and tackle him.

"When the ball left my foot, I saw it wasn't gonna hit the target," Cox says. "You know you messed up, so you wanna correct it and get the ball back as quickly as possible. So you find a little extra and get it back."

Cox's "little extra" then and throughout the match saw him

adjudged Collingwood's best on ground. After the siren, Cox and Holmes embraced and engaged in some friendly banter.

The two men's footy fates again intertwined seven weeks later, on Saturday, August 22. St Kilda had announced to the footy world two days earlier that Holmes would make his AFL debut in a night match at Etihad Stadium. Cox, meanwhile, would be playing the same morning at the Collingwood VFL team's home ground, Victoria Park against Richmond's reserves, while Collingwood's varsity would take on Richmond's in the afternoon, at the MCG.

Before Cox left the apartment he was sharing with his teammate Darcy Moore — a promising forward who had made his AFL debut earlier that season — the two made a friendly wager. Whoever kicked the most goals that day would get a free dinner at the other's expense.

Cox booted a season-high five in his side's 72-point win and was judged Collingwood's second-best player.

Across the globe, late in the afternoon on a Texas highway, Cox's big brother Nolan was live-streaming the match via his car radio while driving 200 miles north from Austin to Dallas. After each goal his little brother kicked, Nolan Cox was yelling to himself in the car in celebration. Their father, Phil, was also listening in as the match unfolded.

In a role reversal from their driveway basketball games, now it's baby brother Mason who is influencing big brother Nolan. While Mason was playing his inaugural VFL season, Nolan started playing competitive footy in the USAFL with the Austin Crows, as a ruck and center half-forward. Not only would Nolan win his club's best first-year player award, he also earned a USAFL regional tournament's most valuable player honors.

Back in Melbourne, just as Moore was arriving at the MCG, he was unaware of the score from Cox's game — until Cox called him to let him know.

"Bullshit!" said the astonished Moore, who that day went goalless in his side's 91-point loss. "You didn't kick five!" Moore was likely still surprised while treating Cox to dinner at Meatmother, an American-style barbecue restaurant.

On the evening of Cox's big day, he was too "physically dead" from his own match to attend Holmes's that night against Geelong. But he watched it on TV and tweeted his compatriot a congratulatory message. Suddenly, two Americans were making news playing Australia's game.

But for Cox, neither the Sandringham nor the Richmond match is the one he most treasures from his first season. It was from an early-season match at Victoria Park, a win Collingwood sealed in the last minutes over a determined Footscray side. Late in the match Cox marked the ball inside 50, close to the boundary line. He faced a tight angle if he took a set shot for goal, so instead he kicked the footy to a teammate close to the goal square, who marked and then kicked an easy goal. It was the side's first win of the season.

With Holmes debuting, Cox's stock rising and the Collingwood seniors set to miss the finals, the media began speculating about a possible call-up and AFL debut for Cox. There were two rounds left in the season, but it didn't come to pass.

"Collingwood didn't feel the need to rush me, so it didn't really bother me," says Cox, who rates his season performance as a seven out of 10. "Obviously I want to play AFL, but I wasn't freaked out."

Cox entered the 2016 preseason feeling more settled. He could report to training at the same time his teammates would. He had fully assimilated to the Collingwood club culture. Schuman — Cox's close friend and roommate from his college days — again moved in with him, the two sharing an apartment in Richmond.

"His being here is a mental help," Cox says. "It's good to have someone from outside footy. Footy's a small aspect of life and sometimes you need a break from your surroundings."

Cox has been known to take off-the-grid breaks both during bye weeks and after seasons.

"I'm just an ordinary guy who wants to see the world," Cox says. "I'm comfortable in my own skin."

On the footy oval, Cox appears to have many miles to go before riding off into the sunset.

7

The Hustler

Alexander Aurrichio

Thanksgiving is tailor-made for a large family like the Aurrichios of Dix Hills, New York — a Long Island community about 60 miles east of Manhattan. It's 26-year-old Alexander Aurrichio's favorite holiday of all. For as long as he can remember, it's been him, his three brothers, his sister, parents, aunt, uncle and great-aunt gathered in the dining room. Aurrichio's mother, Jill, is usually directing his father, Lou, to help set up the house for the occasion. When they sit around the table around 5 p.m., they tuck into a smorgasbord that Jill has made: turkey, cranberry relish, stuffing, brussels sprouts, pumpkin, mashed potatoes, sweet potatoes with apples, cornbread, peas and carrots. For dessert, there's cheesecake, gingerbread cake, an apple crumble and cookies.

NFL football is on all day, and Alexander and his brothers usually organize their own football game in a local park with some of the neighbors from their block. Back inside, after dinner, their aunt puts together an American history trivia game, which for Alexander in particular is usually great fun — because he generally wins.

But for the family Thanksgiving Day in 2014, Aurrichio's place at the table was empty. He had flown to Australia to chase his own AFL dream.

Through his dogged determination, a strenuous workout regimen that would put Arnold Schwarzenegger to shame, and a sociable and genuine personality that wins him fast friends in influential places, Aurrichio earned a roster spot on the Northern Blues, of the VFL.

The first-year ruckman started the 2015 season on the team's Development League squad, then was promoted and played 11 matches, in which he averaged 27 hitouts and seven tackles. At the end of the season, Aurrichio won Northern Blues' "Best Clubman" award, a traditional honor that footy squads at all levels bestow on the player who best exemplifies team play on and off the field.

It was a tremendous achievement for someone who had walked through the door of the club without a Category B International Rookie AFL deal. It was an even bigger feat for Aurrichio for many more reasons. Unlike Wallace, Holmes and Cox, he hadn't played NCAA basketball. In college he played first base on the baseball team and was the soccer team's goalkeeper — both positions with small, defined regions, especially compared to the huge expanse of an Aussie Rules ground covered by a ruckman. Aurrichio had attended the AFL's 2014 U.S. Combine in the Los Angeles area, as word of his height, strength and kicking ability — from his time playing soccer — had reached the AFL's scouts. In fact, before the U.S. Combine, Aurrichio had tried out as a goalkeeper for both the Portland Timbers and the New England Revolution, of Major League Soccer. That didn't pan out, and there was something about footy that fascinated Aurrichio.

Six weeks before the combine, Aurrichio found the USAFL website and called its president, Denis Ryan, who told the young man he could help him with fitness and footy skills before he went. Ryan advised Aurrichio to download an app, Coach's Eye, which would help Ryan teach him how to kick an Aussie Rules ball. For good measure, Ryan also emailed Aurrichio and mentioned elite AFL kickers such as the Gold Coast Suns' superstar Gary Ablett Jr., the Western Bulldogs' Matt Suckling, the West Coast Eagles' captain Shannon Hurn, and the recently retired Eagles and Blues great Chris Judd, as players to pattern his kicking after.

Ryan instructed Aurrichio to run a 3-kilometer time trial, and to record his results in a journal. In his first effort at the distance, Aurrichio ran it in 13 minutes, 25 seconds. The next day he cut that to 12 minutes, 42 seconds.

Over several weeks the two men exchanged videos in which Ryan taught, Aurrichio followed and Ryan critiqued. Ryan also connected Aurrichio with a USAFL footy club, the New York Magpies. Three weeks later, Aurrichio drove into Manhattan from his home in nearby Long Island City for his first training session with them.

He left the club to attend the U.S. Combine, but when he returned, weeks went by and he didn't hear anything from the scouts. They didn't pick him to continue on to Melbourne.

So Aurrichio played on for the Magpies, who deployed him in the ruck and at full forward and fullback. Aurrichio played a handful of games for the club, which went on to capture the USAFL's National Championship.

Even in his short time, Aurrichio's performance and his developing passion for footy motivated New York Magpies' head coach, Glenn Ormsby, to get in touch with his VFL contacts. He encouraged them to find him a club to train with.

Aurrichio, to boost his chances, posted a three-minute YouTube video of his newly acquired footy skills for prospective VFL clubs. He went to a local high school football field and baseball diamond, where he demonstrated his handballing, kicking and marking skills — booting goals through American football goalposts. After a few clubs showed some interest, Aurrichio told himself, *Let's run with this.*

"My goal has been to play professional sports," Aurrichio says. Then — perhaps unintentionally — he harks back to his college baseball career: "With footy, the man upstairs threw me a curveball."

The New York Magpies believed in Aurrichio so much that the club's alumni took up a collection to help him get to Melbourne. It was just before Thanksgiving and when he told his mother he would be missing the big day — and that he'd be gone for nearly a year — she was not happy.

"It put a dampener on the holiday," Jill says. "It was tough to get through without him. We were very lucky that when he was in college, we saw him about every week because we never missed one of his soccer games. We were really fortunate like that. We'd rather have him home."

Instead, Aurrichio's Magpies teammates arranged accommodation for him in Melbourne at the home of an alumni member. Aurrichio's roller coaster Australian adventure began moments after his plane touched down at Melbourne's Tullamarine Airport.

"I didn't have a clue when I got to Melbourne," Aurrichio recalls, smiling and chuckling. "It was overwhelming. It was crazy. I didn't even know they drove on the other side of the road. When I got to Southern Cross station [in the heart of Melbourne], my mobile phone didn't work. I mistakenly deleted the address where I was going. I ended up getting Wi-Fi at a Red Rooster, found the address of where I was supposed to stay, then asked for directions. It was the New Yorker in me that figured it out."

In fact, Aurrichio, who is a solid ball of muscle at 240 lbs. and occasionally wears a beard and hair that reaches the nape of his neck, is a living remedy for any homesick New Yorker living in Melbourne. Everything about him exudes the spirit of the Big Apple. He talks like a New Yorker, walks like one, always keeping his wits about him on the streets, and jokes like one, never being afraid to show affection for someone by matching wits.

And like any New Yorker worth their salt, he's not easily intimidated, is thick-skinned and resourceful under pressure, and equally loves challenges and adventures. He doesn't complain — he just plays the cards he's dealt and finds a way to win. Although he's not boastful, Aurrichio also has a likeable swagger about him — one maybe only a fellow New Yorker could appreciate.

Aurrichio worked the phones and organized a rigorous fitness and footy skills regimen, which had him training with three VFL clubs — Sandringham, Coburg and Collingwood — simultaneously. "That was great, but it was tough as hell," he says. "I was doing four different 3-K time trials in a week."

Along the way, Aurrichio met Joel Daniher, who works in financial services at a company called PwC, and is a member of one of footy's best-known families, having several men who played professionally. During the Christmas pre-season break, Aurrichio hit the weights at a local gym and kept his footy skills sharp by training with Terry Daniher, who had played more than 300 AFL games with two different clubs. Joel Daniher then put him in touch with Carlton assistant coach John Barker, and through Barker, Aurrichio sought to connect with someone at the Northern Blues to book a training session, but most team officials were away on holiday leave.

Besides being resourceful, New Yorkers also know how to recognize a lucky break when they see one. So while Aurrichio was at the gym one morning, wearing a Sandringham Zebras tank top, he asked a man nearby to spot him before he started a set of military presses. His new spotting partner introduced himself as Craig Skicko, a Northern Blues assistant coach. He asked Aurrichio if he played for Sandringham. Aurrichio then told Skicko his story and his footy ambitions. A week later, Northern Blues general manager Gary O'Sullivan rang Aurrichio and training sessions were arranged. Aurrichio was now training with four different VFL clubs.

The American then hired AFL player agent, Tim Hazell. Soon, Aurrichio hoped, an AFL club affiliated with one of the VFL clubs would take notice of him in training and sign him to an international rookie contract.

Collingwood showed interest in bringing Aurrichio on board, but there was a condition. "They wanted me to not play VFL for a year, then work out with them the next year and assess the situation," Aurrichio says. The AFL rules stipulate that a player can be signed to a Category B International Rookie contract — which is worth $180,000 Australian per year for two years, although the money is excluded from the club's salary cap allowance — only if he hasn't played in an Australian football competition in the last three years. If Aurrichio went along with Collingwood's plan, he would remain eligible for this lucrative beginning to his football career.

But with the knowledge, skills and increased footy fitness Aurrichio had built in just a few weeks of VFL training, and the promise of live matches against a higher caliber of competition than he could find in the USAFL against lesser talent, it seemed like a no-brainer. "I thought that was way too risky, especially when Coburg and Northern Blues made it known they wanted me." Also, Aurrichio would turn 26 the next year and there was no guarantee Collingwood or any other AFL club would be interested in an untried American ruckman of his age.

Accepting a VFL club's offer would earn Aurrichio significantly less money: match payments of under $500 Australian (about $360 US) for playing in the VFL Development League, where he was likely to start, and just under $1,000 Australian (about $720 US) for the VFL seniors. Aurrichio would need to find extra work to make ends meet and would lose his Category B International Rookie eligibility.

With Joel Daniher and his family opening up their home to Aurrichio, and with some of Aurrichio's new friends helping line up odd jobs for him — including part-time gigs working as a collections agent for a major Australian telecommunications company and bartending at a pub near one VFL club's headquarters — he found the peace of mind he needed to make his life-changing decision. He signed with the Northern Blues.

*

Midway through the 2015 season, over lunch at Squires Loft, a steakhouse in Melbourne's Albert Park neighborhood, on a weekday afternoon, Aurrichio takes a moment to laugh at himself, recalling a funny moment on the oval — his first VFL goal, in a game against the Frankston Dolphins.

He whips out his smartphone and shows the clip: Aurrichio lines up for goal from 50 meters out, the wind at his back. He kicks and the footy sails between the posts. As the first of his Northern Blues teammates, Daman Aujla, gets to him, he raises his hands for a congratulatory high-10. But instead of slapping Aujla's outstretched hands, Aurrichio flattens him with an NBA-style chest bump — an odd choice, considering Aurrichio stopped playing competitive basketball after high school.

That wasn't Aurrichio's only adventure in front of goal. "There was a time I lined up for goal 20 meters out and the wind was harsh," he recalls. "A teammate came running over to me and said, 'Aim for the left goal post.' I did — and I missed by three meters."

While all developing ruckmen — especially newly converted American hoopsters — face the big challenge of improving their endurance, this is especially true for Aurrichio. "My third VFL game," he admits, "I was gassed by the end of the third quarter. In other sports I was accustomed to short, five-meter bursts. In that game, I couldn't get off the field for a rotation. We were on the far side of the field and I could never get a stoppage to come off. The timing is a challenge, too, and knowing where to run and when."

Early on, Aurrichio says, he often was a kick behind in his thinking. Now he's progressed to thinking one kick ahead and is striving to reach the point where his mind is two ahead. The game in which he got "gassed" was against the Werribee Tigers, in which he had the difficult assignment of rucking against a fellow American, Eric Wallace. That encounter left him especially sore from all the physical contact.

"This sport is the toughest on the body," he says. "I've had issues with my elbow, knee, neck and finger. Nothing ever fully heals — there's not enough time. The first legitimate hit I got was kneecap on kneecap in the ruck. That took two months to get better."

Aurrichio also got a harsh lesson from AFL-experienced ruckman Jonathan Giles in a Blues home match against Essendon. Giles also had a day out against Aurrichio, collecting 17 hitouts, taking six marks and kicking two goals. "He makes me look small," Aurrichio says of his 6-foot-8 opponent. "He dominated me in the first half. My coach tells me you have to have front position against opponents. You can dictate the spot on the ground by getting in front."

Getting coached on his ruck craft has also been an issue for Aurrichio. VFL coaches must prioritize developing the players on their lists who also are on their parent AFL club's senior or rookie lists. Darren Flanigan, a VFL Academy coach, has mentored Aurrichio, often reviewing video of his matches.

"I'm not on an AFL list, so I get it," Aurrichio says. "[Fellow Northern Blues ruckman] Robbie Warnock has more time to help me before and after training sessions than the coaches. I've had to learn a lot by myself and by watching [Carlton Blues'] Matt Kreuzer and [Greater Western Sydney Giant] Shane Mumford, who's a bit undersized and a little heavier than other ruckmen, like me. I'm working a lot by trial and error."

Aurrichio hopes to get to know the other VFL-playing Americans, but says he only had time for a quick hello and a handshake with Wallace after their match. Another countryman introduced Aurrichio to Cox at a 4th of July dinner event at Misty's Diner, a kitschy American 1950s-style restaurant in Melbourne's stylish Prahran neighborhood. But even after a night out in that American oasis, Aurrichio misses home.

He loves playing at the VFL's small suburban grounds — especially his own team's home ground, Preston City Oval, which has a special breed of passionate fans who sit or stand mere meters from the playing surface. "It's like playing in minor league baseball stadiums," Aurrichio says. "And the fans coming on the field near the huddle after quarters to hear the coaches? My dad would eat that up. He'd be right in the middle of it."

Once, an old friend from home who was living in Melbourne and playing for an amateur baseball team showed up at one of Aurrichio's VFL games, stood near the Northern Blues' end of first quarter huddle and gave Aurrichio an American-accented pep talk. But his friend's voice is about the only familiar one Aurrichio has heard in his time living in Melbourne — except for characters on the TV reruns he watches of *Seinfeld*. Aurrichio has warmed to Melbourne, but there are things he still misses about New York.

"I like all the suburbs — we'd call them 'towns' — and the cafe culture," he says. "But I've learned you can't compare New York to Melbourne. I don't like the public transportation here. The trams stop every five feet and they have to stop at all the lights. There's one lane. It takes a long time to get around here. New York is triple the size and you can get around fast."

So, like a true New Yorker fed up with any type of delay, Aurrichio altered his morning commute to his day job, borrowing a bicycle to travel nine miles to Albert Park. But that wasn't without misadventure: an accident in which he fell across the tram tracks. Aurrichio wasn't badly hurt; the bike copped the worst of it. The Northern Blues also helped him borrow a Holden SUV, which Aurrichio affectionately calls "The White Buffalo." Even with that, there was a mishap. One day, while Aurrichio was driving it, the car got stuck in neutral on the side of the road. The battery died and the key would no longer work.

But none of this fazes him. As Aurrichio puts it, "I'm enjoying the rollercoaster ride."

*

Aurrichio temporarily got off the roller coaster at the end of the 2015 VFL season. He returned home to see family and friends, and set about earning some cash to fund a second footy campaign. He coached a middle school soccer team and a high school baseball team, which won a championship. He also runs his own small business, All American Landscaping.

"With the student loans for college, I owe Columbia a lot of money," Aurrichio says. "But I'm a hustler, and it's not as if I haven't thought of backup plans."

While she longs for her son to return home permanently, Jill Aurrichio respects his tenacity and accepts his decision to chase his footy dream. "In the beginning, when he left, I thought, 'He'll be home in a year,'" she says. "He's so good at coaching. I told him there are a million things he could do here and stay in sports, but he wants to be a player. He's a very hard worker and if he wants to do something, he's gonna do whatever it takes. I knew I wasn't gonna dissuade him. He's like a lot of New Yorkers in having the attitude, 'You want something done, you get it done.'"

Aurrichio would've loved to have been at the family's dinner table for Thanksgiving in 2015, but again he had to leave for pre-season training in Australia. As it happened, the American holiday coincided with the most important event for Aurrichio's footy prospects in Australia: the AFL Rookie and Pre-Season Drafts. A pool of available players, mostly those who've been let go by AFL clubs, or guys like Aurrichio who have been on VFL rosters but haven't yet been signed by them, hope to get picked.

"It's a hustle lifestyle if I don't get drafted," Aurrichio says, knowing he might once again be stringing together jobs while playing VFL football.

Three weeks before the draft, Aurrichio posted another video on YouTube, this time a professionally made, four-minute highlights package of his 2015 season. His statistics and the mention of his Best Clubman award flashed on the screen. To make it as easy as possible for scouts to spot him, the reel momentarily pauses and a blue circle appears around his image. He runs down ball carriers with strong tackles, takes some strong marks over his head and with his kicks, deftly passes to teammates. But the footage of Aurrichio tossing around taller opposing ruckman in ruck contests like ragdolls and winning ruck battles against battle-tested AFL ruckmen is the most impressive part. At times the way he shoves them out of contests, making him look like a bulldozer clearing trees.

Still, with an hour to go before the clubs make their selections, Aurrichio posts on Twitter about his chances of being picked. "I'd be lying if I said I wasn't doubtful," he tweets, "but you never know."

From his workplace, Aurrichio follows the draft on his smartphone. It is a cruel numbers game: a maximum of 72 players total can be chosen across the 18 clubs, over nine rounds. Some clubs, because they fully stocked their rosters through trades or selections in the AFL National Amateur Draft, involving only the country's top 18-year-olds and held a few days earlier, won't use all their allotted picks.

Every few seconds, a new draftee's name is revealed on the screen. The fourth player picked is a ruckman — one who footy experts were convinced was unlucky not to be taken in the main draft: Gach Nyuon, an 18-year-old, Sudanese-born standout. Essendon claimed him. Majak Daw is re-drafted by North Melbourne with pick 33. A total of 65 players are picked; Alexander Aurrichio is not one of them. He was prepared, though. The Northern Blues wanted Aurrichio back, and that's where he's playing his footy in 2016. In the Northern Blues development squad's first preseason game against Box Hill, the club's match committee named Aurrichio team captain for the day. Still, Aurrichio's keeping his day job. It's back to the hustle, but for now it beats the alternative.

"You can work a desk job for 50 years," Aurrichio says. "But I'm young, athletic and I have the ability to do this."

8

The Tutor and the Pupil
Denis Ryan and Marvin Baynham

An aspiring screenwriter might pitch the following scenario to a room full of Hollywood studio executives. A former college basketball player wows scouts at an Australian Rules football scouting combine and gets an all-expenses-paid invitation to Australia five months later, where he has the chance to earn a contract with a professional club. Only one problem: the player is in America, and there's seemingly no one who is qualified to train him before his big demo. But wait! An Aussie expat and footy guru emerges from the shadows and offers to put the player up in his own home, while at the same time putting him through an intensive, six-week boot camp that will have him AFL-ready by the time of his Australian audition. Besides the action, there'll be some drama, laughs and tears. Best of all — and much like *Rocky*, *The Karate Kid* and *The Blind Side* — this film is an inspirational underdog story.

It stars Marvin Baynham as himself — a gracious 22-year-old, fresh from graduating Georgia Southern University with a bachelor's degree in child and family development and a pedigree as a hardworking, athletically gifted basketball player. Baynham's co-lead is Denis Ryan, a 47-year-old Aussie expat from Melbourne's southeastern suburbs, whose American wife says he lives, eats, breathes and sleeps footy.

In his younger days Ryan played amateur footy in Melbourne's eastern suburbs. He was travelling the world in 1998 and ended up in Baltimore, where a mate was starting an Australian-themed bar called the Boomerang Pub. He and his mates watched that year's AFL Grand Final an hour's drive south at the Australian Embassy in Washington, where a bunch of expats from the two cities had gathered. They chatted eagerly about getting a match going, and ultimately Ryan recruited players from the Aussie and American regulars at the Boomerang to play the Washington group. After the first match between the two sides, Ryan spearheaded an effort to merge the two clubs and enter the USAFL.

That's how the Baltimore-Washington Eagles were born. Ryan played for the club and also served as its captain, senior coach and vice-president. Three years later he became an assistant coach, then senior coach of the USA Revolution, America's first national representative side in the AFL's International Cup. He later developed coaching programs for the USAFL, and today is the league's president.

But that job isn't full-time or paid, so Ryan works a handful of jobs to pay the bills, including managing a furnished apartments business in Baltimore, which he operates remotely with his wife, Crystal, and working a part-time job as a baggage handler for Delta Airlines at Northwest Florida Regional Airport. He attends the AFL's U.S. Combines, willingly working as a "gofer" for Kevin Sheehan and Mick Ablett and the various club scouts who attend.

It was at the 2014 U.S. Combine that Baynham and Ryan met, although their story really begins the moment the combine ended. The invited prospects and scouts exchanged handshakes, smiles and thank yous. Discreetly, because he feared the league might frown on his idea, Ryan sent emails to all the recruits a few days later, thanking them for participating and adding: "If you really want to pursue this, contact me." Ryan also included this hopeful message: "If you get chosen, you have a 50 per cent chance of being signed." The numbers clearly supported Ryan: of the six combine athletes the AFL had flown to Melbourne in its first three years, three had been signed by AFL clubs.

Ryan is adamant that the American prospects the AFL picks to fly to Melbourne must continue building their skills in the weeks and months leading up to their trip. "Why aren't they coached?" he asks. "The AFL's job is to make them elite. The AFL has told me they don't want them to learn bad habits, but if they're taught the basics of kicking and get a grounding, then by the time they go to the Australian combine, they'll wow the recruiters."

Baynham, the second eldest of five children who grew up with their mother in several South Florida cities, was then living on the state's east coast, in Fort Lauderdale. He had impressed the scouts with his vertical jump, agility, sprint and basic footy skills tests. The AFL had impressed Baynham with its professionalism and the game intrigued him. Sensing a possible fit, Mick Ablett devised an endurance running program for him, and gave him a footy.

But whom would Baynham kick to? Surely not his fellow athletes at Georgia Southern, from where he was about to graduate. They would never have seen a footy, let alone know how to kick one. Even after graduation, when Baynham planned to head home to Fort Lauderdale, the USAFL's Fort Lauderdale Fighting Squids were in his backyard, but it wouldn't be worth risking injury with them. Baynham needed someone, *anyone*, to help shape him into a better prospect, if he was serious about chasing this new dream.

So a month after the combine, Baynham decided to email Ryan. "I remember you," he wrote. "I've been watching AFL on YouTube. I think I can be really good at this game."

Two days later, after he'd read the email, Ryan rang Baynham on his car's speaker phone while driving west, past Mobile, Alabama — en route to Baton Rouge, Louisiana, some 340 miles away, where he arranged to play in a USAFL match with a club there called the Tigers, the closest one to his home. Ryan asked Baynham to send him his combine test results, so they could then discuss "options and a pathway" to a potential AFL career.

He also asked Baynham to take a significant first step: spend $20 on an app called Coach's Eye. Through that, Ryan — the self-styled footy *sensei* — could record himself demonstrating how to properly kick the footy and send the recordings to Baynham, who could then film himself applying the lessons and then send it back to Ryan for critiques.

Ryan based his initial curriculum on Kick Builders, an instructional footy kicking technique and program first developed by an Australian coach in the 1980s, who wanted to refine the skills of junior footballers. In Baynham's first video for Ryan, he holds the footy horizontally, like an American football punter before kicking it. Ryan sent back a two-minute critique, in which he showed Baynham the proper way to hold and drop the Aussie Rules ball.

"You've got it backwards a little bit, with the ball out in front of you," Ryan tells Baynham. "You can see here, you're kind of stiff-armed and the ball's out in front of you — it's horizontal, pointing forward ..." The two men exchanged videos for the next two weeks, with Baynham attempting to master the technique. Then one day, in mid-June, Baynham rang Ryan, with big news.

"Jonathan Givony called me," Baynham began. "I've been picked to go."

"You need to come here, then," Ryan replied, holding in his excitement.

The AFL's three-week Draft Combine would be in September. The league also invited Evan Bruinsma, the University of Detroit power forward Givony first called a few months earlier. While the idea of a trip to Australia and competing in the Draft Combine in four months greatly excited Baynham, he still had very limited footy knowledge.

Ryan offered to train Baynham — free of charge — in his own, private six-week footy academy. Baynham could have a room in their home, sharing the house with the couple and their two sons, 7-year-old Quinn and 5-year-old Eddie.

The couple has been married for more than a decade, after first meeting in Baltimore, where they were both living at the time. Crystal Ryan is an American who was tending bar across the street from the Boomerang Pub. When they met, she had a roommate from South

Australia, although she had no idea about footy. That soon changed. Denis taught Crystal how to kick, and she later adopted his favorite AFL team, the Western Bulldogs, as her own.

With his new student, Ryan worked out a plan. Baynham would live and train with Ryan in two, three-week blocks, with a five-week interval in between. "All I want from you is to respect my family," Ryan told Baynham, "and to chip in for groceries."

Baynham agreed to show up in the first week of July. But a week before that, when Baynham originally planned a visit to his mother, he suddenly changed his mind. He would go to the Ryans' house immediately — but even as he hit the road at 3 a.m., leaving States-boro, Georgia, home of his alma mater, Georgia Southern University, for the 400-mile, 7-hour, southwest drive, he hadn't yet told Ryan. Baynham's journey to Fort Walton Beach would be adventurous, but not in the way Baynham expected.

After sunrise, Baynham appreciated the stability and order in the Ryans' household, telling him that instead of arriving in a week, he'd be there in a few hours. Ryan was caught off-guard but, being eager to get his student out on the field, he was okay with the sudden change. But there was just one problem: the room the Ryans had earmarked for Baynham wasn't anywhere near ready. They were using it as a storage room, so piles of clothes were strewn across the bed, sand tracked in on flip-flops from countless beach strolls had to be swept, and footballs were scattered everywhere. Pieces of long, narrow plastic tubing — the USAFL's improvised goalposts — had to be put away. "I was frantically cleaning up for hours," Ryan recalls.

About three hours from the Ryans' home, one of Baynham's tires blew out. He called for help and got someone to patch and pump it up. He thought he'd be right the rest of the way, but the patched-up tire lasted only 20 minutes before it, too, ruptured. This time, Baynham called a tire shop and had a replacement put on. He was good to go.

At about 4 p.m., while Ryan was relaxing at home, he was abruptly jolted out of serenity. Booming, rattling, vibrating sounds were blasting out of a car stereo's speakers. Before even getting up from his seat, Ryan had a feeling and smiled and laughed to himself. A quick look out the window confirmed his intuition: his new houseguest was announcing his arrival. Ryan saw a black Crown Victoria sedan — with orange rims and a matching, Mohawk-like, narrow orange stripe from hood to trunk — lumbering to a stop on the street, alongside the house. This was Baynham's ride, and this was how he rolled.

"I started laughing, seeing him in his 'hooptie'," Ryan says. And he also thought of the incongruity: *How many white couples with two little boys have a black stranger driving up to their home in that type of vehicle?*

Baynham had pulled up to the home, but not quite all the way. "He was so respectful, he didn't park in the driveway," Ryan recalls. "I told him, no, no one here parks out in the street."

After Baynham strode up to the front door, where Ryan greeted him, the coach led the young man through the living room, but before they reached the simple — and hastily tidied — room he'd soon call his own, furnished with a bed, a dressing table and a TV, Quinn and Eddie immediately raced to him, wanting to show him their Skylander action figures. Crystal was worried the guest bed might be too small for Baynham to sleep in, but it turned out it was a perfect fit — if Baynham slept diagonally.

*

Not long after Baynham arrived, Ryan took him aside for a private chat. He asked him a pointed question. "Are you *really* serious about this?"

"Dead serious," his eager pupil replied.

Then, as if laying out a club culture for Baynham to follow, Ryan gave him a memo he had written, with bullet points, outlining his expectations:

- Other than food (& possibly utilities), you do not owe me any money. Not now, not if you get an AFL contract.

- Respect for wife & boys — their sacrifice.
- Work hard & clean up after yourself.
- Training — kicking & handballing — 100 a day — could get boring — quality is better than quantity. 4 × 25?
- Study the game.
- No girls.

When he read the last bullet point, Baynham laughed, telling Ryan, "I've had the same girlfriend the last 10 years."

Ryan required his new student to keep a daily journal of his training regimen, filing notes on the slightest details. As part of Baynham's comprehensive footy education, to help him understand Australian sporting culture, Ryan ordered him to read author Ray McLean's book *Team Work: Forging Links Between Honesty, Accountability and Success* and to write responses to every chapter. Ryan also organized "study sessions" in which Baynham would research the AFL clubs, their rosters, their coaches and especially their ruckmen.

Ryan instructed Baynham to keep tabs on the progress of the VFL's American ruckmen, Eric Wallace and Jason Holmes, plus top AFL ruckmen Nic Naitanui, Brodie Grundy, Todd Goldstein and Mike Pyke. Ryan wanted Baynham to become a disciple of his ruckwork philosophy: develop a relationship with his midfielders, identify the "tap zones," for hitouts and time his leap to meet the footy at its highest point, over his opponents.

There also was an exercise Ryan expected Baynham to do at home in front of a mirror with a footy, for 30 minutes each night. Ryan calls it the *Karate Kid* drill, a reference to the 1980s movie's "wax on, wax off" scene, in which Mr. Miyagi teaches his teenage student hand-to-hand combat by making circular motions without actually throwing blows. In this drill, Baynham would practice kicking without putting boot to ball.

The exercise involved a series of fluid movements. Ryan instructed Baynham first to stand, holding the footy vertically with both hands, and then to move the ball to a 45-degree angle. Next, he told Baynham to take his left hand off the ball, moving it up to shoulder height, to make a "stop" sign — the way a traffic cop signals "halt!" to drivers — while keeping a grip on the ball with his right hand and guiding it down to the release point above his boot.

"The purpose was to practice the upper-body motions of kicking, without actually kicking the ball," Ryan says. "The theory is, if that part becomes second nature, all he has to concentrate on is the timing of his foot swinging through."

Ryan told his student that if he gave it his all, he could become at least 90 per cent of the footy player the AFL would want to see at the Australian Draft Combine.

Ryan outlined for Baynham the daily schedule they'd follow. They'd wake before dawn, then drive to Fort Walton Beach Landing Park, on the shores of Santa Rosa Sound, by 6 a.m. They'd kick the footy around for 30 minutes. Immediately afterward, they'd have 90-minute running sessions, doing 20-meter and 30-meter sprints, and kicking practice during the rest periods. Ryan told Baynham he'd also be doing the "beep test" — a repetitive, seemingly endless series of physically and mentally draining stop-and-start endurance runs, covering 20 meters. The AFL has since replaced beep tests with 3-kilometer time trials. As Ryan reasons, "Mentally you can give up and quit a beep test, but you probably won't quit a 3-kilometer run."

Baynham's explosive running had been unquestionably strong since his high-school days. There's a 2010 YouTube video of Baynham running a nighttime 4 x 400-meter relay high school championship race. For the first 200 meters, Baynham outpaces his opponents at three-quarter speed. For the last 200, he scorches the track, completing his segment in 47 seconds.

So on his first training day with Ryan, at nearby Choctawatchee High School, it wasn't too much of a surprise that Baynham ran a 20-meter sprint in 3.20 seconds. The beep test, however, proved a much greater challenge, especially in Florida's merciless, slow-boiling summer heat and humidity.

In a beep test, the higher an athlete's score, the better the performance. The AFL's U.S. Combine record, at the time, was 16.4. The average American recruit's score was 13.3. The AFL, Ryan said, would expect the American draft prospects to reach at least level 12. Baynham's first score, under Ryan's tutelage, was a shocking 4.1. "I was fuming," Ryan recalls. "It was atrocious. A 10-year-old should get that score. I hadn't done one in years and I went and did it in front of him and I scored a 10. Then we did a 3-kilometer time trial. I told him he needed a time of 11 minutes, 30 seconds. He got a 16:01. He hadn't done much since his last basketball season."

Ryan was stern when he started coaching Baynham, verbally pushing him, testing him to see how he'd respond. The teacher took this approach based on an earlier, intimate conversation the two had about their respective core values. Ryan wanted to learn what made Baynham tick. Beside their heart-to-heart chat, Ryan used a motivational program called Yes for Success, which his twin brother, Gary, a high-performance coach, had created. Ryan extracted two of the program's components to help him learn how best to teach Baynham: asking him to list, in order of importance, his top 10 values, and to share three life-changing moments that led him to make a major decision.

Baynham listed trust, honesty, and loyalty as some of his values. But he named just one life-changing moment: getting verbally humiliated for his poor play by his high school basketball teammates after his freshman season. Baynham decided he'd never again be embarrassed like that, so in the months before his sophomore campaign he trained with an unprecedented vigor. His improvement led to a remarkable year on the court and, ultimately, a college basketball scholarship. From that story, Ryan recognized Baynham's defining value: pride. So Baynham's poor first week led Ryan to get stuck into his student there, where it hurt him most.

"The AFL expects to see an athlete," Ryan admonished, "and right now, I don't see one."

Baynham responded. The second week, he trained six hours a day — two and a half in the morning, and one and a half in the afternoon, plus two more hours at home. He improved his beep test time to a more respectable 10.5. His kicking was also improving: his drop was better, but he was getting frustrated at his slow progress. He trimmed his 3-kilometer time to 13:53.

"I hit a nerve," Ryan says. "I got his value of pride right. It's an inner pride — the good type. Not one where you brag about how great you are, but where you quietly resolve to leave a good impression and win people's respect."

Still, Ryan had other expectations of Baynham that were going unmet. Every night, Ryan would show him videos of AFL matches, but Baynham was struggling to watch. For the first three weeks, he'd tune out after a half.

Away from training, inside the Ryan household, Baynham was happy. Baynham appreciated the stability and order in the Ryans' household. Baynham's parents separated when he was a toddler and he and his siblings moved with their mother to several south Florida cities, including Fort Lauderdale and Miami Gardens.

Baynham's affinity with Quinn and Eddie, whom he came to call his "little brothers," only grew stronger as time went by. They'd play with action figures or play hide-and-seek together. At the dining room table, when Crystal would bring out dinner, Baynham was often so impressed he'd take pictures of the food with his mobile phone.

"I was eating healthy food," he says. "Different varieties. On the whole journey, I was eating something different every day — lasagna, chicken, steak, stuffed bell peppers, fish. But half of the stuff, I don't even know the name of what it was. It was different in the Ryans' house. They're real close-knit."

Yet as comfortable as he felt, it would be several days before Baynham brought his things inside from the car and unpacked.

"He had four or five really big duffel bags of his athletic training gear," Ryan says. "I told him, 'Don't leave them in the car. You don't want your car broken into.' It seemed like he thought he'd be imposing on us if he brought his things in."

When Baynham returned for his second three-week session, not only did he unpack, but he became much more disciplined too. At night, after training, Ryan showed his student episodes of longtime footy journalist Mike Sheahan's *Open Mike* TV show, which the aspiring ruckman eagerly watched. "I discovered he liked learning the history of the game," Ryan says. "He started understanding the game through the eyes of the players. I spoke to him about the cultures of AFL clubs. I gave him an AFL Global Pass and then he really started watching the games online."

Ryan assigned Baynham to write summaries of another of Sheahan's shows, *On the Couch*. Around this time his journal responses to McLean's book grew more elaborate and thoughtful.

"Relationships [are] not only one of the most important things while being a part of a team, but also in life," Baynham wrote. "The trust model also stuck out to me. When people put trust in you they are counting on you to come through for them. I like for people to feel they can count on me and when I come through for them [it] makes me feel even better. Also when a group develops trust, individuals will sacrifice themselves and do what's best for the teams and you usually find this in winning teams."

Now, when Baynham sat down to watch an AFL match, he was giving it his full attention for four quarters. And as if living his own footy training journey wasn't enough, he also grew to love watching the Aussie longshot footy dreamers featured on the Australian reality TV show *The Recruit*.

Baynham's training became progressively more spirited. Once, at the beach, Ryan challenged him to swim out and back. Baynham picked a visual target and set himself a challenge of reaching it. That target was further than Ryan thought he'd go, however, and he had to jump up and down on the shore and yell at Baynham to come back. When Ryan had to go out of town, Baynham did his kick-to-kick sessions with Crystal, who would also challenge him to do extra 3-kilometer runs on a loop in the neighborhood.

Baynham was diligently working himself into becoming the AFL prospect Ryan believed the league expected. But there remained one last hurdle to clear before Baynham headed off to Melbourne: a significantly improved 3-kilometer time. That wouldn't be easy, as he battled occasional hamstring soreness.

Ryan researched the surface and circumference of the track Baynham would be running on in Melbourne, and he coached Baynham on how to pace himself for the all-important run. Ryan designed a running program for his pupil and set a date for a trial, a little less than a week before Baynham was to depart for Melbourne.

The day was gloomy, gray and muggy, with steady rain falling on the black asphalt track at Fort Walton Beach High School. Baynham had to run 7-and-a-half laps to reach 3 kilometers. He started. After each lap Baynham glanced at his wristwatch to see if he was hitting the times he and Ryan forecast. After the first lap, the display read 1:32. Just as they'd been practicing, Baynham had established a strong pace of about 90 seconds per lap.

After the seventh lap Baynham looked at his watch — 10:55 — which meant he was on track to reach his elusive goal of 11-and-a-half minutes. As he finished he checked his watch one last time: 11:31. Baynham's improvement over the distance since he first started training with Ryan was a remarkable 4-and-a-half minutes.

As gratifying as this was for Baynham, he didn't overreact. "I was humble," he says. "I expected to hit my time. I was seeing the results, incrementally. Denis spoke a lot about Australian culture and footy culture and what it was about. Being humble was a big part of it. There's always a bigger picture. He'd always make sure I'd checked my ego."

*

A few days after running that personal best time trial, and with his AFL opportunity close at hand, it was time for Baynham to check out of his room at the Ryan home. Two years later, Quinn and Eddie were still calling it "Marvin's room."

It was an emotional goodbye for everyone involved.

Baynham says he still misses learning from Ryan — and not just about kicking, marking and ruck positioning. "He taught me a lot about an athlete's makeup," Baynham says. "As we moved in the process and grew with each other, he became more like a teammate. We just always had a good time in conversation. He taught me a lot about life."

Although Baynham has moved out of "his" room, there's a lasting memento of his presence in the Ryan home, which wouldn't have happened if not for his intensive crash course in footy. Crystal Ryan thumbtacked the souvenir to the cork bulletin board in her home office. It's a tan-colored greeting card Baynham gave her when he left. The inscribed message reads, "Just a little note to bring the warmest thanks for everything."

But it's Baynham's own words on the opposite page that mean the most to Crystal. "I read it and then I was crying," she says. "I wouldn't say that he's an outspoken person. He's shy and keeps things to himself, but he was able to express himself very well."

Early on, hearing Quinn and Eddie calling their mother "Mom," Baynham playfully followed their lead. But the card shows Crystal's maternal touch directly reached Baynham's heart.

"I felt like I was your son while I was here and this was my home," he began. "Also, when you kicked with me those days, those were the biggest gains I made the entire time. I learned a lot from you these last three weeks that'll make me better in life ... Love you, and thanks for everything."

Baynham then signed his name, adding "#10" next to it — an allusion to the uniform number he wore during his college basketball career.

He still sends Crystal Ryan cards on Mother's Day. "I think," Crystal says, "Marvin was the son I never had."

Baynham also presented a card to Denis Ryan. It's clear from his words that whatever skills Ryan taught Baynham, and however well he mastered them, was of secondary importance, even with the Draft Combine in Melbourne looming. To Baynham, their newly forged partnership meant something far greater.

"When I first decided to come train, I didn't know what to expect,"

Baynham wrote. "It actually ended up being one of the best decisions I ever made … How you interacted with your family taught me how to be a father, husband and a man. You treated me like I was your own and pushed me to the max day in and day out … Living with you these past three weeks was about much more than footy."

Strangely, Ryan is now a little reluctant to ever train another American footy recruit from the U.S. Combine. "It was such a great experience," he says. "It couldn't have been better. It was exceptional. I went in with no expectations. But if I were to train someone else, I'd be expecting it to be just as special. But it can't be. If I trained more people, I'd be forever doing it, hoping the same connection I had with Marvin would happen again. It probably wouldn't."

Through footy, the two men fully invested in the game — and each other. It was a sizeable investment for each man, without money ever changing hands. "I'm not involved in footy to make money," Ryan says. "I'm just trying to grow the game."

9

The "Couldn't Quites"

The unofficial competition to become the first born-and-bred American AFL player ended on the night of August 22, 2015, when Jason Holmes ran out at Etihad Stadium to represent St Kilda.

But this race, which began in 2009, had plenty of other aspirants who ultimately came up short of their goal of becoming AFL players. But the stories of the Americans who gave footy a go but didn't get the prize — the "couldn't quites" — are some of the most compelling.

Shae McNamara: The Original "American Pie"

Old-school lab experiments usually involved a guinea pig — an unwitting test subject. In 2007 Shae McNamara, of Milwaukee, Wisconsin, became one. In three weeks the Marist College graduate would be flying to Munich to make his professional basketball debut. Unbeknown to him, though, McNamara had attracted the attention of an influential person in the footy world — not for what he had done in basketball but for what he *might* do in the AFL.

McNamara's phone rang. It was Matt Brady, McNamara's coach at Marist. "You need to call Digger Phelps," Brady told him.

The mere mention of Phelps's name had McNamara's heart pounding. The college basketball legend — a man with an illustrious 20-year coaching career at Notre Dame University — wanted to talk to *him*. A positive conversation would help McNamara get a ticket to just about anywhere in the basketball universe.

But Phelps might have detected McNamara's flinch after he started their phone conversation by asking him, "Have you ever heard of Australian Rules football?"

"No," McNamara politely answered. What he was thinking was: *You've gotta be kidding me!* "What is it?" he asked after an awkward pause.

Phelps gave McNamara a brief description. "You could be the first American to play it," he concluded.

McNamara let that thought sink in. "I started thinking it'd be special to be the first," he recalls, "to help people to draw inspiration from that. I thought, *I'm athletic and blessed and want to be as unique as I possibly can.* I did some research on Aussie Rules on YouTube and saw the guys wearing the short shorts. I loved soccer and saw some of the same strategy. I saw some of the same skills used in basketball and I saw why they might be looking for an American player. I was impressed."

Still, McNamara went ahead to Munich. Months later, after he came home, he rang Paul Roos. Roos then contacted Chris Olson, coach of the USAFL's Inland Empire Eagles. Olson rang McNamara to arrange a meeting in St. Paul, Minnesota, so they could work out and record McNamara's first attempts at footy on video. Distance didn't matter to McNamara. He made the five-hour drive and met Olson on the St. Thomas University football field. Olson planned to record parts of the workout, edit the footage and then email it to Roos.

"I didn't think [McNamara] wanted to go back to Europe," Olson says. "His experience in Germany put him off. It looked like they were playing in glorified middle school gyms, so the AFL appealed to him immensely. Everything about this game really spoke to Shae."

A few weeks before McNamara made the trip, his personal trainer gave him a warning about Aussie Rules. "That sport's *intense*," he said. "You're going to work your tail off."

But during the workout, Olson realized something wasn't right: his device had failed to record. "How bad do you feel when the kid makes a five-hour trip and that happened?' Olson recalls. "That it was the dumbass recruiter who couldn't record it?"

Still, McNamara had trained with Olson for six hours. After McNamara drove back home, he called a buddy to meet him at a local high school football field and film him replicating the workout he'd done with Olson. McNamara didn't have a footy with him so he kicked, marked and handballed an American football. McNamara sent the tape to Roos.

While McNamara waited for a response from Roos or anyone else at the Sydney Swans, his agent did ritual negotiation dances with several European basketball clubs. Finally, the Swans called. They'd watched the video. They were impressed. But they'd decided instead to sign another North American prospect. He was a Canadian convert from rugby union — Mike Pyke.

McNamara didn't get mad — he got viral. He sent his video to all 15 other AFL clubs. Only one emailed him back, expressing interest — Collingwood.

"The video he sent was goofy," Olson concedes. "It was shown on [the weekly, Australia-wide televised] *The Footy Show*, and someone made a sideways crack that it was amazing that it was taken seriously. But then we took more video and he was kicking and handballing and you could see the progression."

McNamara found a trainer in Orange County, California, to work with him. Then he flew to Las Vegas, where the Pies ran him through five days of physical and psychological testing at a strength and conditioning expo, under the direction of the club's renowned athletic performance manager, David Buttifant. "We'll get back to you in two weeks," the Collingwood officials told McNamara.

By then, a half-dozen pro basketball teams from Portugal to Luxembourg were chasing McNamara, and growing impatient when he didn't commit to them. "One Italian team had an offer of 1,000 Euros a month [$1,430 US], tax-free," McNamara recalls, "and they told me I had 24 hours to decide."

Next Buttifant and the Pies trialed McNamara in Australia for two weeks. Finally, in November 2009, McNamara made history, becoming the first born-and-bred American to be drafted by an AFL club.

"I was stoked for Shae," Olson says. "It was the first time an American was going to get on an AFL list. The way he did it made it that much more special. It was the first time somebody at an AFL draft mentioned an American's name. How cool was that?"

At first, the Pies offered him a two-year deal, worth $32,000 [then about $29,000 US] per year. He and his then girlfriend, Kari, whom ultimately he would marry, would have to make that money stretch in Melbourne. But for McNamara, the decision was a no-brainer. "I was all-in," he says. "Collingwood was a powerhouse club and I wanted to get out and see the world."

Three weeks after he arrived, Collingwood upgraded his status to that of a Category B International Rookie, and increased his salary to the stipulated $65,000 a year. Melbourne's footy writers, playing on the title of Don McLean's iconic 1970s folk-rock song, dubbed McNamara "American Pie." The nickname stuck.

Shae and Kari settled in to a high-rise apartment building in Southbank, a fashionable neighborhood along the banks of Melbourne's Yarra River. McNamara purposely chose a 19th-floor unit, high enough to have a view of the MCG. Waking up every morning, McNamara literally could visualize his goal. "I wanted to remember why I came," McNamara said. "It was a quirky little thing I had to have."

McNamara was assigned to Collingwood's VFL side, and at 24 would compete just one level under the big show, against players who had practically emerged from the womb with the kicking skills he was striving to master. "I had my age going against me," he says. "I also had being a 'project' going against me. The coaches didn't have time to baby me. They didn't really coach me; they sent me to the wolves."

Still, McNamara impressed some teammates by quickly learning to kick accurately with each foot, and by building his endurance and developing the versatility to play different positions. After playing the 2010 season in the VFL, McNamara earned a spot in a nationally televised 2011 preseason game, against the Swans. Late in the match's first quarter, playing full forward, McNamara shoved his opponent aside and took a contested mark in front of the goal square. Thirty seconds later, he drilled home a goal and all his teammates rushed over to congratulate him.

McNamara had a solid VFL season, but Collingwood didn't call him up. In 2012 McNamara played in all three of Collingwood's preseason matches, but still no call-up. In late August, with the VFL season ending and the seniors preparing for the finals, McNamara was told after a Monday training session that he would not receive a new contract offer. He was being delisted. It was, to paraphrase McLean's tune, "bye bye, Mr. American Pie."

In footy, just as in life, there's often a wide gulf between one person's perception and another's. Even today, McNamara and the Magpies differ on why he never got his big chance.

McNamara — now a certified performance, wellness, and confidence coach — insists he was a victim of the club's success and was deprived of the coaching he says he sorely needed. Derek Hine, the Magpies' recruiting manager, tells a different story: one of a foreigner who put his own needs before the club's, couldn't adapt to the club's culture and wasn't willing to put in the extra work.

"I was unlucky to be on such a good team," McNamara says. "If I played on a lesser one, I would've had an opportunity. I did well in the preseason, but [the coaches] didn't have the guts and the courage to put me out there on the big stage."

There's no denying McNamara was on an elite team. The Pies won the 2010 Premiership, during McNamara's first VFL season, defeating St Kilda. In 2011, McNamara's second campaign, Collingwood lost the Grand Final to Geelong. In 2012, when McNamara narrowly missed the cut, Collingwood finished fourth. Sydney beat the Hawthorn Hawks in the Grand Final that year, getting important contributions from Pyke, the man Sydney chose over him.

Hine insists Collingwood's success wasn't why McNamara was delisted. He says McNamara was self-centered, which turned off his teammates. "Shae had enormous talent and we gave him three years," Hine says. "But he wasn't humble when he came in. We talk a lot here about a new player earning respect within the playing group. In Shae's first week with us, he was talking to us about getting shoe contracts. We have some players in the off-season working hard all day, from eight to eight. Shae was more of 'a 9-to-5 player.'"

McNamara was shocked at the timing of getting the sack. "That's not 'side by side'," he says, referring to the Pies club anthem's famous line, "side by side, we stick together," about team unity. "It was the most exciting time of the year and you're not allowed to be part of it? It's quite the opposite of brotherhood. A lot of other [VFL] guys started their vacations. I'm a team guy. I wanted to be part of the team and not say, 'Boo hoo, me.'"

McNamara had a pass that would allow him free entry to the MCG, where he could watch his suddenly former teammates play in the finals. But he had to go to the club to retrieve it. Seeing club officials and his former teammates would've been about as awkward for McNamara as it would've been for a jilted lover to visit an ex's house. So he retrieved the pass late one Thursday afternoon, when few people were at the club's headquarters.

With his agent, McNamara explored his options. Hawthorn invited him to train with its first-to-fourth-year players, in advance of the AFL Rookie Draft. His chances of earning an AFL gig — and making American sporting history — remained alive. But as a backup McNamara also trained for a basketball club, the Sandringham Sabres, of the South Eastern Australian Basketball League.

The Hawks' training sessions went well, McNamara felt. One of his competitors was a former Collingwood teammate, Jonathon Ceglar, a ruckman five years younger, who had also failed to get a senior game with the Pies in several seasons. The contest for Hawthorn's final spot, McNamara knew, would be between him and Ceglar.

In his heart, McNamara knew, after playing three VFL seasons and four preseason NAB Cup games, that he was good enough for the AFL. On the December day the Rookie Draft was held, though, he purposely avoided news of it, not wanting to drive himself crazy. Instead, he worked out with the Sabres. When he was showered, dressed and about to exit the gym, he glanced down at his mobile phone. There was a text message from his agent: "Hawthorn picked up Ceglar."

Are you kidding me? a disbelieving McNamara thought to himself. Instantly, he became emotional. Then he bumped into a Sabres executive on his way out of the building. "Hey, what's the news?" the executive asked him.

McNamara showed him the text.

"But the good news is," the executive said, "*we* want you." The two men shook hands and made a verbal agreement: McNamara would sign with the Sabres.

Minutes later, once McNamara got to his car, he checked his voicemail. It was from the head coach of the VFL club, Port Melbourne. He told McNamara there was a spot for him in the VFL club's ruck division, and that he'd love to have him. It was a footy lifeline — albeit a thin one — that could possibly get him back into the AFL system.

But McNamara didn't grab it. He left the coach a voicemail, thanking him for the opportunity. McNamara wanted to go back to basketball, his first sporting love.

Later, after getting over his initial disappointment, McNamara says he came to understand Hawthorn's decision. "Nothing against 'Cegs' — he was my teammate — but I thought I was ready then, and he wasn't," McNamara says. "But there was a future with him. I only had two to four years left in me, but he had two to 10. It was a smart investment on Hawthorn's part."

Ceglar has footy skills in his DNA. His father, David, had his own brief AFL career with North Melbourne in the late 1980s. Ceglar played 31 games through Hawthorn's "three-peat" Premiership years, from 2013 through 2015, and did well enough to earn a contract extension with the team through to 2017.

McNamara doesn't watch footy much anymore but says he admires Mason Cox, the new "American Pie," and the other U.S. recruits.

The day Cox was making his memorable Anzac Day AFL debut, McNamara Tweeted love to both Cox and his former team: "Great job @masonsixtencox! Wishing you the best today brother! #gopies."

"The AFL is still a great opportunity for guys who couldn't play basketball in Europe, to go to Australia and embrace the culture, see the world," McNamara says, "and not have to work a day job they don't like."

Patrick Mitchell: The Muted Swan

At the time the Sydney Swans were playing in the 2014 AFL Grand Final, one of the club's rookie list players was, in absentia, being inducted into his high school alma mater's sports hall of fame, a continent away.

The inductee, Patrick Mitchell, was being honored for his basketball feats at Dowling Catholic High School in Des Moines, Iowa. He had averaged 15 points a game, the most by any player at the school in nearly a decade. Mitchell is from the city's blue-collar, modest-income east side, and every day he'd travel to its affluent west side to attend the prestigious private school.

Mike O'Connor, Mitchell's high school basketball coach and mentor, remembers how Mitchell, now 27, was a lanky, uncoordinated kid of about 5-foot-7 who grew into a 6-foot-7 dynamo and became the best player he ever coached. O'Connor got to know Mitchell well, driving with him on long road trips to Iowa's neighboring state, South Dakota. He learned that Mitchell has a quick wit — and vulnerability. During Mitchell's high-school senior year, around Christmas, O'Connor noticed the young man was uncharacteristically avoiding him.

"I finally called him over," O'Connor recalls. "I noticed he was wearing an undershirt. He lifted it up and he's got this big 'M' tattoo on his right shoulder. He thought if he got it I'd think less of him. But I knew him well enough to know he's a free spirit."

O'Connor also learned that Mitchell loves a challenge — which perhaps explains why he would take up a new sport and relocate halfway around the world to play it. As a young player, Mitchell desperately wanted to attempt three-point shots during games, but O'Connor wouldn't allow it. But at practices Mitchell kept making a point to try, with O'Connor watching. "If you can prove you can do it," O'Connor told him, "I'll let you try it." Eventually, Mitchell proved to O'Connor he was up to the task. He got his chance.

Mitchell remained in close touch with O'Connor after he earned a basketball scholarship to the University of North Dakota. They talked at least once a week over the phone, and O'Connor continued to mentor Mitchell when he faced tough academic and personal challenges.

After Mitchell's 2013 college basketball season ended, he attended an NBA Summer League tryout camp in Las Vegas. But what he didn't know was that some of the scouts there weren't basketball people. They were from the AFL. One approached Mitchell after his sessions, and invited him to the AFL's U.S. Combine.

When they next caught up, O'Connor was expecting Mitchell to email him a video of his basketball tryout. Instead, Mitchell sent him a link to vision of a sport O'Connor had never before seen. "This isn't basketball," O'Connor told Mitchell, in a phone conversation. "This isn't what you went out there for."

But Mitchell was intrigued by what he had seen of footy and went to the U.S. Combine. He performed so well in testing that the AFL flew him and two other athletes to Sydney to work out for three weeks at the Sydney Swans Academy. Shortly afterwards, the Swans offered a contract to Mitchell, preferring him to the two other candidates: Mark Cisco — a former Columbia University basketball player — and Jason Holmes. Mitchell had a cleaner bill of health and was also a year younger than Holmes.

"I was a bit shocked when they picked Patty Mitchell over me," Holmes recalls. "But he marked and ran better than I did and he followed up more afterward, with workouts."

After Mitchell signed on with the Swans, he moved into a home in the beachside town of Coogee, after first living in Roos's old house. Through preseason running, Mitchell's frame transformed, taking him from chiseled to super-lean. Mitchell and his new teammates did recovery sessions in the Pacific Ocean in January, the time of the year America's Upper Midwest becomes tundra. "It's nice to finally have winter without snow or it being freezing, like in North Dakota," Mitchell would say.

At the club's daily training sessions, Mitchell had only to look at Pyke for an example of someone fairly close to home who successfully converted to footy. The Swans sent Mitchell to play for its NEAFL team, under senior coach Jared Crouch, a former Swan who was no stranger to perseverance. Having been drafted in 1995, Crouch took three years to make his AFL debut, but he eventually played 223 matches, including an AFL-record, 194 straight.

Mitchell often reported to the ground at 8 a.m. for three hours of skill sessions with a development coach — and that was before his conditioning work started. Mitchell tirelessly worked on his kicking — off each foot — and handballing.

"It's a rude awakening of how hard the work is," he said after his first season of training and playing in the NEAFL. "There's no resting. You're always moving. There's tons and tons of running."

Mitchell experienced a moment common to all American footy newbies: their first embarrassing onfield "stuff-up," in which their inexperience is laid bare before the eyes of teammates, opponents, umpires and fans. His initiation happened in an early-season match, immediately after an opponent took a mark against him.

"Move on!" a field umpire yelled to Mitchell, instructing him to yield 3 meters to a player who just marked the ball in front of him, as rules require. But the umpire's unfamiliar accent, plus the game-speed adrenaline coursing through Mitchell, made him hear, "Play on!" He stepped over the mark and tackled his opponent. Immediately, the umpire issued a 50-meter penalty against him, giving Mitchell's man an easy, point-blank shot at goal from the goal square.

"One of my teammates really got into me for that, for giving away that free kick," Mitchell says. "He said, 'That's a dumb play, mate!'"

Still, Mitchell says for the most part, his teammates stayed patient. "They were amazing throughout the whole time," Mitchell says. "They understand where I'm coming from. They all help me out with advice. The training — all the time you spend together — builds a really strong bond."

That showed after Mitchell kicked his first goal. He lined up and calmly kicked the footy through the big sticks, then was mobbed by his teammates.

"I showed the video to the whole senior team," Crouch said, shortly after the season ended. "It was inspirational and exciting — definitely a highlight of his short career. We'd love to see that four or five times a game — he'd be dangerous."

Mitchell proved to be just that, but not in the way the club dreamed. In another match, as the ball was flying towards the 50-meter arc from the wing, Mitchell was alongside Sydney's prized new acquisition, Kurt Tippett, who was playing in the NEAFL to get back into AFL-playing shape after an injury. Mitchell leaped for the footy and his knee crashed hard into Tippett's side, breaking one of his ribs.

"Accidents happen," Crouch said near the end of the 2014 season. "From then on, we told everyone not to get anywhere near [Tippett]."

Crouch says the Swans had low expectations of Mitchell in his first season. They understood he was learning the game. Even with all the preseason conditioning work, he struggled to run out a full game and often would cramp up by three-quarter time. Mitchell also knew he was on a strong team, but he was already 24; both he and Crouch knew he'd have to quickly rise through the ranks.

"It's absolutely a race against time," Crouch said, as he prepared his side for the 2014 NEAFL Grand Final. "He has some advantages, such as pure size, but he's got guys who are 19, 20 and 21 competing against him. The learning curve is steep."

Mitchell was omitted in the team's Grand Final lineup. A week later, the Swans issued a terse, three-sentence media release: Mitchell had decided to return home.

Still, O'Connor, Mitchell's longtime mentor, says his former player's effort to become an AFL player was "a great lesson to me and to young kids." "I'll tell them to get out of their comfort zones one day and have an experience like Pat," O'Connor says. "What he was doing takes tremendous courage."

Marvin Baynham: The Star-crossed Scholar

For months before he arrived at the Draft Combine in Melbourne in September 2014, Marvin Baynham had lived, breathed, eaten and slept footy. His newfound footy *sensei* Denis Ryan's impromptu, six-week Australian football boot camp had produced truly wonderful results. Baynham knew more than just handballing and kicking. He could talk about AFL history with footy scholars. He could break down the techniques of the AFL's leading ruckmen. Baynham became a "footyholic," and he now had his chance to impress AFL scouts and land a coveted contract. Eric Wallace had done it two years before. Jason Holmes did it the previous year. Both Ryan and Baynham were confident that 2014 would be Baynham's turn.

"Just show us athleticism," the AFL scouts told Baynham.

He did. Emphatically. Baynham smashed the existing Draft Combine record in the standing vertical jump, ascending to just under 3 feet, and ran the 20-meter sprint in 2.82 seconds, an astonishing speed for an athlete his size.

The results didn't surprise Ryan. The American recruits, he argues, are older and more physically mature than the Australian 18-year-olds. "The guys in the Australian system are scrawny little kids," he concludes.

The AFL website's video reports on its Draft Combine were all about Baynham's performance. Tadhg Kennelly, the Irish former Swan who converted from Gaelic football, appeared in the video and said of Baynham: "His speed's unbelievable. He [beat by] 10 centimeters [the] all-time vertical jump record. He's a great guy. He's done a pile of homework on the game. It's incredible. He's got the character to make it, so our fingers [are] crossed."

A number of AFL clubs approached Baynham: the Port Adelaide Power, Richmond Tigers, North Melbourne Kangaroos, Essendon Bombers and Adelaide Crows. But most of his meetings were brief, lasting between five and 10 minutes. Adelaide's chat with Baynham, however, went for about 20 minutes.

"They seemed like they were really serious," Baynham says. "They asked if I felt homesick, asked me about my endurance and asked about my family. They asked what I knew about the game. I thought there was a 75 to 80 per cent chance they'd offer me a contract."

The Crows didn't, and Baynham went unselected in the draft. But there still was hope for him to get picked up in the Rookie Draft, three months after the combine. A few weeks beforehand, St Kilda featured Baynham in a short "Draft Hub" video for its website. In it, Baynham praised Holmes, saying he had encouraged him, given him insights and had been a great role model.

AFL national talent manager Michael Ablett then urged North Melbourne to ask Baynham to train with some of its players at its high-altitude camp in Utah. It was held Thanksgiving week, though, and proved fruitless for both parties. Baynham arrived two days before the holiday, the day when the club broke camp, so he could only train with the team just once, on Wednesday. Still, the club posted video of his workout on its website. On camera, Baynham said he has fallen in love with the game. North Melbourne veteran Daniel Wells partnered with Baynham, working with him on basic skills, and in the video he offered some positive words.

"He's pretty athletic," Wells said. "I did some skills with him. So far, he's not too bad. He hasn't kicked [the footy] too much, but he definitely has some talent about him. If he wants to have a crack at it, it seems like he's really determined. That's half the battle."

A week after the Kangaroos' Utah camp, the Rookie Draft was held. Baynham went unclaimed. None of the clubs that circled him during the Draft Combine or sent out feelers acted on their interest.

That completely frustrated Ryan. "Those clubs were all interested and had different reasons why they didn't take Marvin," he says.

Port Adelaide already had one Category B International Rookie on its list, Irishman Daniel Flynn. Flynn played on Port's minor league affiliate in the South Australian National Football League (SANFL), but left Port Adelaide in January 2015 and return to Ireland for good. If Flynn had left a month or two earlier, perhaps the Power might've drafted Baynham. North Melbourne already had its own Category B rookie, Eric Wallace.

After his strong combine showing and the Utah camp, Baynham was left perplexed and peeved. "The clubs never told me where I went wrong," he says. "They asked me to be an athlete. And what did I do? I broke the vertical leap record, ran the 20-meter sprint in record time. What else did I need to do? I'm pretty sure no one did what I did, all that training and learning."

Unexpectedly, in January 2015, the AFL once more reached out to Baynham, inviting him to train with its Australian Academy under-18 recruits at the IMG Academy sports complex in Bradenton, Florida. The recruits did full footy drills with established AFL stars such as Geelong's Tom Hawkins and Joel Selwood and Sydney's Luke Parker and Dan Hannebery.

League officials told Baynham and the other American athletes to "bring your gear" — but the meaning of this might have been lost in translation. As Ryan notes, if they'd told Baynham to "bring your *cleats*," he would've known to bring a pair of footy boots. Baynham showed up with different footwear, which Ryan says disappointed AFL scouts.

"Mick Ablett told me he was disappointed that Marvin's kicking hadn't improved since October," Ryan says. "But he had an unrealistic expectation about how he was going to improve. How was Marvin supposed to improve when the AFL hasn't assigned anybody to mentor him?"

Ryan invited Baynham back to his home to train again, but by then Baynham — who had graduated college eight months earlier — needed a full-time job to support himself.

At the 2015 U.S. Combine, draft expert Jonathan Givony also expressed frustration that no AFL club signed Baynham. "Marvin showed the most willingness to do it, of anybody," he says. "It was disappointing he didn't get a chance. But Marvin fell into a year where there weren't many teams looking for guys like him."

Ryan and Baynham remain in contact. They hold out hope that

Baynham can somehow continue his footy journey — and perhaps find a way into the AFL — by playing in the NTFL, the SANFL or the WAFL. But that would mean Baynham getting a full-time job in one of those states to support himself while playing.

AFL clubs may have questioned Baynham's footy ability, but Baynham doesn't question his own resolve. "I never played basketball until my first year in high school, and in four years I was able to get a university scholarship," he says. "I was confident. I've always been strong-willed and confident."

Alex Starling: The Best There Never Was
Of all the athletes involved in the AFL's seven-year American Experiment, only one has inspired a club's complete adulation. Only one has stoked a club's hopes that it had unearthed a precious diamond, a game-changing force. That's why it was so shattering for both the player and the recruiting staff when the footy fates conspired to snuff out a career before it got started.

Talk to any Sydney Swans recruiter who was at the club in 2011 and they'll tell you: Alex Starling not only could've been the first born-and-bred American in the AFL, but also should've become an Australian household name. This man, they believed, had it all: athleticism, aptitude and attitude.

"I have no doubt Alex would've been a star," says Paul Roos, who coached Sydney from 2002 to 2010 and was head coach of its academy from 2010 to 2013. "He was in the 1 per cent of athletes, like [recently retired, probable future AFL Hall of Famer] Adam Goodes and [current Swans' superstar] Buddy Franklin. He would've been a fantastic AFL player."

For Starling, the youngest of three children, who grew up in Miami's impoverished and violence-ridden Richmond Heights neighborhood, his path to the AFL started in 2011. He was attending Bethune Cookman University, in Daytona Beach, Florida, and was working towards a degree in business administration and management. He also was having a strong basketball season. Starling had earned a reputation on the court as a hard-working, uncompromisingly physical player. He played under coach Cliff Reed, known for conducting college basketball's most physically demanding practices.

Jonathan Givony floated Starling's name and those of three other players to the Swans as the club prepared to conduct its own U.S. Combine in Redondo Beach, California, bankrolled by Swans former part owner Basil Sellers. Then Givony contacted Starling via Facebook to invite him. Starling was intrigued, said yes and flew to Los Angeles.

Bethune Cookman's basketball media guide listed Starling as being 6-foot-6. But when Chris Olson first saw him from out his car window, while picking him up at Los Angeles International Airport the night before the combine began, he felt he had been deceived.

"There was no way he was that tall," Olson says. "Unless he was standing on top of a New York City phone book when they measured him. My first thought was, *We wasted a trip on this kid.* He didn't tick the box of being as tall as 'Roosy' and the Swans wanted. But he had this humble confidence. He told me in the car, 'You realize these other guys you invited don't even need to show up.' But I didn't take it as his being overconfident and cocky. What he was telling me was that nobody else was gonna come at it like him. Alex wanted the other candidates to regret even showing up [and] competing against him. When we tested him, he went absolutely flat out."

Olson says Starling "murdered" a 3-kilometer time trial, completing it in 11 minutes, 21 seconds. "He lapped everyone else," Olson says. "Some of the other guys just ended up quitting, but Alex *sprinted* the last 100 meters."

Starling was channeling a sporting icon's words to propel him. "The quote that was in my head," he wrote in a blog for the USAFL website about his experience, "was Muhammad Ali's, 'Don't quit. Suffer now and live the rest of your life a champion.'"

Starling also logged the best time in the 20-meter sprint, running it in 2.82 seconds. But his and the other invitees' initial footy skills left so much to be desired that the Swans' staff nearly admitted defeat and conceded the experiment was a disaster.

Before the athletic tests began, Roos and the Swans' head of player personnel, Kinnear Beatson, had decked the prospective recruits out in the team's red and white gear, then brought them into a hotel conference room and showed them video of how footy is played — or *supposed* to be. They then took the recruits to a park near the Pacific Ocean, with members of the USAFL's Los Angeles Dragons and some assorted footy-loving Aussie expats, to try the kicks, handballs and marks they'd just watched.

"They looked like complete spazzes," says Olson, who fell in love with footy the moment he watched it in the 1980s on late-night ESPN telecasts, then, a decade-and-a-half later, took up playing the game with a USAFL club. "It was so sad. Roosy and I got back in the car and he asks me, 'Is this how Shae started out?' These guys didn't look like they were ever gonna get it. I could tell Roosy was thinking, *What did I just do? How am I gonna tell Basil?*"

But when Olson and Roos returned to the hotel lobby, they found Starling waiting for them. He demanded more practice time. So the three men went back outside. "In the next hour, he advanced so much," Olson says. "There was something about him, that he just wanted to do it *right*."

But beyond demonstrating improved skills, Starling showed Olson and Roos something much more meaningful. "We sat down at a picnic table and talked to Alex and really got to know what a special kid he was," Olson says. "It wasn't just his athleticism. It was his character. The light bulb went off in Roosy's head and it confirmed what he thought about recruiting American athletes."

Starling, too, was excited by the prospect of learning and excelling in a new sport. "I fell in love with Australian football immediately," he wrote in another of his USAFL blog posts, "and knew that if I was given the opportunity to play AFL I would do everything to make the most of it."

A little more than a month later, the Swans flew Starling to Sydney to train for three weeks, both at the Swans' Moore Park facility and at the Sydney Cricket Ground. Starling worked out with Roos, senior coach John Longmire, Beatson and development manager Stuart Maxfield.

"He was fanatical about the way he went about it," Roos says. "He was unbelievably dedicated. He surprised everyone in the coaching group."

The Swans were smitten with Starling. They developed big plans for him.

First, in January 2012, they signed Starling under the AFL's International Scholarship Scheme, which allowed the club to periodically train him in Australia during his college breaks. George Stone, the development coach who greatly helped Tadhg Kennelly convert from Gaelic football to Aussie Rules, would train and mentor him. At the end of 2012 Sydney planned to draft Starling as a Category B International Rookie, which would mean he could start playing in the Northeast Australian Football League (NEAFL) in 2013.

The Swans posted a 90-second highlight video of Starling working out at the SCG on their website. Watch it and it quickly becomes obvious why the club was so enamored.

While all the American ruck prospects are athletic, they still look as if they're growing into their roles. No matter how much experience they gain, they may never look like footy naturals because the sport hasn't come to them naturally. Not so for Starling. He looks almost *too* natural, if such a thing is possible. Starling is fluid in the training sessions — he looks like he already has "silky skills," which every player works hard to develop. The Swans were re-thinking their initial idea of playing Starling in the ruck, and instead began planning to deploy him in the forward line.

In the video, Starling effortlessly scoops up a loose ball on the run, then balances himself and slots a goal from 40 meters with a kick that couldn't be straighter. In a marking contest he "bodies" Roos with ease, then gracefully leaps to take the ball overhead, landing balanced and calm. He shakes and shimmies around Roos like an NFL running back, before booting another goal. He brings deft touches to handballs and his kicks appear expertly weighted. Toss the "American" label out the window — Starling looks like a man who has played footy well all his life.

"I've never seen a bloke cover ground like him," Roos said of Starling at the time. "I've never seen a guy run from center half-forward to the goal square as fast in my life."

But during one of the training sessions that year, something went terribly wrong. Something physical that had been nagging Starling for months reached a tipping point.

Starling told the Swans' coaches his left shin was very sore. The Sydney medical staff thought enough of his complaint to perform some precautionary tests. The results confirmed something far worse than soreness: Starling had a stress fracture, a small break in a bone, caused by repetitive activity. Stress fractures are usually self-healing, but only after several months of rest. According to medical studies, most athletes who have stress fractures have a high chance of suffering them again in the future.

Roos and the Swans' medical team were flummoxed. Why hadn't Starling's condition been previously diagnosed while he was in college? How could he have been allowed to continue playing basketball?

"He'd been carrying the injury for about a year," Olson says, "but he was pushing through."

After deliberating on Starling's footy future, Sydney management finalized its decision a week before the 2013 Rookie Draft, when it originally planned to pick him. The club issued a media release saying it wouldn't draft Starling. "The seriousness of the injury," the release read, "would negate Starling from training at AFL level."

Both Starling and Roos were crushed.

Still, Starling wouldn't give up. A December 9, 2013 story in a small Melbourne-area newspaper, the *Frankston Standard Leader* reported that Starling would join the VFL's Frankston Dolphins in 2014, and quoted club senior coach Simon Goosey describing Starling as "one of the best athletes I've ever seen." The accompanying photo showed a smiling Starling in the Dolphins' red, white and black kit, alongside Goosey. But the apparent deal soon fell apart.

Starling then moved to Adelaide, where his agent was living. Port Power invited him to train with its reserves squad, the Port Adelaide Magpies, hoping he could heal, recapture his magic and then be available to sign. But Starling gravitated back to basketball.

He joined the Premier League's Woodville Warriors, and immediately dominated the competition. Besides helping his new club to the 2014 premiership, he was named the Grand Final's most valuable player, he earned league all-star honors and won its "fairest and most brilliant player" award. Off the court, Starling utilized his business degree, running a basketball camp for kids aged seven to 18.

In 2015 Starling moved to Warrnambool, Victoria and joined the another Australian basketball competition, the Big V League, signing on with a team called the Warrnambool Seahawks. He won the team's most valuable player award for the season, and on his off-days coached basketball at a primary school and umpired other youth games.

Starling's Australian adventure has turned out far differently than he could've possibly imagined. His journey wasn't supposed to take him full circle, back to basketball. But it has.

The footy world never will know what "might have been" with Starling. Olson still wonders what he could've achieved as an AFL player. Roos says he became — and remains — good mates with his former star student, which is why it was so hard to cut the professional ties they were developing.

"As a friend, it was disappointing," Roos says. "But Alex understood. As a professional athlete, he knew the risks."

10

Baby Steps
The 2015 U.S. Combine

Already, the sun is blistering hot and the humidity is smothering. It's a few hours before noon on Florida's Gulf Coast, on the wide-open grassy fields at the IMG Sports Academy in the town of Bradenton. The faint hum of a distant lawnmower and the calls of seagulls provide the soundtrack. Sprinklings of tiny black gnats dot the air, causing the group of men here to swat them away from their faces and bodies. The closest weather the group of Australian recruiters assembled here might have experienced to this back home would likely be a summer's day in Australia's tropical Far North Queensland region. This is the AFL's 2015 U.S. Scouting Combine.

These fields are only a mile or two away from the air conditioned conference room where, about an hour ago, 15 young men — whose common denominators are their college basketball experience and their average height of 6 feet, 7 inches — began their crash course in Aussie Rules football. Just weeks ago these recruits played their last games as NCAA hoopsters. Shortly they'll graduate from their universities and be thrust into the "real world." This is about the time the anxiety kicks in for American college seniors who don't have employment waiting for them after they walk across a stage to collect their diplomas, then shift the tassels on their academic caps to signify their status as graduates, and finally, toss their caps high into the air with their classmates.

For the young men here on the IMG fields, brought together from universities across North America, the only certainty they have after graduation is uncertainty. They're not on the radars of the NBA clubs, and won't be drafted a few months from now. If they are fortunate, they might attract the attention of professional basketball clubs in Europe, the Middle East or Asia. And if these guys want to enter the corporate world — good luck. They'll have to get in line with the hundreds of thousands of other graduates of the class of 2015, float their resumes out among the sea of others, and hope the subject they majored in, their grade point average and anything else they may have going for them will win them an interview.

But that's not why these men are here, sweating in the sweltering conditions. They are here because they are dreamers. They are working to earn the two-word descriptor of "professional athlete" and this combine might be both their first and last chance at that dream. For many of the recruits, this is their first in-person interview with a potential post-college employer. Over the next few days, the AFL recruiters, constantly taking notes in their minds and on paper, will take stock of everything about each prospect, from their coachability to their adaptability to their athletic and academic smarts.

These athletes, all of whom thrive on competition and have garnered success in a sport they love, must now start from scratch and experience the frustration of unfamiliarity and failure. They are taking baby steps. And of these 15 young men, three at most will be invited, a few months from now, by the AFL recruiters to train for three weeks in Melbourne. If they make it that far, they're in the best position to hone their skills and perhaps earn a contract with a club as a "Category B International Rookie."

The first day's very first drill begins with something familiar. The hopefuls, whom the AFL recruiters collectively refer to as "the boys," are all outfitted in black compression tops and shorts, with white numbers on the fronts and backs of their shirts. Mick Ablett, the AFL's national talent manager, Matthew Capuano, the Carlton Blues' ruck coach of the last five seasons, and Kevin "Shifter" Sheehan, the AFL's national talent and international manager, whose own 102-

game career lasted from the mid-1970s into the early 1980s with the Geelong Cats, lead this drill, as they will all the others.

The trio assembles the boys into pairs and has them toss the unfamiliar footballs up above the heads of their partners, who must then practice tapping it down. To these guys, who have done countless jump balls and opening tipoffs as centers or forwards in basketball, this must look easy enough. The object of the exercise is similar to a ruck contest in footy: win the contest and successfully give a teammate first use of the ball. But less than a minute into the drill, just as some of them might be thinking the technique is too simple, Capuano stops the activity and commands everyone's attention.

"I don't want you to jump at the ball," he instructs. "You want to hit the ball at its highest point, so you can get your hand on it."

After this drill, the instructors then get the recruits in five groups of three, with the third man acting as a tap-down target.

"Do it a little softer," Ablett tells Jalen Carethers, a 21-year-old, 6-foot-8 invitee who played his college basketball at Radford University, Virginia. Ablett then compliments the handiwork of Matt Korcheck, a 23-year-old out of the University of Arizona. Everyone's laughing it up in this competition, shoving each other around while jockeying for position, trying to put Capuano's instructions into practice with this strange red ball that some have never even seen before.

"What play is this?" Carethers asks Capuano, seeking to learn about ruck contests and their importance in footy matches.

"It's called a ball-up," Capuano explains.

Marking — which the AFL instructors explain means "catching" in American sporting lingo — is next. Capuano demonstrates the correct technique for marking by holding his hands alongside each other, his thumbs forming a "W." The boys respond, but hold their hands up as if they are showing their claws.

Capuano and Ablett drill stab passes at their new charges as the hopefuls run towards them in two lines. The players must mark the kicks, handball back to the kickers, and then sprint back to the line for more. All the while, the boys talk it up, encouraging their new-found comrades.

"Good hands, 15!" Carethers shouts to Korcheck, referring to the number on his jumper, after he cleanly takes mark after mark.

After running American combines for four years, the recruiters are sure of one thing: handballing may look like the easiest footy skill for a new player to master, but it confounds many American prospects. Many drop the footy entirely and strike it awkwardly and underhand-edly, as if serving a volleyball.

"I see a lot of you guys, when you start, want to take your hand away and punch it," Capuano says. "You want to hold the ball low and then hit it like an uppercut. Catch your fist with your hand. It makes it easier for someone to receive, with backspin."

Once the drill gets underway, Shifter chimes in: "Follow through towards your target."

The pupils, lined up about a meter apart, are doing about as well as can be expected. Several repetitions in, they're making progress. James Johnson, a 6-foot-9 Canadian who played basketball at Virginia's Liberty University, quickly gains Ablett's praise as the group's best handballer, with Capuano giving him a pep talk.

"Hold the ball up more," Capuano says. "That's it! That's better! Once you get confident in the ball position, you can hit it harder. Are you punching it? Set yourself. Make sure you get that handle right."

With a blow of his whistle and a cry of "Listen up!" Ablett announces the start of a handball game. The recruits must successfully handball to their partners, then take a step back for every time they receive a handball on the full. The winning pair will be the one that can handball the furthest without spilling it.

"Off we go!" Ablett yells, starting play.

"Pressure time!" Junior Fortunat, another Canadian, shouts as he tentatively handballs to Capuano, who is acting as his partner.

After a few minutes a winning pair emerges: Zachary Reynolds of Northern Arizona and John Crnogorac of the University of Mississippi. But this pair has a decided advantage: Crnogorac is an Australian who grew up in Sydney and so has had a lifetime of exposure to Aussie Rules football.

Somehow, when the guys split into two groups and handball while quickly running towards each other, the skill becomes easier. "Good job!" they yell to each other. One of the North Melbourne recruiters takes out his mobile phone to record the drill on video.

"All right, lads, hold it there," Capuano yells out. Then he divides the recruits into four groups, for a "five-star" handball drill, which has them running diagonally towards each other, handballing while crisscrossing and dodging the oncoming — and sizeable — human traffic. "Don't wait for anybody!" he shouts, exhorting his charges to keep pace. While the handballs aren't perfectly executed, the young men surprise themselves and laugh in celebration as they avoid collisions.

When Ablett calls for a short break, he speaks to the group about developing game awareness. "When you're receiving the ball, you want it between your waist and your chest," he begins. "You try and get it up *here*," he warns, holding his hands high above his head, "and someone's gonna break your ribs."

The drill continues, and so does the boys' talk and clapping, which pleases Shifter. "We really want the noise," he says. "You have to get used to the sound of your teammates. Voice recognition is important in footy. It's the awareness of your teammate around you. We play our game in such tight situations."

Simulating match situations is a big step forward from the morning session in the conference room where the group first assembled, after they were ferried over by bus from their temporary digs in a neraby apartment complex. Capuano did his best to explain what the ruckman's role entails, while the group sat around a table and watched video of some of the AFL's current ruckmen in action.

"It's a very physical weekend for a ruckman," Capuano begins. "There may be 110 to 120 contests. How well can you direct the ball to your teammate while your opponent is smashing the hell out of you? You have to have a strong body but soft hands. It's a one-step run off, using one driving leg. You guys might be used to driving off both legs in basketball in a jump ball."

Ablett chimes in: "Boxing out for a rebound, trying to use your strength, is very similar. We find a lot of you guys transition very well. I heard a lot of guys asking, 'How long does it take to transition?' There's no set time, boys. Be open to that."

*

Being open to the reality that there's no timetable to adjust to a completely foreign sport is a big ask of young men with uncertain futures. They're all chasing the dream of playing a professional sport, one that has become more remote since their college basketball careers ended. So the Aussie Rules combine — organized and paid for by the AFL — seems to many a great proposition.

"You can't lose coming here," says Daquan Holiday, a loquacious Brooklyn-accented 6-foot-8 recruit with a knack of playfully needling his new teammates. He played basketball for the New Jersey Institute of Technology. "What's the worst that can happen? If I don't get picked, I can at least say, 'I tried.' It's a great opportunity. I looked [footy] up on YouTube and it looked pretty crazy. I saw a couple of hits on players. It's different from what I'm used to. I always look at the excitement of the game by how many people are in the stands, and from what I saw, it was packed."

For Carethers, his time at the Combine is his first-ever encounter with anything — or anyone — Australian. "It's my first experience, even hearing the accents," he says. "When I got the email from Jonathan [Givony] inviting me, I thought it was some human-trafficking scam. It was the randomness of it. I'd never heard of Australian football. I looked up Mason Cox and some of the other people who tried to play and then I researched the AFL. It's really physical, you have to be smart and you have to run so much. I didn't think it'd be that much running."

That realization is all too common among American footy hopefuls. But they can take heart in the fact that even some of the best AFL ruckmen faced challenges to develop their endurance. AFL recruiters point to the beginning of the 21st century as a major turning point for ruckmen. That's when a select few began to play the position more athletically and more skillfully, which then led to a new set of expectations for Australian and international recruits.

The recruiters point to one AFL ruckman in particular as a game-changer: Dean Cox, the former West Coast Eagles star, who is now the club's rucks coach. Cox, whose 6-foot-8 stature is comparable to many of the American recruits at this combine, played 290 games over 14 seasons, kicking 169 goals and earning All-Australian honors six times, including in 2006, when the Eagles won their last Premiership. But as Nick Byrne, a North Melbourne scout who attended the Florida Combine along with that club's list manager, Cameron Joyce, remembers of Cox's early days, "He couldn't run a lap around the ground when he started." But that would change and Cox would soon set the standard.

"Dean Cox was a pioneer," Joyce says. "He was a ruckman who could find a lot of the ball. He was like an extra midfielder. He also could take marks in the forward line. He had a real aptitude for finding the ball."

To a lesser degree, Byrne cites Corey McKernan as another influential ruckman. McKernan enjoyed a 237-game career with North Melbourne between 1993 and 2001 and again in 2004, with a 41-game stint at Carlton from 2002 to 2003 sandwiched in between. He booted 310 goals on his journey and earned two Premiership medallions with North Melbourne, in 1996 — the year he tied for first in the Brownlow Medal but was ineligible for the award because of a suspension early that season — and 1999. At Carlton in 2002, McKernan led the club in goal kicking and earned the club's "best and fairest player" award. "Corey McKernan changed the ruck position with his dynamism and kicking goals from the forward line," Byrne said. "He had natural athleticism and he had the ability to ruck, then follow on to the ball."

Hours after their initiation to the Australian game on the field, and after lunch at a nearby country club's dining room, the boys are bused a few miles to the sprawling IMG Academy campus. It's a small village of indoor and outdoor tennis courts, weights rooms, basketball gymnasiums, a wellness spa, a covered turf training center and dormitories for the visiting amateur athletes who train here. The prospects' first order of business this evening is a skinfold test (in which their body fat is measured), followed by 20-meter sprints, standing and running vertical jumps, and agility drills, all with the recruiters watching.

The skinfold testing takes place on the second floor of one of the indoor basketball courts. While the boys wait for sports dietician Kate Burks to break out the tape measure, the calipers, and the grease pencils to gather data on their chests, shoulders, triceps, biceps, waists, abdomens and thighs, it doesn't take long for three of the recruits to embrace being back in their natural sporting habitat.

Crnogorac, fellow Australian James Hunter, who has just wrapped up his college basketball career at the University of South Dakota, and Deji Adekunle, an Englishman playing in his junior year at Northwestern State, Louisiana, can't resist grabbing a basketball and taking turns dunking and sinking jump shots. Hunter, sporting a fluffy brown Mohawk, is a big, bearded, smiling ball of energy. He's a hard trainer, but when out of training mode he's a jokester. He grew up in Sydney and played some footy, but Hunter had much more fortune playing basketball and rugby at Cranbrook School. He hadn't thought about footy in years, though, until getting the email inviting him to the combine.

Brian Hornstein, a recruit from Dallas, Texas, stands 7 feet tall and is the combine's tallest hopeful. He played at Florida International University and, like most of the other recruits, was a center, also known as the "five-man." "Usually the five-man is the goofiest guy on the team," Hornstein says, then he breaks into a chuckle. "And here we all are!"

Hornstein's unexpected excursion into footy began just weeks ago, when his coach, Michael Curry, asked him to come to his office for a meeting. Hornstein thought Curry, who had mentored him on and off the court, wanted to talk about opportunities to play pro basketball in Europe. Instead, coach and player watched a video on a computer about the AFL and the combine. "It was a little disappointing," Hornstein recalls. "I've been playing basketball so long. I know the coach is helping the other guys on the team do their thing, and I was thinking that I don't work any less hard than they did. But there are no hard feelings. I knew my college basketball days were coming to an end eventually. In my mind I thought I could play overseas, but I didn't know if that would benefit me in the long term. Now all of us are here seeing what could happen. Nobody here is threatened by anyone else. We all respect each other. It's like we're on a new team."

Seeing video of Mason Cox training for Collingwood has helped Hornstein. "It really hit home, seeing Mason," he says. "That made it real."

If neither the combine nor European basketball opportunities pan out for Hornstein, he has hopes of pursuing another dream. During a break from college, he started working for the Omni, an upscale Dallas hotel. "I kind of fell in love with the idea of working in hotels," he says. He became so enamored that he worked part-time at the Omni for two years. After the combine, Hornstein even has an interview lined up with a Marriott hotel in another part of Florida for a manager-in-training position.

As he waits to take his skinfold test, Hornstein reflects on another kind of testing he and everyone else had earlier in the morning: psychological. Representatives from the AFL clubs — North Melbourne, Essendon, Richmond, and Carlton — each administered short questionnaires to the recruits, hoping to learn about their personalities. Word got around that clubs, if they were interested, might ask the boys for a follow-up interview. But it's only one day in and it's too early for them to get any indication if they're impressing the recruiters, who are giving nothing away. As Hornstein notes, "They're holding their cards close to their chests."

Kye Kurkowski, a soft-spoken 23-year-old from Grant, Nebraska, isn't too stressed out by the proceedings. That's likely because he has stared down far more harrowing situations than whether he'll be picked for a follow-up audition.

With a population of just over 1,000 people, Grant is a dot-sized speck on the rolling plains near the Colorado border, in a region known for producing an abundance of wheat, corn, soybeans and sunflowers. Not long ago, if someone had said the word *combine* to him, Kurkowski would've immediately thought of a combine harvester. He's been around those machines all his life, growing up on a family farm with five siblings.

Kurkowski can hardly remember a time in his life when he wasn't riding around on tractors, which he started doing at age 2 or 3. He also remembers the hard times, when his parents, like many other farmers in the region, fell into debt and had to sell their farms. Kurkowski's mother, Judy, went to work for the U.S. Department of Agriculture, while his father, Kelvin, now buys and sells tractors. Grant's agricultural riches are always at risk because of its location in "Hail Alley," a swath of land where North America's most dangerous hailstorms occur. When dark thunderheads form in the Platte River Valley, local farmers know the forthcoming hail could trash a good wheat or corn crop. As Kurkowski says, "It's a race against time."

Away from the farm, Kurkowski, who majored in agricultural engineering at the University of Nebraska, grew up playing basketball. But it's also his soccer background that has the AFL scouts intrigued. They believe that both his height and his kicking skills will give him a competitive advantage over many of the other hopefuls. There's also Kurkowski's understanding of teamwork, which seems uniquely suited to AFL football.

"On a farm, as a family, you're a team," Kurkowski says. "Everyone's got a part to play. AFL seems like the most fun of the sports out there. I'd be a tall, athletic guy with a specified role. In the end, it's part of being part of a team, being able to compete."

*

It takes the Essendon scout a second to comprehend the number he's just heard inside one of the IMG basketball gymnasiums. He gasps in amazement and then says four words barely loud enough for anyone else to hear, as he jots the number down in his notebook: "You can't be serious."

The incredulous man is Marty Allison. Along with the other AFL scouts he has been watching, the recruits run across the parquetry floor, their sneakers emitting high-pitched squeaks as they go. They are running 20-meter sprints between towering parallel light fixtures. Motion sensors mounted on tripods detect their movements at the five, 10 and 20-meter marks.

As each recruit finishes, Ablett calls the final number aloud, as much for the benefit of the watching scouts as for the recruits themselves, who are anxious to hear about their own performance. There is no emotion about Ablett's voice, no matter what the number — no indication of awe or disappointment. He's leaving that to the scouts as they record the data. Richmond's scout uses a yellow notepad and a pen, while the North Melbourne and Essendon men use their mobile phones.

"Two point seven nine," Ablett calls. This is the figure that has prompted Allison's amazement. It signifies how fast Jalen Carethers has run the course. The first time he did the test this evening, Carethers ran it in 3.02 seconds. His new mark of 2.79 seconds is two-tenths of a second off the record for the 2014 Combine, and just four-tenths of a second off the all-time Combine record.

"That's *too* quick," Allison says excitedly. "Normally that time is for someone much smaller. To come off and reduce the score by that much makes me question the validity of the test."

However improbable, the result is legitimate. Korcheck has run the next best time, 3.03 seconds, while Christian Behrens, of the University of California Berkeley, earned the next fastest mark, at 3.04. James Hunter runs times of 3.25 and 3.26.

Carethers also stars in the standing vertical leap test. The prospects all launch upwards and attempt, at the apex of their leaps, to swat back a set of plastic strips that look like the teeth of a comb. With Ablett literally raising the bar at the top of the apparatus after each recruit's turn, they reach heights ranging from 2½ to 3 feet — that is, until Carethers soars to surpass 3-feet-1 inch with his three attempts. He scores well in the last test of the day, which measures agility. It's a series of six sprints, with a recorded voice from a machine prompting when the group should start. It's still too early to tell which of the boys the AFL scouts will invite to Melbourne a few months from now, but Carethers certainly hasn't done his chances any harm.

*

Threatening dark gray skies, blustery winds and steady rain greet the recruits and scouts on the morning of the Combine's second day. It seems like Mother Nature has unleashed her own teaser trailer for "the mean season," the annual six-week period in America's southeast Atlantic region in the late summer months of August and September, in which furious and damaging thunderstorms and hurricanes ravage the sea and the land.

One of the athletic trainers assigned to work with the squad has been advised by a scout that the players may have to be evacuated because of lightning spotted 7½ miles away. After a short primer on kicking by the scouts, the pupils are testing their ability to kick the Australian ball. Most of their kicks are ragged. Many hold the footy like an American football — horizontally — and kick it off the sides of their feet. A short time later the outdoor training is postponed: the lightning poses too great a risk. Everyone seeks shelter in the bowels of an outdoor track and field stadium as the combine's organizers figure out a Plan B.

Boredom and restlessness grip the group of competitive athletes. Hunter and Korcheck are using their smartphones to find out the "lightning capitals" of the world. Small groups of other recruits sit and talk quietly at picnic benches under the stands. The recruits are relieved and amused when Holiday and Carethers launch into an impromptu debate over which rapper is better — Drake or Fabolous. "You are *blasphemous!*" Holiday animatedly shouts at Carethers, with a half-serious, half-joking expression on his face, after Carethers argues in favor of Fabolous. "Drake makes *all* the hits, boy! I bet you can't name two songs off Fabolous's album!"

The Australian contingent looks on, smiling, not knowing what to make of the discussion. The Americans, whose number include the athletes, Givony, a *New York Times* reporter and a freelance photojournalist, all gather round to soak up the entertainment. It's the kind of verbal jocularity commonplace among young men on a city basketball blacktop or in an African-American-owned barbershop.

Holiday and Carethers reach a stalemate and start another debate on a topic all the boys know well: who the NBA's best players are, position by position. Holiday, the most vocal of all the athletes, looks through a pro basketball magazine, checking the rankings of various NBA point guards. He spars with Carethers about whether Golden State's Stephen Curry is a better point guard than the Los Angeles Clippers' Chris Paul. When the two recruits can't break the deadlock after making their cases, they ask the photojournalist for her opinion. She pivots, asking the two what they think about veteran big man Kevin Garnett deciding to return to the Minnesota Timberwolves, the team he started his career with.

At last Givony and Ablett announce that the program will continue inside the conference room, but not before Holiday and Carethers square off one last time on another basketball matter.

"[The New York Knicks'] Carmelo Anthony is the best scorer in the league," Holiday confidently declares.

"Nah, Carmelo's on the downside," Carethers retorts, and the entire contingent laughs.

Cameron Joyce's moment has now arrived. The North Melbourne general manager for football operations and list management will be making a presentation in the conference room with Mick Ablett. Joyce plugs in his laptop computer to a television monitor so he can project images onto the big screen. He'll be giving them four things: a broader and more detailed guide to Aussie Rules footy than what the invitees could find on YouTube; a look inside his own club; an insider's guide to the culture and life of an AFL footballer; and, lastly, motivation for the boys to keep pushing themselves, fighting for the remote reward of being picked by an AFL club to undertake an extraordinary athletic adventure.

The first video Joyce plays is a 2½- minute mini-documentary on Jason Holmes's journey, produced by St Kilda Football Club. It was shown as part of the 2014 Virgin Australia Film Festival, and it soon went viral. It's an inspiring video, chronicling Holmes's transformation from NCAA power forward to VFL ruckman. It shows his performance at the 2013 U.S. Combine, his subsequent tests at the Melbourne Combine, his signing a two-year deal with St Kilda in October of that year, and game footage of him playing for the VFL's Sandringham Zebras. The hopefuls watch silently as strains of the song "Symphony of Emotions" by Audioctane accompany Holmes's voiceover narration. As the video fades to black, the words "Everything's possible" flash in white letters.

Moments later, Joyce explains what every prospect is anxious to hear. "The AFL will bring two or three of you out in a few months," he begins. "But in the meantime, if another club wants to fly you out or make you an offer to sign, they can."

Joyce's presentation, "A Day in the Life of an AFL Player," gives the boys their first detailed look at what might eventually be in store for them. He asks them to speak up if any of the terminology he uses is unfamiliar. None do. These guys are used to team meetings with their head coaches, spending days lifting weights, recovering from games, doing injury-prevention exercises, studying video from previous games and meeting with advance scouts to discuss opposition teams' tactics.

But "professional development," as all AFL clubs conduct with their players, is different from what these athletes have experienced.

At North Melbourne, as Joyce explains, four hours one day a week is set aside for time away from football. Players take university studies, work part-time or involve themselves in a trade, preparing for work they'll do in the off-season or after their footy careers are over.

These young American athletes also are unlikely to have endured any preseason as physically rigorous as an AFL one, Joyce tells them. It begins in November, with three-hour conditioning and craft drills three times a week, until the start of the season in March, with only the Christmas season off.

Joyce's favorite part of his presentation is the video on North Melbourne's facilities at Arden Street. As the traditional club anthem, "Join in the Chorus" (set to the tune of an early 20th Century Scottish folk tune) plays in the background, he jokingly tells the recruits — all members of the hip-hop generation — "Don't judge the club on the song." It's doubtful that phrases in the video such as "Shinboner spirit" (a reference to the club's unofficial 19th Century nickname, which it acquired because some of its players toiled hard in a slaughterhouse, separating meat from animals' shinbones) and "the North way" or the images of former 1990s glory years captain Wayne Carey and his legendary coach Denis Pagan will have any great impact on the hopefuls, but many of them smile when they see that the Arden Street facilities include a basketball court. And they become engrossed when photos and video of Eric Wallace follow. In between highlights of a few of Wallace's best marks for North Ballarat and an interview from the Kangaroos' website, the recruits learn that Wallace, at the 2012 U.S. Combine, ran a 2.93 in the same 20-meter sprint trial they did the night before.

When some of the recruits ask how Wallace is doing now, in the North Melbourne system, Joyce is frank. "He kicks the ball quite well," he begins, "but his weaknesses are around the endurance side and game sense."

"I don't reckon he ran a lap without stopping when he first started," Mick Ablett adds, "but the improvement he's made has been incredible. If you have the drive and work ethic, success will come."

But it's the all-important quality that statistics can't measure — game sense — that Ablett says is just as valuable for a ruckman as the ability to give his teammates first use of the ball, or follow up ground balls, or be a tall marking target in the forward line. "Game sense is knowing where to position yourself around the ground," Ablett says. "Will you go forward or back to defense to help? Game sense is something that takes time. You have to go to and watch as many games as you can and talk to people about that. The game starts with you guys, as ruckmen. The coaches will often go up to their ruckmen and say, 'It starts with you today.' It takes competitiveness. You wouldn't be here if you didn't have it."

It's not hard for Joyce to cite an example of a current AFL star ruckman who wasn't a readymade talent, and who made a name for himself on basketball's hardwood rather than on a footy oval. Joyce simply looks to his own club's list. "Todd Goldstein played basketball and didn't start playing footy until he was 18," he says.

After the 2015 season, Goldstein, the star Kangaroo, would not only earn both his club's award for "best and fairest player," but also All-Australian (All-Star) honors. Before taking up footy, Goldstein had played on Australia's national under-19 basketball squad. "Todd's involvement in the game has improved," Joyce continues. "He's multifaceted. He's also marking and tackling too. He rarely goes forward, but he spends up to 85 per cent of the game on the ground."

At this point Ablett takes over the presentation, showing clips of various aspects of the game. The spectacular marks — "speckies," in Australian parlance — get the most *oohs* and *aahs*. They also motivate the recruits to ask a question all Americans seem to want to know after seeing the aerial acrobatics. "We just saw players jump on other players' backs," recruit Christian Behrens begins. "Is that legal? Is that a skill you can practice?"

Marty Allison, the Essendon scout, assures the group that, yes, leaping on another player's back is legal in footy. It's a shame the AFL scouts couldn't have brought over some marking bags, he muses, so the Americans could practice the craft.

Ablett asks them if they want to see more highlights, and the young men clamor for a YouTube video on footy's "hardest hits." This clip may have the least to do with the AFL, and it's neither produced nor sanctioned by the league, but it gets the loudest reactions and the most enthusiasm from the boys, who are used to watching bone-crunching tackles in American football. It will take time, apparently, for footy's finer points to be fully appreciated.

Day 2 at the combine unfolds without great fanfare — nothing emerges as eye-popping as Carethers's 20-meter sprint time, but Carethers does nail his first-ever shot at goal, during a "set-shot" simulation drill on a turf practice field at the IMG campus. While Zachary Reynolds of Northern Arizona and Holiday run this evening's fastest 20-meter sprints, Kurkowski registers the next fastest times of 3.08, 3.12 and 3.11 seconds. And while it may not mean a contract is in the offing, the Richmond scout has done a follow-up interview with Alan Wisniewski, a 6-foot-10 hopeful from Penn State University, and Allison has given out Essendon player handbooks to Carethers, Korcheck and Crnogorac.

*

No one knows the precise origin of the expression "You never get a second chance to make a good first impression," although some scholars attribute it to Irish poet and playwright Oscar Wilde. The time to have made that first impression for this year's crop of footy hopefuls has long past, but on the third and final day of the combine they're hoping at least to make a lasting impression on the scouts.

They will have their first opportunity after breakfast, when they run a 3-kilometer time trial. It's the test that in the last decade has become the clubs' barometer of their players' fitness on day one of each preseason. The hopefuls will do the trial outdoors, under the slow-building Florida heat and humidity, running seven laps around a blue synthetic track.

"The distance best replicates a comparable amount of running without rest in a footy match," Nick Byrne says. "It's a rudimentary test. It's a good way to test endurance without grinding them into the ground. Any less distance would be too short, any more would be too much."

Around 11 minutes would be a great time for a big man, Byrne says. If the prospects average about 1:40 or 1:45 per lap, they'll end up with a 12-minute time. Givony has advised the recruits to go light on breakfast before the run, but not many heeded that advice, piling food on their plates.

"Twelve-and-a-half or below is what you're looking for as a baseline," Byrne tells them. 'Midfielders run this in the mid-10s or below."

Before the group starts, Byrne backs Kurkowski, Hornstein and Wisniewski to come out on top, because their best running doesn't come in short bursts, as it does for some of the other candidates. "It's really rare someone that explosive will do well in a distance run," Byrne says. "Look at their body shapes. It's a lot of height and weight for someone their height to carry around. The bigger muscle groups — the quads, calves and core are great for short distances. Carrying those parts around for 3 kilometers requires a lot of effort."

As the boys trudge across the finish line, Byrne isn't too far off in his predictions. With a time of 11:56, Kurkowski scores the second-best time of the recruits. Korcheck is fourth with a time of 12:08. Wisniewski and Hornstein, with times of 12:25 and 12:35, are near the middle of the pack, while Carethers's time of 13:17 comes close to last. The biggest surprise is pulled off by Len Springs, a 6-foot-9 Northern Arizona big man, who runs the trial in an eye-opening 11:14. While other scouts are making notes in their notepads, Byrne, who has keenly watched the race from start to finish, notes that Springs walked two extra laps after all the others had finished.

The combine's two best jokesters, Hunter and Holiday, although spent, can't resist more playful banter after they leave the track.

"Would you do this again?" Hunter asks Holiday.

"Gimme a hundred dollars and I would," Holiday answers.

The closing combine activity, after a marking drill takes place, is hard to describe. It's not quite footy, it's not quite American football and it's not quite the Australian-Irish hybrid "International Rules" game that meshes Gaelic and Australian Rules football. It's a creation of the AFL scouts that involves handballing and tackling, played on a field with non-players serving as boundaries on two sides, with Aussie footballs serving as boundaries on the other two sides. Ablett demonstrates the correct tackling technique. He coaches the boys to stay low and bend at the legs, but not to lead with their heads, as often is done in American football. Half the prospects put on yellow mesh vests and assemble on one side, forming one of the teams. The object of the game is for a team to successfully handball its way from one end of the ground to the other without being whistled for holding the ball.

It's impossible to tell who "wins," but the boys' spiritedness and competition can't be missed. They don't like to lose at anything, and it shows.

The banter continues, and Holiday gets off two of his best quips. "Everybody tryin' to be Superman, but all we got are Clark Kents out here!" he yells to his teammates after he sees them not sharing the ball. At another juncture, after his team has turned the ball over, Holiday turns to his teammates and reminds them of his prowess at finding free space: "Call me 7-Eleven, 'cause I'm always open!"

The game ends after 15 or 20 minutes. Three of the boys, including Carethers, get their knees iced by the trainer. Korcheck, who took the best grabs in the marking contests, has ice on his right ankle. On the opposite leg, inside his calf, Korcheck has a tattoo of a basketball with the word "*PASSION*" spelled out in capital letters, in calligraphic script. Like the other boys, this strange, improvised version of footy has been his first attempt at playing any version of the game. "I was just glad not to get called for a foul," he says. "I've never been told to tackle before. It's surprising how tired you get playing in such a short space."

After the athletes get cleaned up and eat lunch, the U.S. Combine ends. The scouts tell the boys they're proud of them. They're thankful the young men gave up their time to come to the combine, and took part with such enthusiasm. Now, for them, the waiting begins.

Hours later, at Tampa International Airport, Behrens stands in line to board a short flight to Atlanta. After that, he'll catch a connection to the San Francisco Bay Area, where he'll return to business as usual at the University of California, Berkeley. In just over two weeks, he'll graduate. Even during the hyperactive last three days in Florida, Behrens, who majors in American studies, was able to punch out an assignment for a media and marketing class — a response to a question about Charles Babbage's analytical engine, which many scholars believe was the world's first computer.

Behrens still holds on to his professional athletic dreams. "I have some agents I'm talking to," he says. "I'm seeing about playing basketball in Italy, Germany, Spain or France. I've also been talking about playing in a Scandinavian country."

Behrens is close to his mother, a retired radiographer, but dearly misses his father, who died when Behrens was 17, before he went away to college. He wishes his father could've lived to see his AFL tryout. "My dad would've been thrilled at this opportunity," Behrens says. "It exceeded my expectations. I want to exhaust all my basketball opportunities, but my intentions here at the combine were to impress the scouts — to show them I'm interested."

11

No Rucking Way

Americans Forge a Different Footy Pathway

With the American Experiment still in its infancy, U.S. athletes pursuing AFL careers generally fall into three categories: long shot, real long shot, and super long shot. But it's fair to say Brandon Kaufman, Rory Smith and Billy Mallard have established a fourth category, uniquely off the scale of unlikelihood.

That's not because they aren't talented sportsmen. Kaufman once fiercely competed for an NFL roster spot. Smith played basketball, American football, soccer, rugby and volleyball in his teens and early 20s, and has an abundance of athleticism. Mallard, after a brilliant high school career, played NCAA football at a small Utah university. A CFL team considered signing him.

But the trio's unorthodox pathways to Aussie Rules are completely different from those of the other American footy hopefuls. None played college basketball, or attended the AFL's U.S. Combine. Because of their size — Mallard stands 5-foot-10, and Smith 6-foot-2 — neither could ever be considered ruck prospects. They're also both in their late 20s. Their only hope of reaching the top level of the sport lies in convincing Australian scouts and coaches that they can play positions on the ground other than the one most every AFL scout and development coach has targeted Americans for, and do it without many years' preparation.

Though they're countrymen, Kaufman, Smith and Mallard couldn't have had more different upbringings. They're from varied geographical, religious and socioeconomic backgrounds. Kaufman is 25, from Denver, and Jewish. Smith, 28, is white and from small-town, middle-class Exeter, Rhode Island, while the 27-year-old Mallard is an African-American from Westmont, an urban working-class Los Angeles neighborhood that has long struggled with gang-related violent crime. Their paths to Aussie Rules were also wildly different: Kaufman played three years as an NCAA wide receiver and a full preseason with the NFL's Buffalo Bills before getting released. Smith played in the USAFL and parlayed that connection into a spot on a West Australian Football League side; an Aussie expat entrepreneur to audition for a proposed American reality television show, which led him to play for a VFL club, recruited Mallard.

Kaufman's 2015 reality was running his own personal training business. He'd rise every morning before dawn and drive 20 miles from his Denver home to a gym to train clients before they started their own workdays. Evenings and weekends, Kaufman operated a "wide receivers' academy," coaching high school and college football aspirants. The mentoring was rewarding — but exhausting.

"I was run-down," Kaufman says. And, having played high-level American football, basketball and running track and field since childhood, he was itching for action. "I still had my athleticism and it didn't feel right not playing a sport — especially when I felt I could still play. I needed the competition."

Opportunity beckoned on a late August 2015 morning, a week after Jason Holmes made his historic St Kilda debut. Tom Ellis, senior coach of the USAFL's Denver Bulldogs, sent Kaufman a message via social media: "I would love to talk to you about Australian Football. I think you would be a great player. It's not Rugby. We just had the first American convert play professionally in Australia. I recruit and also coach for the USA National Team … Hope to hear back sometime."

Seventeen days later Kaufman responded, telling Ellis he'd hear him out. Ellis had suspected — correctly — that he wouldn't have to twist Kaufman's arm. His homework on Kaufman's athletic prowess and character told him he'd be a good fit.

Kaufman had enjoyed a stellar football career at Eastern Washington University, where he studied sociology and met — and later married — a woman named Lauren Jacobsen, one of the school's women's soccer team's best players. Kaufman left EWU in his third year, 2013, because he expected an NFL team to draft him. None did. But a few months later, before preseason, the Buffalo Bills signed him as a free agent. He played well in an exhibition game, making a spectacular catch from the first pass thrown his way. But Buffalo cut Kaufman before the regular season.

In 2014 the CFL's British Columbia Lions trialed Kaufman, but a nagging left knee injury spoiled his opportunity. In 2015, with the injury healed, Kaufman had a month-and-a-half preseason audition with the CFL's Edmonton Eskimos. He felt great and was in his best form, but the team axed him. So did the 13 other North American pro football teams that tried Kaufman out, before Ellis contacted him. Only rugby teams and ones in the indoor, Arena Football League were pursuing Kaufman.

"At that point his NFL dream was over," Ellis recalls. "I had a feeling he might be open to footy."

Kaufman had never seen or heard of Australian football before Ellis emailed him some video clips. Sensing his last chance at a professional athletic career, he agreed to attend a weeks-long basic footy training camp in Denver in October 2015. American AFL player agent Zach Frederick convinced the AFL's Gold Coast Suns to monitor Kaufman and John Peters, another former NCAA football standout and recent NFL hopeful, at the camp.

"My kicks were pretty disgusting at first," Kaufman recalls with a laugh. "I had no business doing it. In [gridiron] I never dropped a pass in my life, but I looked terrible marking the footy."

Occasionally, the pair trained with the Bulldogs and played in in a nine-on-nine intrasquad match. Though they both were still footy newborns, Kaufman's and Peters' raw talent indicated potential beyond that of all the Bulldogs' experienced players. "With their athletic ability," Ellis recalls, "they were head and shoulders above everyone else."

Following from afar, the Suns were impressed — especially with Peters, because of his 6-foot-8, 260-lb. frame. They were looking for competitive tall talent in the forward line, the backline and the ruck. The club agreed to bring Peters to Gold Coast to train. Frederick and Ellis lobbied the Suns to trial the 6-foot-5 Kaufman, too, and the Suns officials relented after Frederick told them that if they trained Kaufman, he'd pay his airfare.

In January 2016 Gold Coast temporarily moved Kaufman in with two of its emerging young stars: midfielder Touk Miller (whose father is American) and tall forward-ruckman Peter Wright, the number eight pick in the 2014 AFL National Draft. The three were getting along great, although one morning Kaufman got the scare of his life. While waking up and pulling back the bedsheets, Kaufman recoiled in shock when the biggest spider he'd ever seen emerged to greet him.

Wright and Miller were so amused by their roommate's reaction that they plotted to "take the piss" out of Kaufman. A few days later, as Kaufman opened his bedroom door, he was spooked again. This time, a snake was slithering on the floor. Kaufman was relieved to discover that the serpent was actually rubber, and his prankster teammates were manipulating its movements with a fishing line. Kaufman laughed, but still he moved to the couch for the rest of his stay.

At the Suns' Metricon Stadium, in Carrara, Queensland, Kaufman immediately impressed development coach Dom Ambrogio. He scored 14 on a beep test, and ran a two-kilometer time trial in six-and-a-half minutes. In drills and match simulations, Kaufman was eased into the backline. It was just like his school football days when he played cornerback, which required him to man up on wide receivers. Ambrogio — who had sent Kaufman video of the Sydney Swans' superstar forward Buddy Franklin, telling him, "That's who we'd want you to guard" — started seeing Kaufman in a brighter light.

"He's agile, has really strong hands to mark and is super competitive and super driven," Ambrogio reflects. "He has qualities for a tall defender or tall forward, but could go into the midfield in a pinch. We had him in match simulations and he looked natural."

To Kaufman, the Suns' warm, collegiate club culture, which reminded him of being back at Eastern Washington, was a far cry from Buffalo's icy, cutthroat NFL pre-season camp. "An AFL club has much more of a team atmosphere," he says. "It's how they develop their players. They don't cut them and leave them. In [an NFL] meeting room, you're so used to going in and expecting to see someone one day and then they're not there the next, because they've been cut. In the AFL, you have coaches who care about you and who you care about."

Still, with just two days left in his two-week audition, Kaufman doubted he'd get signed. He felt he hadn't improved his kicking, especially while running. Ambrogio told Kaufman from the beginning that his kicking had to be elite. But the American pupil felt he was nowhere close. "I was ready to go home without a contract," Kaufman says. "But when we did our intrasquad match, I felt like they saw that I could learn."

Early on in that game, Kaufman showed clean hands and poise, marking a kick in the backline and then smoothly feeding a handball to the Suns' superstar captain Gary Ablett Jr. Later in the match, Kaufman shined brightest. With the opposition attacking and Kaufman at the back of the center square, he correctly read the cues and left his man just in time to intercept a handball. But instead of kicking or handballing to a teammate, Kaufman reverted to his American football instincts. He audaciously charged straight through the corridor with the footy, trying to get separation from a defender in hot pursuit. Kaufman accelerated and, just before he had covered 15 meters — after which a player must either bounce the ball or touch it to the ground, or be penalized for "running too far" — he attempted a bounce. The footy flipped around in midair, but miraculously fell back into his hands.

Then Kaufman really stepped on the gas, and was still eluding the defender after another 15 meters. He bounced again. This time his technique was better but he fumbled the footy after he attempted to grasp it. He was stopped by a defender's run-down tackle before he could get a handball away. The whistle blew and Kaufman got pinged by a coach playing the role of umpire for not disposing the football by hand or foot after having prior opportunity ("holding the ball"). But the watchful coaches didn't care. They were too pleased with the initiative he'd shown.

"We couldn't believe someone who went from playing one little practice game in Denver to playing in his first-ever Australian scratch match was so confident to attack the game," recalls Sean Clarke, the Kick Builders coach who trained Kaufman in Denver and watched the action unfold. "Not many people in that situation would have the courage to run and carry. It was very ballsy."

After the trial, the Suns made their own ballsy move, telling Peters and Kaufman they wanted to sign them. In doing so, the Suns would be the first AFL club to have two born-and-bred Americans on their roster. Peters opted out, though. The NFL's Cincinnati Bengals, for whom he played in the 2015 preseason, offered him a practice squad spot, which gave him a shot at making the team. Kaufman, disillusioned by his NFL experiences, was all in, and the Suns signed him to an International Scholarship. If he showed enough potential in minor league AFL Queensland (QAFL) games, and perhaps later in the NEAFL, Gold Coast told him, they'd draft him as a Category B International Rookie.

"He has a lot to learn," Ambrogio concedes. "But his tools are pretty good. We may have an exciting player on our hands."

*

On the AFL talent evaluators' radar, Rory Smith is about as visible as a pebble on the ocean floor. That's okay with Smith, who has a good sense of humor. It's good enough, in fact, for him to have landed an acting role on *The Bean Bag Series*, a comedic YouTube program produced by an American accounting firm, quirkily celebrating its 50th anniversary. Smith is an information technology recruiter by trade. Improbably, in 2015 he found himself lining up with the reserves of the eventual WAFL premiers, the Subiaco Lions, at Perth's Medibank Stadium for a clash against the East Perth Royals.

Smith, who graduated from Quinnipiac University, came to Australia knowing the likelihood of his playing AFL were beyond astronomical. That he rose so high in the footy hierarchy after only discovering the existence of Aussie Rules five years ago — through playing the popular video game *Halo 3* on Xbox — defies logic.

After playing for a campus rugby club in his senior year of college, Smith was burned out on sports. So he satisfied his competitive hunger by playing team doubles of *Halo 3*. Another player was an Australian university student, whom Smith only ever knew by a screen name. While online chatting through the TV screen, the student told Smith about footy, saying the game had components of three sports Smith had played — rugby, volleyball and basketball — and that he should check it out.

Smith never heard from that gamer again, but a seed had been planted. In 2014, three years after the gaming episode, Smith was living and working in Boston. He found the website for the USAFL's Boston Demons and emailed the club. The Demons invited him to training and he did well enough to get a game in Canada, when the club played a Montreal-based AFL Quebec team. Later in the season, the Demons started him at half-forward in an away game against the New York Magpies.

In that match — in which Alexander Aurrichio lined up in the ruck for New York — Smith, then a relative footy first-timer, had a blinder. To the amazement of his new teammates, he booted four goals.

"I kicked one that was a quick snap from a tough angle; another, I got ahold of the ball and slotted it in; then I kicked one that was a torpedo," he recalls, sounding incredulous about his stunning display, including his "torpedo punt," a seldom-used footy kick which when in flight, spirals like an American football and indeed looks like a projectile fired from a submarine. "I didn't even know what a 'torp' was — my teammates told me later. I made a lot of tackles, too. We lost, but everyone was really complimentary."

Less than a year after he first laced up his boots, Smith was encouraged by his new teammates — Jeremy Humm, who played 23 AFL games for West Coast and Richmond, and Russell "Rusty" Smith, Subiaco's former talent development manager — to relocate to Perth. They and the other Demons closely watched his USAFL progress. He mostly played as a center halfback or in the midfield, and only occasionally in the ruck. "I always played hard," Smith recalls. "I got a lot of touches and everything kinda clicked."

Smith played out the whole season, which included the Demons' appearance in the USAFL national tournament. But even more impressively, Smith won the club's best and fairest award. At the team's post-season "Mad Monday" party in Boston (modeled after AFL clubs' end-of-season, costumed, comical affairs), he started talking with the club president about travelling to Australia to have a crack at playing footy at a higher level. Both Humm and Russell Smith hit up their West Australian contacts to find clubs that would have a look at their club's unexpected star. Rory Smith researched programs that allowed foreigners to work on rural farms on working holiday visas, which would also allow him to train with a footy club.

Smith got as far as meeting a shepherd, but that's as close as he came to working on a farm. Instead, he got a job at the Perth office of Chandler Macleod Group, then one of Australia's largest employee recruiting agencies. After temporarily living with Russell Smith's family, he got his own place with a couple of Irish guys. Rory Smith's Boston Demons teammates convinced the Lions to invite him to train with them. Smith says the sessions were "the highlight of my day."

While Smith was training with Subiaco, he was getting valuable game time with Scarborough, a club in the West Australia Amateur Football League. He used his strength, speed and tackling ability in the club's backline. But his game still needed some polish. The first time he tackled an opponent in a match, Smith led with his head and launched into his opponent's mid-section, like an NFL defender. "Everybody freaked out," he recalls. "I almost got written up in the [umpire's] book. But I learned my lesson."

Smith found a home as the Scarborough third-team's center half-back. He loved controlling the backline and being an enforcer. He calls himself a "one-percenter kinda guy" (a complimentary nickname for a footy player who excels at doing the little things necessary to helping a team win) when describing his style of play. The Subiaco braintrust noticed.

"He totally committed himself to the program and we had faith and trust in him," says Luke Sanders, the club's football operations manager at the time. "His skills lacked a little bit, but he had a good pace. He's a big body and was able to play as a defender. He could also mark the ball, which is a handy skill."

With a late-season match against East Perth approaching and Smith still training with Subiaco, a couple of unlucky injuries to his teammates turned out to be his good fortune. Two days before the match, he was promoted to the Lions' reserves squad. The club posted a feature about Smith on its website, and a local radio station interviewed him. In America, Smith grew up dreaming of being a professional athlete and now, in Australia — for at least a day — he would be. The Lions played him in the backline.

"The best thing about playing there was that he could run with and man up on his opponent," Sanders recalls. "His opponent would lead him to the ball and he could understand how the ball moves."

Smith's time on the ground — and indeed his professional footy career — appeared to be the equivalent of a cameo appearance in a film. About a month before he arrived, a large Japanese firm, Recruit Holdings, announced it had acquired the Chandler McLeod Group. Nearly four months into Smith's employment there, staff layoffs began. His job was one of the ones that got cut.

Smith scrambled to find another job and nearly landed one, but it didn't come to fruition. With no income on the horizon, he had to use part of his last paycheck to fly back home. In mid-August, on the day his six-month working visa expired, Smith departed Australia.

"It was a heavy decision to make and a lot of thought went into it," he says. "The Scarborough thirds' season had ended. I played the last game with them, and we won, so I was able to give a nice, strong goodbye there."

Subiaco, meanwhile, was approaching the last part of its season, and was making a run for a back-to-back WAFL Premiership, which eventually it would achieve. Smith could've continued his professional footy quest by training with the Lions, but after assessing his chances and out of respect for the club, he chose not to.

"I didn't see myself getting another game," Smith says. "They would likely be practicing much higher-level footy strategy, which I still didn't have a great grasp of, or at least not anywhere near their level. I have no regrets and feel very fortunate to have experienced what I did. I have a lot of love for Subiaco FC."

Smith also still had it for the Boston Demons, where his improbable journey began. So after he resettled in the Boston area, he played in two matches for them. The team lost both. When he was interviewed for new jobs, all his potential employers were impressed after he told them about his Australian adventures. Ultimately Smith landed a job at Boston University, although he says he'd like to return one day to Australia and try to get some more amateur games in Western Australia or Victoria.

"He didn't get to showcase all his skills, and he would've needed more time to develop," Sanders says of Smith's time at Subiaco, "but he embraced the opportunity."

In the reserves game he played against East Perth, Smith got just one touch and made just one tackle. And one kick. Still, Smith says: "I have no regrets."

*

On a midweek December 2015 evening in Inglewood, in South Los Angeles, Billy Mallard takes a seat at a table at Roscoe's House of Chicken and Waffles, one of the popular African-American soul food eatery's many locations around Los Angeles. Mallard is three months removed from his own professional footy adventure, which had him playing in both an Australian state league team and in a country one.

It's also the day after yet another mass killing in America — this time in San Bernardino, just a 90-minute drive from the restaurant. Two gunmen murdered 14 people and wounded 17 others at a health department holiday party.

Tonight, though, Mallard isn't thinking about that. He has alongside him his pride and joy, his 9-year-old son, Trayce, who can't stop smiling. Of all the American athletes who recently have come to Australia to pursue a footy career, only Mallard is a father. He orders a plate of scrambled eggs, grits and a chicken wing for his son, and then he orders his favorite item for himself: the "President Obama Special" — three chicken wings and a buttermilk waffle.

"Maybe it was meant to be for me to go over there," Mallard says of his Australian experience, which transported him from Westmont to Port Melbourne and Sandringham, then to the sleepy country town of Temora, New South Wales. "It's different from South Central [Los Angeles]. It was a safer environment. You didn't have to look over your shoulder every minute."

When playing American football, Mallard never had to make any backward glances. He was a talented running back who usually left his opponents in his wake. The speedster was a star at Alain Leroy Locke College Preparatory Academy, in the South Los Angeles community of Watts. Mallard's high school opened in 1967, two years after the devastating Watts Riots, with the aim of providing better educational opportunities for the neighborhood's children. But the school soon fell into disrepair, and gangs and violence imperiled the campus. By the time Mallard attended the school, though, private foundations had spent $15 million to transform it. Mallard and his peers wore uniforms, the campus was renovated and students were performing up to established educational standards.

Mallard attended Dixie State University in St. George, Utah, a small city named for an apostle of the Church of Jesus Christ of Latter-day Saints. The city was infamous for a surge in cancer rates resulting from residual fallout from the U.S. military's aboveground nuclear testing. It was there that Mallard continued his football career.

After graduation, Mallard had NFL dreams but no team drafted him. So in 2014 he attended a tryout camp at nearby Long Beach City College for the CFL's Edmonton Eskimos. And that was where Miro Gladovic, an Aussie expat living in Los Angeles, introduced himself to Mallard and two other camp participants, Carl Winston and Mallard's high school and college teammate Torrey Harkness.

Gladovic, who grew up in the southwestern Melbourne suburb of Altona but now lives in the Los Angeles community of Marina Del Rey, had spent years as an agent for Australian soccer players, selling their skills to elite professional European teams. He represented two star Aussie soccer stars and helped them land contracts with top German teams. But Gladovic is also a lifelong footy fan and he had a new, big idea: a reality television show for an American audience, about former NCAA football players attempting to learn Aussie Rules football and eventually make it to the AFL. He'd come to the Eskimos' tryout to put his plan in motion.

"I was looking for phenomenal athletes," says Gladovic, who came to the Eskimos' tryouts on the recommendation of a former NFL-playing friend. Both they and the Eskimos marveled at Mallard's pace when he ran a 40-yard dash in 4.3 seconds.

"Billy's a freak of an athlete," Gladovic says. "He has AFL potential. His age is ancient by AFL terms, but if you can get two or three years out of him and the other guys, it'd be worth it."

Mallard says the Eskimos were interested in signing him, but he didn't have a passport and therefore couldn't travel to Canada. (He applied for one but found it would take him three months to get it.) With no other paths to becoming a professional athlete, Mallard listened to Gladovic tell him about Aussie Rules and his TV show concept.

Gladovic calls it *American Footy Star*. He first came up with the idea several years ago. He says American networks ESPN and Fox Sports were interested when they had the rights to broadcast AFL matches, and that marketers from Red Bull energy drink, which viewed Australian football as an "extreme sport," were interested in sponsoring it.

But as Fox Sports developed several channels, in a move to compete with ESPN, it scaled back its original programming, which ruled out Gladovic's proposed show. The Australian says he's shot enough footage for a complete season — he has posted some clips to YouTube — and is still shopping for an American television deal.

"I had European [soccer] scouts laughing at me when I was telling them Australian players could play in Europe," Glaodvic says. "So finding potential American footy players became a challenge, a business plan."

Gladovic helped teach footy skills to a group of players he recruited from the gridiron tryouts, while an American football trainer worked on their fitness. At a testing Gladovic coordinated — which he based on the AFL's Draft Combine — Mallard ran a 20-meter sprint in 2.63 seconds, recorded a standing vertical leap of 3 feet and a scored a running vertical leap height of about 3½ feet. Gladovic also worked with the USAFL's Orange County Bombers and San Diego Lions to get the players some game time. In the end, he chose Mallard, Harkness and Winston as the three best players to market to Australian country, suburban and state leagues.

Making the pitch — and hearing the blunt responses — wasn't easy. First Gladovic sent vision of his American prospects' skills to an AFL agent. Mallard's evolving footy skills at the time were, kindly put, raw and unconventional. In a YouTube highlight video for *American Footy Star*, when Mallard bounces the footy while running, it looks like an odd cross between basketball dribbling and throwing. He holds the footy horizontally, gripping it tightly in his palm. Still, when he bounces it, the ball springs back up from the deck for him.

In the same video, when Mallard kicks, he drops the footy with one hand, tilting it backward instead of vertically dropping it. The point of impact of his kicking foot isn't the ball's point, but an area below its nose. Still, however improbably, Mallard's kicking towards targets is fairly accurate. Harkness and Winston, in their highlight videos, display skills of about the same caliber.

The agent reported back to Gladovic that "a group who saw it was cringing at their techniques. That was a ridiculous attitude," Gladovic says. "I'd want to see these freakish athletes with ridiculous skills learn the game."

Gladovic says he approached more than 50 clubs, including all 18 of the AFL, plus those in the SANFL, WAFL, VFL, NEAFL and AFL Queensland. No takers. One club representative went as far as telling Gladovic, "We don't want that kind of publicity."

Finally, the former Hawthorn Hawks star Gary Ayres, by then senior coach of VFL club Port Melbourne, agreed to have Winston and Harkness train there for six weeks. Gladovic's two protégés learned of Ayres's invitation on America's Super Bowl Sunday. When they arrived at the club, Ayres said, "Carl and Torrey are very strong, explosive, running type players, who have the potential to develop" into small defenders or midfielders.

Meanwhile, Paul Hudson, the Sandringham Zebras' senior coach, became interested in giving Mallard a look. He invited him to train with his team. "I'm massive on development," Hudson said, "and Billy's size and type of player hasn't been given a chance at AFL level, but there's room for one or two types of those players in your side. I enjoy giving guys against the odds an opportunity and the chance to prove people wrong."

The clubs weren't willing to fly the three players in, so Gladovic paid for their airfares to Melbourne. He also rented them an apartment in Port Melbourne, above a pub on the neighborhood's busy Bay Street strip.

At the end of six weeks, Harkness and Winston were faced with a choice. Port Melbourne didn't see them as ready for its senior team, so Ayres offered them spots in the reserves. But the Temora Kangaroos, a club in countryside New South Wales, about 250 miles west of Sydney, promised them more playing time. Australian AFL player agent Ricky Nixon had got in touch with Gladovic and was instrumental in persuading Temora to sign the Americans.

"He showed us testing results from what they did in the US" recalls Darryl Harpley, Temora's president. "Some of it was better than anything done at AFL Draft Combines in Melbourne and we thought we'd give 'em a go. We took Carl and Torrey on, but Billy had a gig at Sandringham."

So off went Harkness and Winston to Temora. Its population is about 5,000 and, like Ballarat, the Victorian city where Eric Wallace started his professional footy career, it first attracted fortune seekers during the 19th century gold rush years. Mallard continued training at Sandringham, the club where Jason Holmes started the 2015 season in his quest to make St Kilda's senior team. The two briefly met during a practice.

"'Huddo' told me about an American they had training and wanted me to meet him," Holmes recalls. "My teammates told me about how much he bench-pressed. He's probably still on the leaderboard. He trained hard and he was fast."

And in a preseason match with Sandringham's VFL Development League team, Mallard made his presence felt. As a player, Mallard compensated for his unrefined footy skills with American football ingenuity. Would-be tacklers struggled to keep up with his speed. His stop-start running in improvised, zigzagging patterns made him impossible to corner. In one of his USAFL matches he had even kicked a couple of goals. So it was fitting that, in a preseason match at Ikon Park against the Northern Blues, Mallard did what came naturally after running on to a loose ball in his team's forward line. "I started running with the ball, made people miss and kicked the goal," he says. "Everybody went crazy. The whole team ran down to me."

Hudson chuckles with delight when he recalls that moment. "It was quite bizarre because we'd put him in the backline so he could learn the game, but then there was a moment I thought we could use him up forward," he says. "He read the play pretty well, then got away from the players in the vicinity. It was even more bizarre that he ran past another American, Alex Aurrichio, who was in the area. Our boys got excited when they saw that Billy had some space to run into and then he kicked it."

While the moment was special for Mallard, it meant even more to Holmes, who, with the St Kilda rookie and senior players, saw the vision of Mallard's goal inside the theatre in the Zebras' rooms. "Huddo showed the whole team the goal he kicked and how excited the boys were, sprinting to him to run from the defensive 50," Holmes says. "I was happy he got to experience the camaraderie."

Ultimately, Mallard was offered a spot on Sandringham's Development League team, but he preferred to join his mates, Harkness and Winston, in Temora. Nixon helped broker a deal and Mallard turned up at his new club just two days before the start of the Kangaroos' 16-game season. Suddenly, Temora — which had won its league's previous three premierships — had three untried American players on its list.

"There was a real buzz around town about their abilities as athletes," Harpley says. "With their speed, they could start 20 meters behind an opponent and beat him to the ball. Their speed was unbelievable. They had a presence. Even the opposition fans were amazed with how high they jumped or how quick they'd get to the ball. Everyone was wondering what these guys could achieve."

The refrain of Temora's club anthem — "Are we good? Are we good? Are we any bloody good?" — seemed especially appropriate for the three new recruits. In the early minutes of the team's first home game, against the team they'd defeated the previous year's Grand Final — with Mallard and Harkness starting in the backline and Winston at half-forward — Temora's staff, players and fans quickly learned how good they were.

"It was game on and both sides were ready to have a go," recalls Christin Macri, Temora's head coach. "Carl was playing in the forward pocket and the ball was around the 50-meter line. He dropped back into the space and one of our boys kicked it to him, and Carl marked it about 20 meters in front of goal. My first thought was: *Please kick it*. He ran in and [kicked] from point-blank range. It was the first kick he ever got. It was an exciting moment."

So exciting that the 1,000 fans that had showed up went bonkers. Those watching from their parked cars around the ground all honked their horns in appreciation.

Meanwhile, Winston, a former gridiron running back for Washington State University, and wide receiver for the New Mexico Stars of now-defunct professional regional indoor Lone Star Football League, staged his own madness. "He got excited, did a jump and fist-pump while all the boys all got around him," Macri says. "He did a double-fisted bicep flex. It was a very American celebration."

That moment, though, would be the lone highlight of Winston's season. He got a few more possessions in that game, but a couple of matches later he limped off the ground. At first his injury looked innocuous — perhaps a rolled ankle — but it turned out Winston had broken a bone in his foot. He ended up having to wear a "moon boot," and the injury cost him the rest of the year.

Harkness, meanwhile, played forward, but it was hard for him to create separation from opponents. Macri then tried him in the backline, but soon demoted him to the Temora reserves. As the season progressed, Harkness worked his way back onto the senior list and ended up playing 12 games.

But it was Mallard who had the greatest impact. Two games in particular impressed Harpley and Macri. In one, Mallard started at center halfback against the eventual league premiers and almost completely negated his opponent. "He was best on ground," Harpley says. "He held a very experienced player to one goal."

In the days before the other match, Macri found himself short — literally — in his ruck division. One ruckman had returned to his native Ireland for a couple of weeks, while the other had travelled to Fiji. Mallard had shown a tremendous vertical leap when Macri tried him in ruck contests during training sessions, so he experimented, starting Mallard on an opponent eight inches taller than him. "His opponent probably looked at Billy and thought, 'Well, I've got him covered,'" Macri says. "But Billy really hit out to advantage. He was amazing." So much so that Mallard actually earned two votes for the Jim Quinn Medal, awarded at season's end to the league's best and fairest player.

Gladovic says Temora's residents treated the Americans like rock stars. In a six-minute video the league produced for YouTube, to coincide with the 4th of July, fans got a glimpse of the players' lives, on and off the field.

"Anywhere you go, people wanna talk," Mallard says. "You get stopped. In the store, just walking down the main street. They just wanna know about America and how we like it here. And they ask, 'Are you gonna stay?'"

Maybe they would have, for the remainder of the season, if not for a tragic event back home. In going to the other side of the world, Mallard and Harkness got a temporary respite from their Los Angeles neighborhood's gun violence. But its specter rose to haunt them once again. In the wee hours of Saturday, July 18, Mallard was awakened by a phone call at the home he, Harkness and Winston were sharing. It was the mother of his son. She told Mallard that his cousin, Kenneth Peevy, had been murdered — gunned down in the early morning, outside a friend's home.

According to news reports, the shooting was gang-related. Depending on who was being quoted, Peevy was either an active, unrepentant hardcore gang member, or a former gang member who had reformed his life and was now devoted to raising his young son and coaching a youth football team. Either way, authorities say Peevy was shot dead by a member of a rival gang, after he posted to Instagram a video of himself beating down someone from that gang.

Although Mallard and Peevy were cousins, their mothers had raised them as if they were brothers. "We did everything together," Mallard says. "He was a funny guy, a character. He was someone everyone wanted to be around. His death affected me a lot. There's still not a day that I don't think about him."

Mallard says that because everyone in his neighborhood knew him as an athlete, he was never pressured into joining a gang. He was away at college when Peevy got involved in gang activity. Peevy should be remembered, Mallard says, not for his gang affiliation but for being a good father. To have a permanent reminder of his cousin, Mallard was planning on getting Peevy's face tattooed on his left pectoral muscle. It would sit above another tattoo, of a pair of praying hands, and opposite a single cursive word on his right ribcage: *Blessed.*

Around the same time, Harkness also lost a cousin and a close friend to gun violence. Losses of their loved ones affected the trio's form. Whatever momentum they had gained as players now evaporated. The trio arranged to return to America, missing Temora's last two regular season and eventual playoff matches. Although their presence was unlikely to have made the difference, Temora didn't win its fourth straight Premiership.

"Billy had body strength and speed to play as a defender, really held his own in the ruck with his explosive leap and really evolved around the ground," says Macri, who, before taking the reins at Temora, had seven years of player development work with the Greater Western Sydney Giants' Academy and with AFL NSW. "Without the tragedy back home, Billy would've been handy to have."

Hudson reckons Mallard still is handy. Late in 2015, he reached out to him, inviting him back to Sandringham for another preseason. He says Mallard's choice to play at Temora was wise, as it gave him an opportunity to learn while playing. According to the Sandringham coach, his awkward kicking style can be fixed with time and practice. "Billy's quite muscly, and because of his physique it's harder to control the ball," Hudson says. "You've got to devote numerous hours to getting the technique right. Twelve months isn't enough. It would take two to three years to refine his habits."

But Gladovic, an avid NFL fan, says his recruits wouldn't necessarily have to have the sharpest of skills to succeed. He is still trying to convince footy clubs' senior coaches and list managers that former college gridiron players can play specialized roles in their sides. "If you gave them the free roaming forward pocket role, they'd break the rules," he says. "They'd be shrugging tackles and could take off on 30-meter runs, running routes like they did in college, not running around chasing and defending in the backline. But even at the state league level, the people at the clubs don't want to rock the boat and takes the risks, because they don't want to lose their jobs. They don't have the foresight to see what these guys could be."

On July 6, 2015, Gladovic thought he'd brought to the Essendon Bombers an elite American athlete they'd be crazy to deny a tryout — Ramses Barden, a 6-foot-6 former NFL wide receiver. He'd played four years with the New York Giants and then was on the Jacksonville Jaguars practice squad, but last saw game action in 2012 — and he was 29. But Barden was fit and had been part of Gladovic's *American Footy Star* show. However, the timing of Barden's pre-arranged training couldn't have been more ill fated. The previous day, with the doping scandal fallout blanketing the Bombers like a toxic fog, St Kilda thrashed them by 110 points, as rumors swirled that Essendon head coach James Hird would be fired.

Still, Barden, donning a practice jumper with the same number 13 from his Giant career, did ground ball, kicking, handballing and rucking drills — for a paltry grand total of about 15 minutes. "It was a miracle we got even that long," Gladovic concedes. "It was the single-worst day in the club's history when we showed up. I could've turned up with the pope and we wouldn't have gotten more time."

Meanwhile, Gladovic says Harkness and Winston have a "hunger" to return to Australia in 2016 and pick up their footy where they left off. But towards the end of 2015, Mallard was undecided.

He smiles when he reminisces about his time in Temora, how friendly the people were and how he enjoyed riding all-terrain vehicles on a teammate's farm and going hunting. Mallard says he misses the beach and cafe scene on Bay Street in Port Melbourne, and the charm of Sandringham, which he says reminds him of nearby Manhattan Beach, California, but without the traffic snarls.

But while he was a world away from home, playing football in Australia, Mallard deeply missed Trayce, his son. He wonders: if he were to return to Australia, could he take him along? Mallard wants to be close to him, and he also feels a duty to be around for Peevy's son, who is close to Trayce in age. Mallard still occasionally drives to Inglewood Cemetery to visit his fallen cousin's resting place and pay his respects. Mallard says footy is a "cool sport," but he didn't watch any of the AFL finals after he returned home. American football, he says, still is his first love.

So Mallard plans to look into possibilities closer to home. A new, professional, developmental American football league was scheduled to begin in 2016, and Mallard says he might attend its tryouts. And the Eskimos are again returning to Long Beach. Still, he wouldn't rule out a return to Australia sometime.

For his part, Gladovic wants a firm deal in place for Mallard, Harkness and Winston for 2016, not just an invitation to a VFL club's preseason training, with a possibility of landing a spot on its roster. "I don't want to send them there on a wild goose chase," he says. "With a VFL pre-season and a year of playing country footy, these guys have served their time. They're more than ready."

12

What Happens to a Dream Deferred?
The Next Act

Early Monday morning in Melbourne, reality is hitting hard, like a bone-crunching tackle. Two days after the 2015 Grand Final, The Beast is wounded.

Eric Wallace is alone in his apartment, which he'll be vacating in a few weeks. His parents and his younger sister had been in town for a week or so, but are now back home. Wacky Wednesday's fun was days ago, and many of his now former North Melbourne teammates are starting their annual leave and going travelling.

It's been a couple of weeks since the Kangaroos told Wallace they were delisting him. His three-year journey from North Carolina to North Melbourne is officially ending. Wallace could see the end coming, and both the presence of his family and the comfort he finds in his religious faith had softened the blow, but still he is hurting.

"I have no idea what I want to do," he says. "I really wanna be an athlete. I want to find a purpose and a direction."

Does he return to basketball? Australia's National Basketball League's season starts in a matter of days, so it's too late to try out for a club. Does he try his fortunes at another footy club? If he wants to play on, he'll have to wait about eight weeks for the AFL Rookie Draft, his last hope to continue his AFL career. Does he try the NFL? He hasn't played American football since high school, but he loves the sport. Perhaps he could coach basketball? That used to be his long-term plan, but not something for his near future. But right now he has no employer, so every option must be considered. Wallace is confronting something that faces every professional athlete one day: the reality that they must wake up from living their dream.

"It's absolutely like what happens in post-traumatic stress disorder," says Shae McNamara, who experienced similar feelings in 2012, after Collingwood delisted him. McNamara now counsels and coaches people who, like Wallace, reach such professional predicaments. "Every athlete has a vision, and that is that they're going to achieve something that technically might not manifest. The individual's reality is completely shocked, because that was their status quo. Athletes are trying to make peace. The biggest issue is, when you get cut, how you respond will dictate everything, and that's based on mindset. People who have the mindset that they'll always learn, develop and grow from every situation will handle it better."

Of course, Wallace's professional career isn't over; it just feels that way right now. The reality is that he completed a master's degree; he has an undergraduate degree in finance; he has an extremely supportive family he can live with; he's saved some of the money he made in Australia; and he doesn't have children to provide for. Still, self-doubt creeps in.

"You second-guess the whole process," McNamara says. "You start wondering, 'Could I have done better?' Egotistically, you're gonna go, 'I suck, I'm a loser, I wasted my time.' But people will realize they needed [to] learn the lesson and needed to grow and needed the lesson in humility. When it comes down to playing professionally, you'll be at peace if you can say, 'I had a good crack and I gave it everything I had.'"

In his time of uncertainty Wallace reaches out to his longtime friend, adviser and American agent, Dwon Clifton. Like Wallace, Clifton also played pro sports overseas, with a Portuguese basketball team. He, too, was living out his own dream, but a severe knee injury forced him into a quandary not unlike Wallace's. He too was forced to contemplate whether to continue as a player, or retire and change paths.

Clifton retired. He had earned a business administration degree at the University of North Carolina, Greensboro, and after a stint as an assistant coach of a college basketball team he started a boutique player agency, which he later sold. Now he's part of an agency called Rival Sports Group. Advising clients such as Wallace is something Clifton takes great pride in.

"When Eric would hit a tough patch, he'd ask, 'Am I doing this because I love this game, or doing it because it's a cool job?'" Clifton says. "He had moments when he doubted himself. I told him that feeling was natural. Australian football wasn't his first love or passion — it was really more of a job. Training was different than what he was used to and it wasn't as smooth an adjustment as he may have made it look on the surface. Still, he wanted to be great and make it on the highest level."

*

Wallace and McNamara, of course, aren't the only subjects in the AFL's American Experiment to have their footy dreams deferred. There are a number of others, including Patrick Mitchell, Alex Starling and Marvin Baynham.

Baynham has begun working to help young people living in unimaginable poverty and violence realize their own life dreams. A side benefit of his involvement in footy led him to a mentor in Denis Ryan, and the opportunity to share his gift of nurturing children with his mentor's two young sons. Footy may yet lead him back down the child development path.

After Baynham's time at the IMG Sports Academy proved a dead end, he was hired as a youth advisor at the Corporation to Develop Communities of Tampa, a non-profit organization dedicated to addressing societal ills in East Tampa neighborhoods. These communities are wracked by substance abuse, unemployment, teen pregnancy and high dropout rates from school.

Baynham was running both a youth leadership program for teens and a "positive action" program for pre-teens, helping redirect them away from violence and gang activity. In 2015, as part of the anti-violence campaign, he organized a three-on-three basketball tournament involving 400 kids on 40 different teams. Baynham remains committed to helping East Tampa residents, who he says are in "dire need." East Tampa reminds Baynham of similar neighborhoods he and his own family survived.

His biggest dreams transcend playing professional sports: Baynham wants to establish and run his own non-profit center for underprivileged families, and he also wants to resurrect a latent childhood dream to become a firefighter. So at the beginning of 2016 he enrolled in a two-year program at Learey Technical College in Tampa.

For several months after his IMG experience, Baynham was intrigued by the idea of living in the Northern Territory and working and playing footy with Aboriginal Australians in remote areas. "I'd like to get back to ground zero and see how people live off the land and live simply and be away from urbanized areas," he said at the time. "I was blessed to be capable and able to play sports at a high level, but being a professional athlete was never my ultimate goal. What means most to me are people."

Baynham says he still follows the AFL, but not as eagerly as he once did. He says the ambiguity surrounding his recruitment and the miscommunication have left an unpleasant taste in his mouth. He no longer has the league's app on his mobile phone, but Baynham occasionally checks the AFL standings and the players' race to win the league's Coleman Medal, the award for most goals kicked. Plus, he has Ryan to update him. And true to the form in which he laughed at Ryan's "no girls" rule while he lived with the Ryans, saying he'd had the same girlfriend for 10 years, Baynham and his longtime sweetheart, Qui Roach, got engaged early in 2016 and started making plans to marry in 2017.

Eventually, Baynham sold the Crown Vic sedan in which he first rolled up to Ryan's house. He now owns three used cars he has had refurbished: a gold 1984 Corvette, a white convertible Camaro and a

2001 silver Mustang. He'll travel in those cars, but Baynham is determined not to go down the road he's seen former teammates stumble onto, when they reach a desperate place, realizing their professional athletic dreams are over. "A lot of them don't have anything and they put all their energy into becoming professional athletes," he says. "When I do something, I put everything into it, so whatever I'm doing, that's my Plan A."

McNamara says he advises American athletes to develop plans for after their pro careers — before they ever start. "I had one," he says. "Think about all the stories about athletes losing their money because they were living in the moment and living beyond their means. Most people, though, have shortsightedness, then the reality hits that they're not good enough to play anymore. I didn't have it in my heart to continue playing. I love my body feeling light and loose, with no aches and pains. I'm happy with that."

Even Jason Holmes, entering the 2016 season in his second year of AFL footy, is contemplating his own future career. "As a kid I wanted to be an athlete," he says, "but I like to debate and play devil's advocate. I enjoy history, and as a lawyer, you study cases and then you have debates. One of my coaches as a kid was a lawyer, and he found the courtroom to be like the basketball court."

Holmes says he probably won't go to law school, but he has dreams of becoming an author and perhaps running an Australian coffee shop in America — if he doesn't hang around in Australia after his AFL playing days.

*

After Wallace left Melbourne and returned home, the funk that had been enveloping him began to lift. "Eric is a very up-and-down kinda guy," Clifton says. "But he's levelheaded. He'll sit down and do his own self-evaluation and can snap right back out of it and know there's a bigger picture."

The day of the 2015 AFL Rookie Draft, Wallace's professional footy chapter ended. But as the names of the rookie picks were announced, it's unlikely he noticed. It was Thanksgiving and Wallace was at home with his family, celebrating as favorite NFL team, the Carolina Panthers, beat the Dallas Cowboys, en route to an eventual Super Bowl appearance.

It's not hard to guess how Wallace, the social media maven, let his American friends and his newly made Australian ones know how happy he was. Along with a photo of himself wearing a Panthers' helmet and a beastly glare, Wallace tweeted to his 3,745 followers: "The look I give my dad and sister (Cowboy fans) after the game today! #PantherNation #Panthersvscowboys #KeepPounding."

The Beast was back, and hunting for the next challenge.

13

Baby Blue

Matt Korcheck

It's an uncharacteristically rainy and humid summer Southern California night, and Matt Korcheck's prospective AFL career is scheduled for takeoff. But after landing at Los Angeles International Airport from a four-hour, cross-county flight from Tampa, his big chance suddenly and unexpectedly appears grounded.

In Tampa, Korcheck had boarded a U.S. Airways flight that pushed back from the gate at 7:14 p.m., local time — just nine minutes late — and was due to arrive at LAX at 9:09 p.m., Pacific time. Plenty of wiggle room, he thinks, to make his 11:55 p.m. Qantas flight to Sydney, after which he would fly to Melbourne for a comprehensive three-week AFL training camp.

Korcheck earned this chance after impressing league scouts three months ago at the 2015 U.S. Combine in Bradenton, Florida. He wowed everyone there with his unusually strong marking hands, his 3-kilometer time and his drive. In Melbourne he'll be meeting up with his combine mates, Jalen Carethers, James Johnson and Kye Kurkowski, the three other athletes the AFL talent evaluators had chosen from the competitive field of 15. Further impress the Melbourne camp's trainers — Carlton Blues' rucks coach Matthew Capuano and the Adelaide Crows' former senior coach Brenton Sanderson — and Korcheck could win a contract with an AFL club.

Before tonight, Korcheck has never been to Australia, so he's excited about experiencing a new country for the first time. At 22, he's fresh out of the University of Arizona, where he played basketball, so the camp represents the most important job interview of his life. He doesn't want to be late — but Mother Nature couldn't care less. She unleashes heavy rainstorms directly in the path of Korcheck's flight. He and his fellow passengers are trapped on the Tampa tarmac, where their plane idles for an hour and 15 minutes.

Finally, the weather relents and Korcheck's flight departs at 8:30 p.m., local time. Even so, with a flying time across the country of four hours, Korcheck should arrive at LAX with time to spare to make his trans-Pacific connection. The plane touches down at LAX at 9:57 p.m., local time. Mother Nature is done messing with Korcheck's plans, but there's still room for human error. There's no available gate for Korcheck's plane to dock in, so he's stuck in a second tarmac turmoil. He waits. And waits.

Meanwhile, at the Qantas counter at LAX's Tom Bradley International Terminal, check-in for Flight 18 to Sydney is in its final stages. Most passengers booked on this flight have already moved through the security screening and are in the departure lounge.

Finally, after 50 minutes, Korcheck's plane roars to life and taxis to an open gate. Korcheck now has to race from Terminal 6 to the Bradley Terminal as if he were running a basketball fast break back on his college home hardwood in Tucson, or better yet, if he were matching the pace of his 3-kilometer time trial at the U.S. Combine. The terminals are 1.1 kilometers apart and Korcheck has precious little time.

At 11:07 p.m. a Qantas check-in counter agent advises a small group of passengers hoping to fly standby that Flight 18 is closing. They're out of luck. Korcheck will be too if he doesn't get here soon.

Moments later, Korcheck — whose short-sleeved shirt and shorts signal his unpreparedness for the cold Australian winter he'll face — emerges from the pack. He holds his mobile phone in hand and anxiously looks around for Qantas's famous "flying kangaroo" logo. He spots it and gallops to the check-in desk.

"Check-in has closed, sir," the agent tells Korcheck, although he does ask for Korcheck's passport. He's still a chance to make the flight.

He fidgets as the agent stares into his computer screen and pecks away at the keyboard. The agent walks away from the desk and disappears through an open door behind him. More waiting. Korcheck gulps down a bottle of water. It seems like forever, but after a couple of minutes the agent returns. He faces Korcheck. "You're good," he says. At last Korcheck can relax and smile his customary big smile.

He's already been up for 18 hours. He'd spent time that morning with his parents and some friends. Every day for the last two weeks he and Denis Ryan have exchanged videos through the Coach's Eye app — the same one Ryan first trained Marvin Baynham with — so Korcheck could arrive at the camp with more polished kicking and handballing techniques.

At 12:10 a.m. Korcheck slides into his economy comfort seat with extra legroom — for which he paid an additional $300 out of his own pocket. This flight, too, is delayed. But who cares? They're finally away at 1:01 a.m. Korcheck now has 14-and-a-half hours in which he doesn't have to race to get somewhere.

*

After Korcheck's experience at the Florida combine, a bunch of player agents raced to get to him. They rang him endlessly, offering to help him land a European basketball playing deal, but Korcheck ignored them.

"I had it set in my mind that footy is what I wanted to pursue," he says. "It was something new and different. I wanted to try something I'd never done and make my own, cool life story. I'm glad I get to live out this opportunity and be part of the first generation of Americans to try it."

A few weeks before Korcheck took off for Australia, some American media online, print and TV outlets reported prematurely that the AFL's Carlton Blues had signed him. Citing a *Herald Sun* piece — which clearly stated that the club was paying for his trip only so it would have first crack at signing him, *if* it wanted to — some American reporters jumped the gun. This particularly annoyed Jonathan Givony, who had handpicked Korcheck and invited him to the U.S. Combine. "They put the cart way ahead of the horse," he said.

Even those American outlets that reported on Korcheck's Australian audition accurately couldn't resist indulging in some tired Australian pop-culture references, or mischaracterizing Aussie Rules as an inherently violent sport. "Crikey!" blared the headline of one Phoenix television station's website. The story that followed twice used the phrase "Down Under" as a substitute for "Australia" and described AFL uniforms as affording players "very little protection."

For its part, Carlton, having just suffered one of the worst seasons in its otherwise storied history — which included its firing of head coach Michael Malthouse, declining attendance at its matches, a poor win-loss record and interim senior coach John Barker calling out a handful of players for giving half-hearted effort — desperately needed something positive to share with fans. The club trumpeted Korcheck's arrival and first few days of training on its website.

Under the headline "The Big American Lands at Carlton," the story was accompanied by footage of Korcheck's training sessions and an on-camera interview. Korcheck was shown performing agility drills and kicking at the Blues' training ground, Ikon Park, mostly under Capuano's watch.

"He impressed me at the U.S. Combine with picking up basic skills," Capuano says. "The other thing that caught my eye was his competitiveness. I liked his body contact in that improvised handballing game at the combine and he performed really well in competitive marking drills, on top of the way he tested. He came across as very impressive. You can only learn so much about them when we have them, but you're also looking at their character. Matt is humble and respectful but confident in his ability. I've got a good feeling about him."

For the next three weeks, with only a few days off, Korcheck and his two countrymen toiled hard, pushing themselves to the brink of their physical limitations. Korcheck still had no clue what his potential employer — or any of the other clubs' scouts who watched him — thought of his effort. But it certainly couldn't have hurt that former Blues great and current general manager Stephen Silvagni and his family hosted Korcheck at home for dinner. Korcheck spent part of the evening shooting hoops with one of Silvagni's sons.

On his second-last day training with the club, after a tough stationary bike conditioning session with Capuano and another Carlton assistant, Silvagni asked Korcheck to come to football operations manager Andrew McKay's office for a meeting. "The whole way walking up the stairs — more like *crawling* up the stairs after the workout — I was like, 'Please offer me something,'" Korcheck says. "I really was hoping to get good news." He was nervous as he sat down at a table with Silvagni, McKay and Capuano. "I figured they'd say something like, 'It was nice to have you here,'" Korcheck recalls. "'We'll call you.'"

Instead, McKay said, "We want to give you a crack."

Now Korcheck was forced to restrain his excitement and stay businesslike. The assembled Carlton top brass discussed the base salary and living allowances of a Category B International Rookie contract. They told him there'd be money set aside for him to fly family and friends in for visits, and for him to return home on leave. They went over the restrictions he'd be under as a professional athlete.

Of course, he would jump at the chance. But the delicate dance demanded that the Blues give him a couple of weeks to think about it.

In August 2015, four months after his trial at the U.S. Combine, it was made official: Matt Korcheck became the fourth born-and-bred American graduate of the AFL U.S. Combine in four years to get signed by an AFL club.

∗

Before Korcheck could begin his new life in Australia, he had an urgent personal matter to attend to: surprising his college sweetheart,

Katie Ellis, with a carefully mapped out marriage proposal.

It was October and Ellis, 24, who had graduated from the University of Arizona two years before Korcheck, had just finished a round of exams at Western University of Health Sciences in Pomona, California, where she was in the penultimate year of a four-year veterinary doctorate program. What better way to let off steam, she thought, than to have a day out with friends at Disneyland, where she has an annual pass? But one of Ellis's friends, it turned out, was a mole. Months earlier, she had been discreetly asking Ellis about what kind of engagement ring she would hope to have, and she reported Ellis's Disneyland plans to Korcheck.

Korcheck, whose father, Michael, was a colonel, rescue group commander and HH-60 Pave Hawk helicopter pilot in the U.S. Air Force, is no stranger to important missions. His father often had them when he served in Air Force Special Operations. Now Matt Korcheck flew out to Southern California from Tucson, where he was still living, and staged his own covert special ops mission in the foreground of Disneyland's Sleeping Beauty Castle.

While getting to the park that day, Ellis noticed that one of her two friends was walking through the entrance much faster than she normally did. Then Ellis saw that her friend's husband was carrying a big, professional-looking camera. When they all neared the castle, another of Ellis's friends pulled out her mobile phone and began recording. Before Ellis could figure out what was going on, she spotted Korcheck, waiting for her.

"I was shaking," Korcheck recalls, "and full of joy."

"Stop!" Ellis jokingly said, the moment she saw Korcheck, and she smiled and turned back to one of her friends. "Did you know?"

The couple embraced and kissed.

"What is happening?" Ellis asked Korcheck.

Korcheck then held his sweetheart's hands, playfully pulling her back and forth. He stared intensely into her eyes. Ellis's friend's camera was busily flashing, capturing the moment. "You know, I've known for a very long time, I've wanted to be with you …" Korcheck began.

By this time Ellis knew what was coming. After Korcheck's speech of about 30 seconds, he reached into his pocket, knelt on his right knee — which put him at eye level with the 5-foot-6 Ellis — and pulled out a ring box. Ellis clasped both hands to her face in surprise. Tears came to her eyes as she repeatedly nodded and said, "Yes." As he took out the ring — a princess-cut solitaire diamond on a silver band — Ellis repeatedly fanned herself with her hands.

"Put on the ring!" a friend yelled.

"I'm working on it," Korcheck said.

Immediately after slipping the engagement ring on Ellis's finger, he exulted just as an AFL footy player might after kicking his first goal — triumphantly, but not outrageously. He smiled broadly and pumped an uppercut fist in the air.

The moment was far removed from when the couple first met, years before. It was underneath a palm tree outside the McKale Center, where Korcheck had just played in the University of Arizona basketball team's Red-Blue Game, an intraclub match before starting the pre-season. Mutual friends had arranged the meeting.

"When I was being set up with him, I was like, 'A basketball player? No thanks.' They told me he had a lot of tattoos," Ellis recalls. "He was so nervous then. He was the most awkward person in the world. It was adorable. We all went to a restaurant and we sat in a booth and he sat far away from me. He would talk to me, but didn't seem super interested. I went to the bathroom with a girlfriend and told her, 'I don't think he likes me.'"

But for Korcheck, though it was impossible for Ellis to know, it was love at first sight. He got her number from one of her friends, then texted her to ask her out to dinner. On the way there, Ellis again got a whiff — this time literally — of Korcheck's awkwardness, riding in his well-worn Toyota 4Runner. There was a fishy smell coming from the back seat, which it turned out was a days-old seafood remnant from a doggie bag Korcheck had neglected to take inside. So Ellis rolled down the window and caught a stiff breeze blowing through her hair, which she had just done for their date.

Ellis won't ever forget the first moments of their dinner.

"What size house do you want to live in?" Korcheck asked, showing that "adorable awkwardness" that was quickly growing on Ellis.

"I thought to myself, *What kind of question is that?*" Ellis recalls, laughing.

There would be many more dates. Hiking in nearby Sabino Canyon. Horseback riding in the desert scrub. Movies. Ellis had expected a basketball player like Korcheck to be cocky and full of himself, because he was playing for a high-profile university. "But he was so shy," she says. "He's so sweet and has a great smile."

Before the proposal, when Ellis knew living across the world in Australia might be in Korcheck's near future, she was torn. She would miss her partner if he embraced the opportunity, but at the same time she was excited for him. She had encouraged Korcheck to go to the U.S. Combine, when, about a week before it was scheduled to happen, he nearly backed out. Korcheck was thinking instead of applying for a job with the University of Arizona's athletic department. But she insisted he go.

And back on that nervous hour-and-a-half on the LAX tarmac, when Korcheck was "freaking out" and worrying that he'd miss his international connection, sending Ellis frantic texts, it was Ellis keeping him calm with soothing messages of her own.

During his three weeks of training in Melbourne, Korcheck and Ellis overcame the huge time difference, speaking every day using Viber on their smartphones. Towards the end of his time in Melbourne, Ellis awoke one morning in California to find a memorable text from him: "I have good news." She called him and he told her about Carlton's contract offer.

"I was excited and confused, because I don't really know anything about the sport," Ellis says. "I just told him, 'If you really like it, I support you a thousand per cent.' I moved away from him after school to take up my passion, so who would I be to keep him from following his? I told him if we wanna keep this going, we can make it work. I'm on board."

After she graduates, Ellis is hoping to do a required rotation at a Melbourne veterinary hospital so she and Korcheck can live together.

She may get some needed connections and assistance from McKay, the Blues' football manager, who studied in veterinary school at the University of Queensland while playing in the Carlton backline. McKay later graduated and was a part-time veterinary surgeon.

Before jetting off to Melbourne to begin his time as a Carlton player, Korcheck also had to part with a very close friend: a pit bull mix he rescued six months earlier from an animal shelter.

"He had a pretty rough backstory," Korcheck says. "He was made to fight other dogs and was left outside by a previous owner. He had some battle wounds. I said to myself, 'I gotta save him.' At first, he was pretty scared of everybody. I think he thought I was gonna hit him because he had [been] beaten. Then he started to get pretty normal."

The dog's original name was Canelo — Spanish for "cinnamon" — but Korcheck wanted to re-christen his new buddy so he'd have a clean break from his nightmarish past. While driving his new friend home in his 4Runner, he took a look in the backseat and saw one of his basketballs, with the manufacturer name emblazoned on it. His mind instantaneously went back to the film *Cast Away*, in which Tom Hanks's character is marooned on a tropical island. Out of desperation, he befriends a volleyball he finds, giving it the same name Korcheck gave his dog: Wilson.

Fortunately for Korcheck, he found a loving home for Wilson with a Tucson couple, which already had a playmate for him, their husky.

Then it was time for Korcheck to say farewell to Ellis. "Anytime we say goodbye, it gets pretty emotional," he says. "When you see each other after long periods of time, it's like a tease. It helps that we're tremendously busy with our careers, to take our minds off being so far apart."

*

Korcheck showed up for his new AFL career two weeks before preseason. He settled in to a three-bedroom house with a fellow Blue, Blaine

Boekhorst, whom he met during his three-week tryout, and another roommate. The set-up is similar to how Korcheck rolled in college, living with two of his best friends.

Once preseason started, he worked extensively with Capuano, new Northern Blues senior coach and former All-Australian ruckman Josh Fraser, and teammates Boekhorst and Dylan Buckley. He very quickly found out how different preseason basketball practices are from preseason footy training. "I think I did more running in one day than I did in an entire preseason in basketball," Korcheck says. "I'm finding new ways to push my body."

The weightlifting and swimming sessions guaranteed that. There was also the challenging mental preparation. Korcheck and his teammates watched hours of video from the 2015 season and began learning new head coach Brendon Bolton's footy philosophy. For Boekhorst and Korcheck, preseason training meant leaving home at 6 a.m. and returning 12 hours later.

"I got the sense that these guys are freak athletes," Korcheck says. "It's amazing how much these guys can do. That's another thing that drew me to the sport, being able to train with the best and do something that wasn't easy. It takes so much effort and discipline."

Mastering kicking remains his big challenge, and like all the American recruits who preceded him, Korcheck still goes to training early so he can do extra skills work. And so far it has been coming along nicely. "They've slowed down the process so that every week we work on one aspect of my kicking," he says. "The biggest thing was that I wasn't following through. I'd lean backwards. Now I'm running and kicking better. I'm really trying to get a feel for the ball. The attention to detail you need to make everything work is like shooting a jump shot in basketball, knowing where your elbow is, maintaining your balance and footwork. In footy, it's about the drop and how every little thing ties in together."

Korcheck's longtime close friend and former University of Arizona roommate Kevin Lohmeier, who now works as a software engineer, witnessed firsthand Korcheck's basketball prowess. Lohmeier was

Korcheck's basketball teammate at Sabino High School and saw his friend's big spurts — not just in growth but also in talent. The team was good and the coach's strategy was two-dimensional: play tough defense and, as Lohmeier recalls, "Get the ball to Matt."

The coach even had a play designed for Korcheck in his senior year called "UTEP" — a reference to the University of Texas at El Paso, which was working hard to recruit him. The coach would pull the other seniors off the floor and substitute them with younger players, who were stronger defenders. The offence would run entirely through Korcheck.

Lohmeier remembers one occasion when "UTEP" worked to perfection. "We were down by 15 points," he says, "and then, with Matt doing all the offensive work, we had the lead back within five minutes."

Lohmeier was surprised but encouraging when his friend's opportunity to play Aussie Rules first presented itself. "He was kinda over basketball at that point," he recalls. "We said, 'You might as well find out. If you hate it, you don't have to do it.' Once we talked to him about it, he got into it like we thought he would."

Like Ellis, Lohmeier also appreciates Korcheck's quirks. He can quote, on demand, dialogue from the cartoon comedy TV show *Family Guy*, and is obsessed with *Star Wars*. Korcheck has an affinity for East Asian culture, too, as a result of the extraordinary circumstances of his birth and infancy.

When Korcheck's mother, Sandra, was pregnant with him, his father was a captain, serving a rescue group at an Osan Air Base in South Korea, 40 miles south of the capital, Seoul. The Korchecks and their two daughters, ages 3 and 16 months, lived off the base, in the town of Songtan.

Matt was due to be born in December, but Sandra went into pre-term labor just over 30 weeks into her pregnancy. She had to be taken via a medevac helicopter to a U.S. Army base in Seoul, but the hospital there couldn't handle a baby that young. She would have to deliver her baby at a hospital that had the proper facilities to help him survive. The nearest such place was a U.S. Marine base, Camp Lester, on

the Japanese island of Okinawa — a two-hour flight away.
The family quickly arranged for their Korean housekeeper to take
care of the girls. With husband Michael alongside her, Sandra was
administered drugs that would keep the baby safely inside her womb
until she could deliver him. Then the couple boarded a McDonnell
Douglas C-9-A Nightingale jet, specially used for aeromedical evacu-
ations. "The pilot asked me what kind of music I liked, so I could try
to relax," recalls Sandra, a nurse by profession. "He asked if he could
play the Beach Boys and I remember saying okay."

So with the group's greatest hits being piped in, and with an incu-
bator on board the aircraft in case Sandra delivered Matt before they
landed, the pilot flew them to Japan, keeping the plane at a low altitude to avoid turbulence. Sandra felt comfortable as, coincidentally,
an American chaplain and his wife also were on board, travelling to
Camp Lester.

Matt was born weighing just over 4½ lbs. He was on a ventilator
for the first four days of his life. After a month in an intensive care
unit, mother and son boarded a military cargo plane to South Korea to
rejoin the rest of the family — but not before making five other stops
on the way to drop off supplies for American troops. The Korchecks
would stay six more months before returning to the US, but it was far
from the end of the family's odyssey. In total, the Korchecks moved 15
times, throughout the southern and southwestern US, finally settling
in Tucson for Matt's pre-teen years.

Korcheck has artifacts and sensibilities reflecting his Asian birth
and infancy. "He has always felt a connection since his birth," Sandra
says. "He knows he was born there. He had things in his room that he
picked up from us from our time there." These include woodcarvings
from Daegu, a city in South Korea famous for its art and a Japanese samurai sword. Sushi is one of Korcheck's favorite foods, and he
arranged the furnishings of his room in his Tucson apartment according to the Chinese art and science of *feng shui*, which aims to balance
a space's aura and energy.

Just as Korcheck has done, by relocating to Melbourne to start a new life chapter, his footy club, having endured dismal seasons recently, hopes to do the same. And while playing in the VFL for the Northern Blues, Korcheck doesn't have to look too far for a reminder of home, as Alexander Aurrichio is a teammate. It's the first time a VFL club has had two born-and-bred American players.

After Korcheck played his first 2016 preseason match, he texted Aurrichio that it was "awesome! Made way too many mistakes but had a blast. The legs just barely made it through." Korcheck knows there will be baby steps, false starts, growing pains, progress, setbacks and small personal victories. And he can't deny that he misses his family, his friends, his pet and — most importantly to him — his fiancée. But Korcheck well knows, as do all the American athletes who have come to Australia, "You sacrifice a lot to come down here."

14

The American Experiment
Lab Results

Merriam-Webster's "simple" definitions of the word *experiment* are these: "a scientific test in which you perform a series of actions and carefully observe their effects in order to learn about something" and "to try a new activity or a new way of doing or thinking about something." Search the same source for the word *successful* and this is what pops up: "having the correct or desired result" and "having gotten or achieved wealth, respect, or fame."

Therein lies the beauty of the English language: words, phrases and sentences aren't always absolute in their meanings. Users are empowered to derive from them their own personal meanings.

So has the AFL's American Experiment been successful? Although the question is complex, and the perspectives of both participants and observers must be considered, the answer is a resounding yes. Producing players like Jason Holmes and Mason Cox, who in a little more than two years each went from having no knowledge of Australian football to playing it at its most advanced level, stands as firm evidence of the experiment's success. So is the now established pathway for more American players to make their way into the AFL each year. An AFL club signed at least one U.S. Combine graduate a year from 2012 through 2015. Outside the league's sanctioned experiment to transform former college hoopsters into ruckmen, some individual clubs — such as the Gold Coast Suns with new recruit Brandon Kaufman — are now conducting their own "lab work" to mold former NCAA and NFL football players into AFL tall defenders and forwards.

The American prospects' ability to transition to the AFL doesn't mean that footy is an easy sport to learn. In fact, Australian Rules is arguably the world's most physically demanding and mentally draining game. It takes a special athlete to possess the aptitude and attitude to grasp a new game with unfamiliar rules, plus a new country's subtle nuances and idiosyncrasies. That there has been at least one born-and-bred American playing at the minor league level from 2010 to 2016 is a tribute to the Australian development coaches who have trained them.

Holmes and Cox have become famous in Australia as the first Americans to play AFL football. More importantly, through their arduous treks, they have earned the entire footy community's respect. But at home, Holmes and Cox remain virtual unknowns. The overwhelming majority of Americans have still never heard of — let alone seen — Australian football.

None of the American athletes who have found a pathway into footy expect instant fame, and certainly not fortune. Compared to the major North American sports leagues, in which even fringe players can pocket millions, an AFL player's pay is paltry. If America's first professional footy players have switched continents to get rich quick, they've chosen the wrong game. Financially, they could've done better for themselves by swapping their athletic gear for suits and ties and "going corporate."

Cox once faced that choice. He rejected what was expected of him and instead gave footy a go, taking up an offer from Collingwood. Then there are guys like Alexander Aurrichio, who just wouldn't — and still may never — take no for an answer, even when no AFL clubs were willing to take a chance on him. Other men such as Rory Smith, Billy Mallard, Torrey Harkness and Carl Winston have also shown the audacity to try and make it as AFL players, while Kim Hemenway and Katie Klatt in April 2016 became the first born-and-bred American women to play in an AFL-sanctioned match, lining up on opposite sides in Sydney in an exhibition clash between the women's academy teams of the AFL's Sydney Swans and the Greater Western Sydney Giants.

Perhaps no other word better captures the American spirit — positively and negatively — than *audacity*. For Americans, it's an essential survival trait. Before his improbable election as the country's 44th president, President Barack Obama authored a book outlining the vision for his presidency and the blueprint for his policies called *The Audacity of Hope*.

Among Australians, Kevin Sheedy, the legendary four-time Premiership-winning coach, probably understands audacity better than most. In 1995 he recruited the very first American born-and-bred athlete to play professional footy, Dwayne Armstrong. If not for accepting a lucrative Australian job offer after playing the 1996 and 1997 seasons on Essendon's minor league team, Armstrong might have earned the distinction of being the AFL's first born-and-bred American, 17 years before Holmes. Sheedy sees a commonality between Americans and Australians, despite the vast geographical and subtle cultural differences. "We have the same language," he says, "and the same desperation to want to be successful."

At the time he recruited Armstrong, Sheedy was good friends with AFL CEO and chairman Ross Oakley, who, with his own unconventional thinking, helped transform professional football in Australia from a suburban competition to a national one. Sheedy's experimentation with international athletes continued in 2005 when he brought Japanese players Michito Sakaki and Tsuyoshi Kase to train with the Bombers, and a year later included Sakaki in a Bombers preseason contest. Years later, Sheedy took the reins as the expansion Greater Western Sydney Giants' inaugural head coach, hoping to establish the AFL in new territory. One of his first moves there also was experimental — recruiting the superstar rugby league player Israel Folau.

Kevin "Shifter" Sheehan, Sheedy's contemporary, who advanced and advocated the American Experiment a few years after Paul Roos began it, offers his own insight into why the U.S. Combine invitees are keen to forge AFL careers. "For some American athletes, it's like a *Survivor*-type challenge that some people thrive on," he says. "We've got a virgin canvas to work with, so we'll see who'll embrace and absorb the game. In three to four years, we hope we could have as many as 10 to 20 American players."

Don't be too quick to dismiss that notion. In February 2016 the AFL pried the door open wider to international recruitment. It dropped the stipulation that capped a foreign athlete's eligibility to be signed by an AFL club in the International Scholarship Scheme at age 22 — the age at which most American athletes graduate from college, with many entering the NBA or NFL drafts.

About a month after the rule change, Gold Coast signed the 25-year-old Kaufman to an International Scholarship contract. Another AFL rule change enacted in February 2016 allows clubs a seven-month period to sign international recruits, from November 1 to June 30, instead of a previous month-long window, from November 1.

Resident footy cynics should hedge their bets on Americans not making it in AFL footy. Thirty years ago, their kind scoffed at VFL/AFL clubs targeting Gaelic football players in the 1980s. One need only gaze at the statue of the legendary Jim Stynes outside the entrance to the Melbourne Cricket Ground to realize how well that experiment worked.

"If the Irish can adapt, then so can the Americans," reasons Grant Hansen, founder and television host of *The Marngrook Footy Show*, a weekly program on Australia's National Indigenous Television Network and a former AFL broadcaster for National Indigenous Radio. "It's just a matter of time. It's a sport they can quickly adapt to. [The Australian-born San Antonio Spurs forward] Patty Mills was a really good footballer before deciding to play pro basketball, so he did both. AFL should be a world game."

Actually, it has been, and for longer than most fans realize. After the turn of the 20th century, some 20 different Australian football clubs were competing in South Africa. On the cusp of the 21st, the AFL was growing the game in Papua New Guinea. The start of the new millennium saw the AFL begin hosting the International Cup, the Olympics-style footy tournament in which 18 men's and seven women's teams, representing 18 countries — including the U.S. — compete for a world title.

By the start of the 2016 AFL season, more than 100 of the league's players — including at least one at each of the 18 clubs — have at least one foreign-born parent. There are nearly 30 foreign-born players on AFL rosters; about a third are from Ireland, while others originated in such far-flung countries as Sudan, Belarus, Fiji and Brazil. With this level of expansion, an observer might reasonably conclude that a foray into North America was inevitable.

But executing it took foresight. It took someone with an innovative footy brain, someone who was unafraid enough — audacious enough — to cop having a reputation in footy circles as an eccentric. It took someone with thick enough skin to defend investing resources in America against parochial thinkers who argued instead for harvesting under-represented Australian regions for talent.

Enter Paul Roos, who over the course of his many visits to America since the late 1980s formulated the idea that would become the American Experiment. "When I was over there, I realized how much talent there was," he says. "It's an untapped area. The talent pool is extraordinary. I knew there would be some rejection for it. I just tended to ignore it."

Roos, who had played for Fitzroy during the years of the Irish Experiment and watched it bear fruit, knew that recruiting American talent would require new methods and a fresh approach. "There are some vast differences between American kids versus Irish kids," he says. "With America, you're not trying to get first-choice athletes. You're not looking for [pro basketball legends] LeBron James or Michael Jordan. You're trying to get first-choice kids in Irish players. The travel factor is bigger for Irish players. Americans love to travel."

Though ultimately he never joined the Swans, Shae McNamara was Roos's first target. Then Roos uncovered a gem in Alex Starling, whose untimely injury was the only thing that kept him from sparkling. Even after Roos moved on from coaching the Swans, his initial foresight lingered at the club. If Holmes and Patrick Mitchell hadn't trained for three weeks at the Swans Academy after the 2013 U.S. Combine, who knows if both men would eventually have earned AFL contracts?

If the AFL really wants the American Experiment to work, that kind of intensive training after the U.S. Combine must continue, according to USAFL president Denis Ryan. That's what happened in 2015, as Matt Korcheck and his fellow U.S. Combine graduates, Jalen Carethers, James Johnson and Kye Kurkowski, got schooled in Melbourne. But it didn't happen in 2014 for Ryan's protégé, Marvin Baynham, and Ryan believes this may have cost him an AFL opportunity.

Ryan says the USAFL, with its network of coaches and clubs and its April-October season, could serve as a bridge between the U.S. Combine and the Draft Combine by improving the American prospects' skills. "It benefits these athletes to have someone on the ground to work with them," Ryan says. "The AFL doesn't think the USAFL can do it. They need to have more faith in us. But they might not have it in the budget."

Ryan has inquired whether clubs at the state league level could help the American Experiment along, providing players with an alternate pathway to the AFL. He says they've told him they don't have the resources to take on American players. And even if American players could be brought on board, if they have a bad experience in Australia it might leave the players with a bitter taste and be negative for the clubs. "I've told them, 'Let's set the expectations low,'" Ryan says. "If we set extended training with state league clubs up as a working holiday, it might work."

As Ryan's statements illustrate, the American Experiment has been characterized by the floating of multiple ideas, and by the use of trial and error methodology. It's produced victories and setbacks, and been driven by idealistic hopes and limited by monetary constraints. The footy "scientists" and their subjects continue to learn from their experiences.

The degree to which the American Experiment has impacted the

American athletes' lives can't easily be quantified. But it has left indelible impressions on every player who has been a part of it.

McNamara reckons his participation was pre-ordained. "It was a sign from God to do this," he says of his footy experience. "It was too unique and crazy for it not to be fate. It's what God needed me to do then. I had the thought that I could make it in something that had never been done before. I had no idea how to do it. There was no template. I believed in myself. It was not a failure."

Certainly not, if achieving a few firsts would be considered successful. McNamara, after all, was the first born-and-bred American to be drafted by an AFL club. By McNamara's criteria, none of the American athletes who returned home after not getting an AFL senior game failed. They all established benchmarks of varying degrees that can never be taken from them. Starling was the first to be signed by an AFL club through the International Scholarship Scheme. Mitchell was the first to play in the NEAFL. Baynham was the first to reach new heights in the vertical leap at the AFL Draft Combine. Wallace was the first U.S. Combine participant to be signed by an AFL club.

Besides these athletic milestones, there are personal ones. For Wallace, the self-described "polymath," coming to Australia helped his horizons to continue to expand. His father, Tremonteo, had never set foot outside the United States until he visited his son in Ballarat.

A week after North Melbourne delisted Wallace, when he was concerned about finding direction and a purpose, he still expressed satisfaction about his overall effort. "Three years ago, I had a dream," Wallace says. "I made the trip over to see if I could do it. I did."

Starling, meanwhile, continues to live in Australia years after his brief time with the Swans. He has made a life for himself in both South Australia and Victoria. Aurrichio is applying his New York "hustler" mindset in Melbourne as he tries to reach AFL level. Mallard, Harkness and Winston momentarily escaped the violence of the 'hood in South Los Angeles through their country footy experiences in rural New South Wales. Smith, for a few fleeting minutes, was a professional athlete. Armstrong, the "prime specimen" in the AFL's first-ever experiment with American athletes, remains in Australia after 20 years, building a successful business career, and helping raise a family with his partner.

If these men had stayed Stateside, the precious moments they lived out in Australia — from which they all learned, developed and grew — would never have happened. Their athletic careers, already stunted by scarce professional opportunities, likely would've been over, and their chance to use their extraordinary physical abilities finished.

Late in the 2015 season, Wallace and Holmes had one last battle in the ruck. It was about a year-and-a-half after their initial contest in Ballarat, and their footy futures were heading in opposite directions. Wallace was desperately playing for a new contract, while Holmes was soaring towards a senior list call-up. In that match, at Avalon Airport Oval, Holmes's Sandringham side beat Wallace's Werribee squad by 13 points. The two Americans' stats were about even. Holmes would soon go into the history books, while Wallace would soon go home. Yet each would say he was inspired by the other's Aussie Rules journey.

If the success of the AFL's American Experiment could also be measured by its ability to raise the prospects' expectations of life and of themselves, and to stimulate their own and the league's decision-makers' imaginations, it has done the job. Australia's footy fans and pundits can debate the experiment's results in pubs, in print, on air and in cyberspace.

By jumping at the chance to be part of the experiment, the American players are all pioneers, regardless of the fame or wealth they accumulate. They've become intimately familiar with Australia, its culture and its people, and they've taught Australians something of what it means to be American. When Jason Holmes ran out with his St Kilda teammates on that August 2015 night at Etihad Stadium, he carried with him all the hopes of past, present and future Americans keen to learn Australia's game and play it at its highest level. There's a positive prognosis for present and future American athletic involvement in AFL footy. The lab results confirm it.

Epilogue
Footy's Future
Femme Fatales Kim Hemenway & Katie Klatt

The moment passes in a flash. It's a blur — two opposing players quickly converging in the heat of a match for, at most, two to three seconds. The scene is a balmy afternoon in April 2016 at the Sydney Cricket Ground, where a curtain-raiser match, ahead of the AFL's "Battle of the Bridge" clash between the Swans and the Giants, is taking place. A medium-sized defender in a Giants jersey lays a solid tackle on a tall Swans tall forward, just as the boot connects with the ball.

The next day the AFL will recognize the importance of this fleeting encounter, posting a photo of it on its website. It's both a glimpse of professional footy's future and a heralding of yet another first in the American involvement in Australia's game.

The Swans forward is 32-year-old Kim Hemenway, born in California and raised in the American south. The Giants defender is 24-year-old Katie Klatt, from a Virginia suburb outside Washington, D.C. The game in which they're playing is an exhibition match between the Swans' and Giants' Women's Academy sides, and thus a showcase for top female footballers hoping to earn a contract in the professional AFL Women's League, which would debut several months later in early 2017.

Hemenway has played eight years for the USAFL's New York Lady Magpies, while Klatt has played 18 months for the league's Sacramento Lady Suns. They are teammates on USA Freedom, America's national women's footy side. At the SCG, the two are the first American women to play for Australian teams in an AFL-sanctioned match. Twenty years after Essendon's senior coach, Kevin Sheedy, tapped Dwayne Armstrong to become the AFL's first U.S. recruit, and seven years after Collingwood made Shae McNamara the first American AFL draftee, Hemenway and Klatt are the first female specimens in a new kind of AFL American Experiment.

Hemenway works in Los Angeles as a respiratory therapist, and first discovered footy about a decade before the Sydney match, in Brisbane. Her U.S. Navy communications vessel, the USS *Blue Ridge* — the United States Seventh Fleet's command ship — docked there. To welcome Hemenway and a shipmate, an Australian family took them to a Brisbane Lions' match at their home stadium, the Gabba. Two years later, while living in North Carolina and working for a healthcare provider, Hemenway saw a Craigslist ad placed by the USAFL's NC Tigers.

"Are girls allowed to play?" she asked the club in an email.

"Yes," came the reply. "But you'll be the only girl there."

That hardly fazed Hemenway. As Jason Cornish — an Australian player on the USAFL's Los Angeles Dragons, with whom Hemenway trains — says, "She plays better than most of the blokes." Later, Hemenway turned up to a USAFL tournament, where she met Andrea Casillas and Christina Licata, the co-founders of the USAFL's New York Lady Magpies. Soon the club was chipping in regularly to fly Hemenway to New York to train and play. At 5-foot-9, Hemenway is one of the USAFL's tallest women, so the Lady Magpies groomed her to play both ruck and center half-forward. She soon earned a reputation, both in USAFL circles and with the Australian scouts who watched her play in USAFL national tournaments and in Melbourne for USA Freedom in the 2014 International Cup, as a strong contested mark and goal-kicker.

Klatt, too, has forged a strong footy reputation, although she has taken a different route to the sport. After graduating from the University of Virginia, where she played on the women's field hockey team, she was introduced to footy by her American boyfriend. That relationship didn't last, but for Klatt, who is a pediatric intensive care nurse, footy became a passion.

Klatt's rise in American women's footy — the history of which dates back to the 2003 formation of the USAFL's first women's club, the Orange County Bombshells — has been meteoric. For Sacramento, the 5-foot-7 Klatt has become queen of the halfback line, shutting down opponents and leading by example and with her voice. Australian footy talent evaluators noticed all that at the 2015 USAFL National Tournament. So did USA Freedom's selectors, who, ahead of the 2017 International Cup, not only named her to the team but also made her vice-captain.

Two months before the Australian exhibition match, both women paid their own airfares to Sydney to attend a two-day AFL national talent search for female footballers to round out the Swans' and Giants' teams. Hemenway and Klatt were the only Americans. The women performed the same fitness and skills tests as the men do at the AFL's various combines. At the conclusion of the event, evaluators named Klatt one of the top five players, while Hemenway recorded the best standing vertical leap, ascending to just over 2 feet. Suddenly, both Americans' chances of getting chosen to play in the Sydney exhibition match grew.

Klatt began seriously considering whether to move to Australia to pursue her professional footy dream. In a blog post for the USAFL's website, she wrote: "Even now, I feel the weight of it as I try to make this life decision. If I decide not to change my entire life for a sport, will I seem scared, or be letting people down, or will I regret passing up this once in a lifetime opportunity? If I don't make the academy, will I seem like a fraud? If I do move and do everything, but don't make it to that highest level, will people laugh at me because I wasn't good enough?"

On a pre-planned Southeast Asian holiday, Klatt acted, deciding to file the paperwork to transfer her nursing license to Australia, apply for a one-year working holiday visa, and in a few months move to Melbourne. On a boiling hot morning over breakfast at her Siem

Reap, Cambodia, hotel, before she and a friend set off to tour the ancient Angkor Wat temple complex, Klatt's decision was validated. She opened an email from an AFL official and got the news that the GWS Women's Academy side had picked her for the Sydney match.

Around the same time, in the United States, Hemenway learned that the Sydney Women's Academy side had chosen her. Because of her age, though, Hemenway couldn't make the same commitment as Klatt; the cutoff age for an Australian working holiday visa is 30, and Hemenway's degree in respiratory therapy wouldn't translate easily to Australia. If she was to pursue her goal of playing in the Women's AFL, Hemenway would have to find an Australian employer to sponsor her.

Immigration issues aside, both Hemenway and Klatt knew that a strong performance in Sydney would help their cause. The two women were switched on once they ran onto the SCG's immaculate surface. *The bar has been raised*, Hemenway thought to herself. *Let's do this.*

Twenty years earlier, in Dwayne Armstrong's maiden Australian match, the footy found him. In the first minutes of the women's match, Hemenway found the footy. She gathered a loose ball in the forward pocket, ran and then kicked long, hoping to hit a target or at least gain territory for her side, but her kick went out of bounds. A few minutes later, Hemenway found space about 25 meters from goal and took an uncontested chest mark. A world away, in Brooklyn, her Lady Magpies teammates, who had gathered late at night to watch a live stream of the match, let out a collective yell.

Hemenway knew this was an easy set shot, but still felt under the pump. *I'd better not screw this up*, she thought, stepping back from her mark, *or everyone in America will give me shit forever and everyone in Australia will write me off.*

She spun the ball once in her hands, looked up at goal, then took a much shorter run-up than the one she practiced in Los Angeles parks, where she'd aim her kick between a pair of plastic tubes she kept at home and planted in the ground as makeshift goalposts. Hemenway knew she didn't need to get a big boot on the footy — she just needed it to go straight. She dropped the ball and swung her right leg. The footy took flight.

"She's slotted it!" Jo Wotton, the live stream's play-by-play commentator, announced triumphantly.

"That is good for footy, Jo," replied her broadcast partner, Craig Starcevich, a star player for Collingwood's 1990 Premiership-winning side. "That's a ripper. First shot on goal for the game."

Hemenway had done just what Armstrong had. But while he had little involvement in the rest of his match, Hemenway was only getting started. Later, she read the flight of a kick towards center half-forward, bodied her opponent, and then reached up and took a strong contested mark. Again she converted the set shot. She would go on to kick a third goal, and narrowly miss a fourth. In Sydney's convincing win, 9.8 (62) to 5.3 (33), Hemenway finished as the match's leading goal-kicker and was one of her side's best players.

While not winning the same accolades, Klatt also did good things for her Greater Western Sydney side. She started at half-forward, then was moved to the halfback line and finished in the midfield. She had 10 possessions, but made her best impact while playing in defense, not once allowing her opponent to take a mark. In the fourth quarter, after taking an intercept mark, Klatt helped set up a goal for her team with a long kick to a teammate.

Afterwards, Starcevich described the American women's presence in the match — and their impact on it — as "a breath of fresh air." In time, his words may well ring true for the Australian footy insiders and fans who once doubted that American athletes could make a go of playing the game.

Gary O'Donnell, the Brisbane Lions' assistant coach and former Essendon captain who mentored Armstrong so many years ago, has a unique perspective on the AFL's American Experiment, from its start, through its evolution, to its future.

"We only need one or two to come through and succeed, and then there might be a flood come across," he says. "It only makes the game better."

*

Dwayne Armstrong, who in 1996 was the first born-and-bred American athlete ever recruited by an AFL club, and the first to kick a goal in an AFL-sanctioned match, lives in Preston, a Melbourne suburb, with his partner, Tracy Coutts, and sons, Tyler and Maddox — both of whom play youth footy. Armstrong works for the Canadian-based sports apparel company Silver Crystal Sports Inc. as its Australasian Development Manager and International Sales.

Alexander Aurrichio started the 2017 season playing in the minor Northeast Australian Football League (NEAFL), with the Sydney University club, before moving to Adelaide and joining the South Adelaide Football club, in the minor South Australian National Football League (SANFL). He missed a chunk of the 2016 VFL season after suffering a broken hand playing for Northern Blues, alongside countryman Matt Korcheck. After Aurrichio won Northern Blues' 2015 Best Clubman award, his teammates voted him to the leadership group — a status no other born-and-bred American has ever achieved at a professional Australian football club.

Marvin Baynham now lives in Tampa, Florida. He has returned to pursuing what he describes as his "original dream," long before he aimed at pro basketball and AFL football — becoming a firefighter. He is enrolled in a two-year firefighter/medic program at Tampa's Learey College. In addition, he is still planning to start a non-profit organization.

Christian Behrens, who attended the 2015 AFL U.S. Combine, moved to Spain in 2016 to play pro basketball for the San Pablo Inmobiliaria Miraflores Burgos. That followed 2015 stints at the Surrey Scorchers of the British Basketball League and at Raiffeisen Wels, a professional Austrian club.

Mark Cisco, a 2013 AFL U.S. Combine attendee, made a last attempt in 2014 at an AFL career as a cast member of the Australian footy reality show *The Recruit*, but was delisted after the sixth episode. He now lives in New York, where he is an account executive for Indeed.com, a website that connects jobseekers with employers around the world.

Mason Cox, a 2014 U.S. Combine graduate, became the second born-and-bred American AFL player in April 2016. He has played 20 AFL matches from 2016 through 2017 and kicked 27 goals. Shortly after the 2017 season, he signed a new, three-year contract to remain at Collingwood through the 2020 season.

Kim Hemenway was nominated for the inaugural 2016 AFL Women's Draft, but went unclaimed. She continues to live and work in Southern California and regularly plays in the USAFL Women's competition. She was selected represent the American women's international footy side, USA Freedom, in the AFL's International Cup competition in August 2017.

Jason Holmes, who attended the 2013 U.S. Combine, in 2015 became the first born-and-bred American to play in a regular season AFL match with St Kilda. He then signed a one-year contract extension after the 2016 season and was elevated to the Saints' senior team. During the 2016 season, Holmes played 14 matches for St Kilda's VFL affiliate, Sandringham and averaging 29 hitouts per match. He played in 14 matches with Sandringham in the 2017 season, but was not recalled by St Kilda. Holmes has finished his St Kilda contract and it remains to be seen whether the Saints or another AFL club will sign him.

Brandon Kaufman, who the Gold Coast Suns recruited and signed in March 2016, kicked a goal in his first professional footy match the following month, for the reserves of the Suns' AFL Queensland affiliate club, the Labrador Tigers. He was quickly promoted to the Suns' NEAFL reserves team and was voted the club's best on ground in his first match for them. However, the Suns released Kaufman in August and he has returned home to the U.S.

Katie Klatt moved to Melbourne in 2016 to live and work — and play for the Melbourne University Women's Football Club. While she continues working at a Melbourne hospital, Klatt in 2017 played on the VFL Women's League club, Melbourne University. Also that year, she played in the Women's Division of the International Cup, the AFL's global amateur tournament, playing for America's national women's footy club, USA Freedom. Klatt, the Freedom's co-vice captain, was one of three Freedom players named to the tournament's Women's All-World team, boosting her chances of getting drafted by a professional AFL Women's League club for the 2018 season.

Matt Korcheck, a 2015 U.S. Combine alumnus, played in 31 matches from 2016-2017 with Carlton's VFL affiliate club, where in 2016, Aurrichio was his teammate. He kicked four goals during that season and averaged 15 hitouts per match. His season highlight came in the last minutes of a late-season match against Footscray, in which he took a strong contested mark, then sealed his club's six-point win by kicking a goal. Before the 2016 season, he and fiancée Katie Ellis broke off their engagement; the extraordinary distance between them had affected their relationship. The two remain in contact. Following the completion of the 2017 season, Korcheck decided to retire from the AFL and return to the U.S.

Billy Mallard lives in the Los Angeles area and still reaches for his professional athletic dream, while raising his young son, Trayce. In early 2016 he attended local tryouts for CFL teams, hoping to earn an invitation to a pre-season camp.

Shae McNamara, the first born-and-bred American ever drafted by an AFL club, and the first to kick a goal in the AFL's pre-season NAB Cup, lives in Milwaukee, Wisconsin. He is a peak performance and mindset coach, and is the author of *Become Unbreakable and Perform at Your Highest Level*.

Rory Smith lives in Boston and is a talent acquisition specialist for Boston University, recruiting IT professionals to work at the school.

On weekends he hunts the footy as a midfielder for the USAFL's Boston Demons.

Alex Starling lives in South Australia, where he is co-captain of the North Adelaide Rockets, in Basketball SA's Premier League. In mid-2017, Starling was among the league leaders in rebounding. Starling has led two other league teams to premierships, including 2016, in which his Southern Tigers dominated the competition with a 21-1 regular season record. Starling was the league's top rebounder, averaging nearly 15 per game, was its third-leading scorer, with 21.6 points per contest and led the league in steals. He also runs the Alexander Starling Basketball Camp, in Adelaide, for boys and girls ages 7 to 18, with other American expat players in Australia as assistant coaches. In addition, he also heads a company called Starling Basketball Training and works as a personal trainer.

Eric Wallace, recruited from the AFL's inaugural U.S. Combine in 2012, and thus the first graduate to be signed by an AFL club, was in mid-2017 participating in training camp with the NFL's Carolina Panthers and hoping to make the regular season squad. The Panthers signed Wallace to a contract in July 2016, as a tight end, then waived him before the start of that year's NFL season. Off the field, Wallace has also been working as a private basketball instructor, and has been officiating basketball games and working with kids at various local parks and recreation departments.

Carl Winston lives in the Los Angeles area. He works in Cerritos, California, as a sales merchandiser for Southern Wine & Spirits, an alcoholic-beverage distributor.

Acknowledgments

All praise to the footy gods. They first appeared in my life in the 1980s, when I was a teenager, using their divine influence to make me see footy for the first time. Airing VFL matches may have just been filling dead hours for you, ESPN, but it aroused my curiosity and changed my life.

Respect to the Indigenous people of Australia, inventors of the "blackfella" ball games, and to Thomas Wentworth Wills, who played, then fused them with "whitefella" games to create the Australian game — one I treasure as deeply as any Australian.

Players of the American Experiment: No matter what your outcome, you're champions. You personify our country's audacious spirit. Thanks for allowing me into your professional and personal lives, letting me shadow you (some of you for years) and trusting me to honestly and authentically tell your stories. Dwayne Armstrong, Alexander Aurrichio, Marvin Baynham, Christian Behrens, Evan Bruinsma, Jalen Carethers, Mason Cox, James Hunter, Kim Hemenway, Daquan Holiday, Jason Holmes, Brian Hornstein, Brandon Kaufman, Katie Klatt, Matt Korcheck, Kye Kurkowski, Billy Mallard, Shae McNamara, Patrick Mitchell, Rory Smith and Eric Wallace — take a bow.

Thanks to the Australian Football Association of North America and to USAFL and member clubs, the San Diego Lions, Orange County Bombers, Los Angeles Dragons, New York Magpies, New York Lady Magpies, Sacramento Lady Suns, Boston Demons, Chicago Swans and Denver Bulldogs. Very warm thanks, too, to the AFL and its member clubs for hospitably granting access to players, coaches and officials: Brisbane, Carlton, Collingwood, Essendon, Fremantle, Gold Coast, Greater Western Sydney, Melbourne, North Melbourne, Richmond, St Kilda, Sydney and West Coast. Thanks also to the VFL clubs Collingwood, North Ballarat, Sandringham, Werribee and Northern Blues; the WAFL club Subiaco; and the NTFL club, the Wanderers.

Many thanks to my Australian media colleagues. Peter DiSisto, see what you started by accepting my pitch to cover the 2012 AFL U.S. Combine for the *AFL Record*? You're a "fair dinkum" editor and an even better friend. Paige Cardona, I originally sought your expertise, but came away with something more valuable — your close friendship. Luke Morfesse and Kasey Ball of the Fremantle Dockers, thanks for the opportunity to write the 2013 "Stateside Docker" columns for the club's official website. Simon White, *WAtoday* sports editor, thanks for having me as a footy contributor. Thanks 6PR Radio in Perth for popping me on air to pop off after Freo's matches. Thanks John Separovich and Gavin Crosthwaite for including me on Big-Footy Dockers podcasts.

Emma Quayle, Peter Bell, Ross Oakley, Kevin Sheehan, Michael Ablett, Grant Hansen and Gill McLachlan, thank you for your advance praise of this book. Glenn Stout, your stellar editing of my article "Footy Dreams: American Hoopsters Give Footy A Go" and Dave Savell, your stunning photos helped this book come to fruition. I'm extremely grateful. Thanks to you, too, Patrick Hruby, for the opportunity to write for *Vice*. Special shout-out to the producers of TV and radio shows throughout Australia who had me appear as a guest in 2016 to promote the book, especially Paul Waterhouse of Channel 7 Australia; Gerard Whateley and Mark Robinson of "AFL 360" for Fox Footy; Gillian O'Shaughnessy of ABC Radio Perth; and the brothers and sisters at NITV's "Marngrook Footy Show": Grant Hansen, Gilbert McAdam, Leila Gurruwiwi and Shelley Ware. You're all *deadly*! Martin Flanagan, you are not only a beautiful man, but also my literary spirit guide. My love to your entire tribe, from Victoria to Tasmania.

Joshua Bilmes, president of JABberwocky Literary Agency, you're a colorful character and a man of character. Thanks to you and Eddie Schneider for your shepherding. Thanks to Nero publisher Jeanne Ryckmans, designer Tristan Main and publicist Kate Nash for your support. Julian Welch, you're a great editor and top bloke. Kirstie Innes-Will and Georgina Garner, your eagle eyes were invaluable.

Paul Medhurst, thanks for your match-sealing goal for Freo in the 2003 Round 23 Western Derby, clinching the club's first-ever Finals berth. I may be impartial as a footy journalist, but as a fan, you made me bleed purple for life. So, much love to every Dockers fan across Australia I've met in person or exchanged a tweet, email, text, Facebook or BigFooty post with.

Here in Playa Del Rey, "Tarps" (the unofficial, Aussie expat mayor), thanks for your "mateship" — and making me a decent kick! I raise my glass at Hacienda to you, Heather and Dennis. Pete Z, Macca, Rupert, Ryan and Sophie, and Mark Vickers-Willis, thanks for being part of this great adventure.

Thanks to my best friends in the U.S. for being themselves: Emmett, Gardner, Chuck and Kim and the entire Brooks family, Mark Nero, Luis, Laurelyn, Victoria, Rodney, Jacques, David Coddon, Ron and Michelle, Marvin, Raoul, Kendra, Marco, Lovella and Rajan, Jose Ruiz, Jimmie Briggs, Tim Dennison, Ken Rosen, Art McCann, Rosanna Llorens, Laura Monjoy, Jamie Meyer, Mike "the Poet" Sonksen and longtime mentors Frank, Connie, Richard Harrington, Tim Gallagher, Susan Taylor, Susan White, Tom Nolan, Ari Goldman and Lee Grant. To all my former students, especially Sam, Sydney, Rudy, Connor, Henry and Ella, who played kick-to-kick with me, joined "SuperCoach" AFL Fantasy leagues and willingly learned the game, thank you. Ethan, Jonah and Henry, you're going to be excellent editors, and Carina and Christine, you're going to blossom as writers.

Huge thanks, Mom and Dad, for everything. It's not easy when your only child's body, mind and soul simultaneously span two countries. I love you both, immensely. Shout-out to extended family: Lucille,

Godfather Al, Carol, and Bob Gore and these branches: the Adamses, Berrys, Chiongs, Grahams, Harrisons, Waymers, and the mighty Buhain clan, from Mama Elma and Papa Maning to my brothers, sisters, nieces, nephews, cousins, uncles and aunties, from the U.S. to the Philippines. May Aunt Charlotte, Uncle Alvin, Grandpa, Grandmom, Lolo Abe and Mamang Puring all rest in peace.

Finally, to my beautiful, dynamic and inimitable wife, Arlene: Honeybee, you're everything in one — staunchest supporter, frankest critic and best friend. I love you. Footy always brings us closer. May it always.

About the Author

Gil Griffin lives in Playa Del Rey, California, and is a journalist and teacher of English and history. He has written for the *San Diego Union-Tribune*, the *Albuquerque Tribune* and the *Washington Post* and has covered the AFL for the league's official publication, the *Football Record*, the Perth, Australia daily newspaper, *WAtoday*, *SBNation*, and *Vice Sports*. Gil fell in love with Australian Rules football in the late 1990s on his first trip to Australia. He has appeared on Australian television as a guest commentator on Australian Rules football on such shows as "AFL360," "The Marngrook Footy Show," "Sunrise," and "Sunday Night."

FOR NEWS ABOUT JABBERWOCKY BOOKS AND AUTHORS

Sign up for our newsletter*: http://eepurl.com/b84tDz
visit our website: awfulagent.com/ebooks
or follow us on twitter: @awfulagent

THANKS FOR READING!

*We will never sell or giveaway your email address, nor use
it for nefarious purposes. Newsletter sent out quarterly.